SCOTLAND'S LOST BRANCH LINES

WHERE BEECHING GOT IT WRONG

· DAVID SPAVEN ·

ORIGIN

First published in 2022 by Origin, an imprint of
Birlinn Limited
West Newington House
10 Newington Road
Edinburgh
EH9 1QS
www.birlinn.co.uk

ISBN: 978 1 83983 019 8

British Library Cataloguing-in-Publication Data
A catalogue record for this book is available from the British Library

Designed and typeset by Initial Typesetting Services, Edinburgh

Printed and bound by Clays Ltd, Elcograf, S.p.A.

To three classic railwaymen – David Prescott, Rae Montgomery and John Yellowlees – without whom this book would not be what it is

And to my late father, Frank, who – personally and professionally – challenged the conventional wisdom on rail closures in the 1960s

Choices . . .

'In 1962 the Marples / Beeching axis began to define their territorial ambitions about rural railways. They laid it down in general that rural railways did not pay, which was true; and could never pay, which was false.'

Gerry Fiennes
I Tried to Run a Railway (1967)

'Did you notice in yesterday's papers that the loss and misuse of tarpaulins in Scottish Region of BR is now costing them more than they will save from branch line closures?'

Frank Spaven
Scottish Office internal memorandum
6 April 1962

'Remedies to combat travel sickness [on replacement buses] e.g. MARZINE AND KWELLS, are readily available . . . On longer bus journeys on buses with no toilet facilities, any juvenile incontinence may be relieved by asking bus conductors to make a short stop.'

BR 'Brief for Liaison Officer' (Aberdeen–Fraserburgh closure)
11 November 1963

'[The Minister of Transport] has not made the slightest pretence of answering the people who argue that there are ways of running the [Deeside] line more economically.'

Editorial column
The Press and Journal
19 October 1965

...and Consequences

'When the train came in, you met people. The line was a link with
the outside world and kept us alive. Now the contact is broken
and the place is dead.'

Duncan Kennedy
The Birth and Death of a Highland Railway (1971)

'. . . only just over a quarter of the former rail users reported that they
did not have their lives altered in some practical way . . . Well over half
their former rail-based activities were affected, as were two-thirds of the
types of destination that they had previously reached by train. Over a
third replaced not only their travel method but also the destination
of some of their journeys, and one in twelve ceased altogether the
activities they had previously reached by the branch lines.'

Mayer Hillman and Anne Whalley
The Social Consequences of Rail Closures (1980)

'. . . the cuts in rail infrastructure caused falls in population in affected
areas relative to less affected areas, loss of educated and skilled workers,
and an ageing population . . . the 1 in 5 places in Britain that were most
exposed to the rail network cuts saw 24 percentage points less growth
in population than the 1 in 5 places that were least exposed.'

Stephen Gibbons, Stephan Heblich and Ted Pinchbeck
The Spatial Impacts of a Massive Rail Disinvestment Program: the Beeching Axe
CEP Discussion Paper No. 1563, London School of Economics (2018)

Contents

List of Maps and Illustrations

Maps

Illustrations

Foreword

Look at a map of the current Scottish rail network and you will struggle to find a single surviving rural branch line. These once ubiquitous feeder routes to Scotland's main lines – typically single-track and less than 20 miles long – had all but gone by 1969, swept away by the infamous Beeching Report and its aftermath. But why did we lose so many railways linking significant towns the length and breadth of the country? This is an important aspect of modern Scottish history, which has never been explored in depth – and it's also been a big part of my life.

I'm a child of the Beeching era. Growing up in north Edinburgh in the 1950s and early 1960s – in a household without a car, and with a father who had a keen personal and professional interest in railways – travel by train on day trips and holidays was central to the life of the Spaven family. And I had been won over by the trainspotting bug before I was even 10 years old.

But I was also realising that the familiar world of the railway was changing – and mostly not for the better. Our local station – Granton Road on the Edinburgh (Princes Street) to Leith North line – lost its passenger trains in April 1962, just two months after another family favourite, the Peebles line, had closed completely.

This was a small foretaste of the sweeping closure programme which would follow Dr Beeching's 1963 report, formally titled *The Reshaping of British Railways*.[1] Soon we could no longer travel by train to Ballater, Crail, Grantown-on-Spey, Kelso and Killin – and worst of all, Melrose, Hawick and Riccarton Junction, when the entire Waverley Route was axed in 1969. And I had a vague realisation of another connection: in the early to mid 1960s my father, Frank, as a civil servant at the Scottish Office, was playing a key role advising on the anticipated regional development implications of the planned Beeching closures.

Neither he nor I ever lost our anger at the short-sighted closure of the busiest section of the Waverley Route between Edinburgh and Hawick, but in the early 1990s we were able to provide advice and encouragement to the first tentative steps to campaign for the re-opening of the railway. By then, on the eve of rail privatisation, I had taken redundancy from British Rail after 18 years in the industry in freight marketing management. Thereafter, while working professionally as a rail consultant, I also spent two decades as a volunteer helping to campaign for a re-opened Borders Railway. Unlike most of the worthy transport campaigns in which I've been involved since my late teens, this one was – famously – successful.

While researching the Beeching Report for an article in *Modern Railways* magazine in the run-up to the 50th anniversary of its 1963 publication, I re-examined the 10 case studies he presented to illustrate the financial rationale for line closures. One of these was the Gleneagles–Crieff / Comrie branch, and my analysis of the line's costs and revenue data persuaded me that the Gleneagles–Crieff section should have been reprieved and then heavily rationalised, rather than closed completely. Would archive material, I wondered, shed further light on this and other examples of what I began to regard as 'Beeching's blind spot'? Most Scottish railway histories – with a few notable exceptions, such as A. Derek Farr's *Stories of Royal Deeside's Railway* – have devoted remarkably little attention to the Beeching era. And historians, other than Farr, when briefly reviewing branch line closures often express a 'regrettable but inevitable' attitude to the demise of the railway. These seemed to me to be major omissions in our understanding of a crucial period in Scottish railway history.

A related point is the neglect by historians – other than Farr – of a key question: how many Scottish branch lines were needlessly axed due to a failure to 1) undertake sensible economies short of closure and 2) implement fit-for-purpose service upgrades? The former aspect had first come to my attention as early as 1967 in *I Tried to Run a Railway*,[2] the seminal memoir by Gerry Fiennes, General Manager of British Rail Eastern Region, who pioneered the concept of implementing major infrastructure and operational economies on branch lines to create 'basic railways'. It was a book which earned him the sack, but also exposed a fundamental flaw in Beeching's treatment of loss-making lines.

The appeal to me of writing a book on the bigger picture of the demise of the Scottish rural branch line was not only in unearthing historical revelations about the mistakes of the Beeching era (as I had explored for *Waverley*

Route: the life, death and rebirth of the Borders Railway[3] and *Highland Survivor: the story of the Far North Line*[4]), but also – given my involvement in campaigning for the Borders Railway – in the consideration of how many of the branch lines might now justify re-opening.

How do we define a branch line?

The 10 line closures dissected in greatest detail in Part Two of this book are primarily – but not exclusively – located in central, eastern and northern Scotland, reflecting my own personal experience and opinions. And some of these routes do stretch the traditional view of the length of a branch line – which prompted me to go back to basics: what is the definition of a branch line? *British Branch Lines*,[5] written in 1965 by that doyen of railway authors, H.A. Vallance, notes that there was a 'marked divergence of opinion as to what constituted a branch line' during a discussion following a lecture on economies in railway operation: 'Neither the lecturer nor any member of his audience was prepared to give a description that would fit all cases, and subsequent attempts to find an all-embracing answer to this question have proved equally unsuccessful.'

In *The Country Railway*,[6] David St John Thomas beautifully evokes the life and times of the typical British branch line, but he does not explicitly offer a definition. After perusing a number of dictionary listings, I concluded that the best came from www.lexico.com: 'A secondary railway line running from a main line to a terminus.'[7] But I would add reference to distance: 'A secondary railway line – *typically less than 20 miles in length* – running from a main line to a terminus.' Such a definition distinguishes it from a 'cross-country' line, which can be defined as a secondary railway linking two main lines; cross-country lines were usually also longer than branch lines.

Eight of the case studies in Part Two involve routes which were, at some stage of their history, cross-country lines – the justification for inclusion being my view that only a shorter, 'branch' element of the through railway merited reprieve in the Beeching era and / or re-opening today. *Scotland's Lost Branch Lines* sticks largely to what might be described as 'rural' or 'semi-rural' railways, so only some of the more significant closures within the 'Greater Glasgow' conurbation and Edinburgh are specifically identified (primarily in Part One).

Sources and acknowledgements

The key primary sources of rarely or never referenced material which have helped to inform this book's analysis of the Beeching era are the National Union of Railwaymen (NUR) archive at the Modern Records Centre of Warwick University, and British Railways' internal 'Brief[s] for Liaison Officer[s]' (produced prior to public hearings on proposed line closures) held at the National Records of Scotland, in Edinburgh. The NUR files have been crucial to a central thesis of the book – that BR chose (or was told) to ignore the scope for infrastructure and staffing economies as an alternative to closure – while the BR briefs reveal much of the 'mind-set' which drove the closure programme in the 1960s. The wider context for the story of Scotland's branch lines has been informed by a variety of histories of the country's railways and of individual branch lines. All of these are referenced in the notes section, and the principal sources are listed in the bibliography. Endnote numbers are used throughout the text, and the vast majority provide references for quotes, etc. However, in some cases the endnotes supply additional information on a topic, and the note number is accordingly italicised within the text.

I am particularly grateful to three friends and former 'industry insiders' – David Prescott, Rae Montgomery and John Yellowlees – for their insights and input. David began his career with British Rail only 11 years after Beeching had reported, and he found that many of the attitudes of that era were still prevalent. He had a long career in the rail industry – in operations, marketing and business management – culminating in senior management posts in the passenger sector. Subsequent work as a senior rail adviser to Transport Scotland allowed him to see the rail industry from the other side of the fence. David brought an acute perspective to aid my analysis of network contraction during and after Beeching, an attribute which has much helped me in our work together in rail consultancy over the last two decades.

Rae Montgomery worked for BR throughout the Beeching era and in the early 1960s held the post of Reshaping Assistant at the Divisional Manager's office in Inverness. He was directly involved in the closure process through compiling the Briefs for Liaison Officers for the Ballachulish and Crieff / Comrie branches (as well as other threatened routes) – not that he necessarily agreed with all the views therein! Rae is particularly well placed to judge the prevailing culture and management imperatives which helped to reshape the rail network. He also has an encyclopaedic knowledge of

Scotland's railways and a keen eye for writing style and spelling, much to my benefit.

John Yellowlees (latterly ScotRail's Honorary Rail Ambassador, or 'Mr Railway' in Scotland) worked for more than 25 years as a professional railwayman, and there is little which he does not know about the history and geography of our rail system. John's eagle eye sharply scrutinised the entire text and made important comments and corrections on both railway facts and my use of English.

My friend and fellow Birlinn author Andy Drummond brought a well-informed perspective to copy-reading late drafts of the book, making invaluable comments on content, structure and style. His meticulously researched and highly-recommended *A Quite Impossible Proposal*, the story of the ill-fated attempt to build a railway from Garve to Ullapool, was published in 2020.[8]

Andrew Boyd knows more about Scotland's railway history than almost anyone else, and he came to my aid on a number of aspects of this book's analysis, as well as supplying some vital documents from his personal archive, notably the BR Scottish Region 'Sectional Appendix' for 1960 and 'The Register of Scottish Signal Boxes'.

I am fortunate that Robert Drysdale was researching a planned book on the demise of Edinburgh's suburban railways at the same time as I was putting together *Scotland's Lost Branch Lines* – he unearthed a number of valuable references for my work from the National Archives, in London, and the National Records of Scotland, in Edinburgh.

My old friends David Fasken and Bill Jamieson played an important part, too, with David reviewing (and improving) the Buchan chapter, and Bill likewise the chapter on Peebles, the analysis of the steam-to-diesel changeover in the North East and all the map and photo captions. Thanks are also due to members of the Great North of Scotland Railway Association, and to railway author Sandy Mullay, for their assistance.

Any remaining mistakes or omissions are, of course, my own responsibility, and I will be pleased to be advised of these via my publisher, Birlinn.

I am grateful to a variety of contributors for the maps and photos, which beautifully illustrate this history of Scotland's branch lines. I have benefited from the considered craft of Alan Young's delightful hand-drawn maps, while the crucial photographic input – as well as my father's and my own collection – is largely the work of the late Sandy Murdoch (courtesy of Transport Treasury),[9] David Murray-Smith, the late WAC Smith (also courtesy of Transport Treasury) and Norman Turnbull.

Last, but not least, my thanks go to Birlinn, for whom this is my second book – in particular to Managing Director Hugh Andrew for our discussions on various book ideas, which finally settled on Scotland's branch lines, and to Editorial Manager Andrew Simmons for his invaluable guidance throughout the publication process.

Glossary and list of abbreviations

'The railway' is a parallel universe, with its own language. For example, in this book, the singular phrase 'the railway' is often used where readers might expect the plural version, 'the railways'. This is because people in the industry tradition-ally say: 'I work on the railway.' They regard it as one entity, even in the era of privatisation, with the industry fragmented into multiple different companies.

Where examples of jargon or abstruse technical terms are deployed in the text on single occasions, clarification is provided in the notes at the end of the book. For words or phrases used more frequently, brief explanations are provided here:

block post: the controlling point (traditionally at a signal box) of the start / end of a *block section* equipped with stop signals.

block section: the length of track between two *block post*s on which only one train is allowed in each direction – or in the case of single-track lines, to ensure that the line between *crossing loop*s can only be occupied by one train at any one time.

bogie: the structure underneath a railway vehicle to which axles (and, hence, wheels) are attached through bearings – as distinct from vehicles such as *railbus*es, which have rigidly mounted axles.[1]

chord: a short section of track connecting two separate rail routes, often creating the third side of a rail 'triangle'.

crossing loop: a short section of second track provided on a single-track rail-way (typically at stations) to allow two trains travelling in opposite directions to cross each other; in modern incarnations it can also be signalled to allow a faster train to overtake a slower one travelling in the same direction.

Diesel Multiple Unit (DMU): a *bogie*d multiple-unit (multiple-carriage) train powered by on-board diesel engines and requiring no separate locomotive as the engines are incorporated into one or more of the units (normally under the floor, between the *bogie*s); confusingly, a DMU formed of, for example, two units (carriages) is typically described as a 'two-car set'. Single-unit 'railcars' (see Chapter 8) are also categorised as DMUs, but, to add further confusion, the battery-powered two-car multiple unit deployed on the Deeside Line (see Chapter 12) was described as a railcar.

heavy rail: '. . . conventional railways forming part of the national network, including commuter, intercity, high-speed rail, rural and freight services, as distinct from metro, light rail and tram lines, people movers and similar.'[2]

long siding: often applied to a passenger branch line which has been rationalised down to a single-track 'basic railway' with no loops, sidings or pointwork on the branch itself (such as the current Drem–North Berwick line).

One Engine in Steam / One Train Working: method of control of a branch line whereby a physical token and signals at the junction permit only one train to be operational on the line at any one time – more flexible than a *long siding*, since points and goods sidings, etc., controlled by the train crew can be retained (as in the case of the St Combs branch prior to its 1960 conversion into a *long siding*, see Chapter 9).

permanent way: '. . . the elements of railway lines: the pairs of rails typically laid on the sleepers . . . embedded in ballast, intended to carry the ordinary trains of a railway. It is described as a permanent way because in the earlier days of railway construction, contractors often laid a temporary track to transport spoil and materials about the site; when this work was substantially completed, the temporary track was taken up and the permanent way installed.'[3]

railbus: a lightweight single-car diesel unit (with four wheels and two rigidly mounted axles), most often associated with those introduced by BR on branch lines in 1958. These had a single central door on each side of the unit, and seats for only 46–56 passengers. The different classes of railbus ranged from 105 to 150 horsepower (hp), and all were withdrawn from service by 1968.[4]

rolling stock: the wheeled vehicles of a railway, such as locomotives, passenger coaches and freight wagons. 'The word "stock" in the term is used in a sense of inventory. Rolling stock is considered to be a liquid asset, or close to it, since the value of the vehicle can be readily estimated and then shipped to the buyer without much cost or delay. The term contrasts with fixed stock (infrastructure), which is a collective term for the track, signals, stations, other buildings, electric wires, etc., necessary to operate a railway.'[5]

single-line token (or 'tablet'): the Electric Token Block system is based on the principle that 'every train passing through a single line section must carry a token, obtained from a token instrument, of which there is one at each end of each section. The instruments at each end of a section are electrically interlocked so that it is possible for only one token to be "out" (i.e., in use) for the section at one and the same time. The token may take the form of a circular tablet, a few inches in diameter, or a metal key about 6 inches long. It is placed in a leather pouch with a large loop handle to facilitate the handover from signaller to driver, and vice versa.'[6]

solum: the land on which a railway – now closed – was located, but with the track and signalling removed.

Telephone & Notice Board: a very low-cost form of signalling for freight-only lines, where stop signals were replaced by a notice board instructing the train driver to phone the designated (controlling) person – often a signalman at a signal box some miles away, but also possibly a shunter at a yard – who would authorise the move past the notice board.

Type 2 diesel: in 1957, with the shift away from steam traction, BR introduced a new 'Type' classification for diesels, based on the power of the locomotive. Type 2 locos (of which there were a number of models, built by different private manufacturers and BR itself) were those with engines of between 1,000 and 1,499hp – and they were the operational mainstay on those of the routes examined in Part Two of this book which did not convert to DMU operation. Other diesel locos were classified as Shunters or Types 1, 3, 4 or 5.[7]

Up / Down directions of travel: On most of the British railway network, 'Up' is the direction towards London, and 'Down' refers to the direction away from London.

List of abbreviations

BR	British Railways / British Rail
BRB	British Railways Board
BTC	British Transport Commission
DMU	Diesel Multiple Unit
ECML	East Coast Main Line
GNOSR	Great North of Scotland Railway
LNER	London & North Eastern Railway
LMS	London, Midland & Scottish Railway
MoT	Ministry of Transport
NUR	National Union of Railwaymen
SCDI	Scottish Council, Development and Industry
SDD	Scottish Development Department
SEPB	Scottish Economic Planning Board
SEPC	Scottish Economic Planning Council
SRDA	Scottish Railway Development Association
TUCC / TUCCS	Transport Users Consultative Committee / Transport Users Consultative Committee for Scotland
WCML	West Coast Main Line

PART ONE

The birth, life and death of Scotland's branch lines

1

Branch lines everywhere in the private sector era

Travelling by car today through the hilly terrain of north Fife, a visitor – and perhaps even a local – would be surprised to learn that trains ever traversed this thinly populated rural area. Few traces are now left of what was, in 1909, the final passenger railway to be opened in Scotland prior to the modern 'post-Beeching' era.

Like a number of the last rail routes to be built north of the border, the line from Glenburnie Junction (near Newburgh) to St Fort essentially went from nowhere to nowhere – although arguably the North British Railway may have seen potential for through traffic from Perth to St Andrews. But, unsurprisingly, given the sparsity of local population and lack of industry, its passenger service succumbed to road competition in 1951 (after a life of only 42 years) and freight in 1964. North Fife was never 'railway country'.

Such late line openings in the first decade of the 20th century – there were a handful, notably branches to Ballachulish, Dornoch, Fort Augustus and Mallaig, and the cross-country link from Dunfermline via Culross to Kincardine – were the tail-end of a Scottish railway-building era stretching back to the late 1820s and early 1830s, when, for example, the noteworthy Dundee & Newtyle, Edinburgh & Dalkeith and Garnkirk & Glasgow Railways were under construction.

The development of the main line system in Scotland, with its sparser population and often more difficult geography, lagged behind England. The Callander & Oban Railway, the Highland Main Line to Inverness, the Waverley Route from (Edinburgh and) Hawick to Carlisle, the West Highland Railway to Fort William, and links to Stranraer only opened between 1860 and 1900. But people everywhere – not just on main line corridors – had been 'clamouring to be connected to the railway',[1] and a significant number of branch lines had opened in Scotland by 1860, notably in the 1850s – many of them either spun off from the Glasgow–Aberdeen main line through Strathmore, or from the nascent Great North of Scotland Railway system radiating from Aberdeen. Among the country towns connected to the network were Aboyne, Alford, Callander, Crieff, Dunkeld (later to be the starting point of the Highland Main Line to Inverness), Jedburgh, Peebles and St Andrews. Typically, such branch lines were built by a local company formed for that purpose, with some, but not all, of the required finance provided by an established railway company which would eventually operate the line.[2]

The 1860s also saw a surge of rural construction, including the Buchan lines to Fraserburgh and Peterhead and a number of branches in the Borders. But each subsequent decade of the 19th century brought only modest additions – other than the West Highland Railway in 1894 – taking the network close to its final size. And the later the opening, generally the lesser were the financial prospects, as a succession of railway companies were to find, literally to their cost.

The impact of the railway

The railway created new mass markets and a changed national identity, with prompt deliveries of national newspapers (as well as the Royal Mail), the creation of 'standard Greenwich or "railway" time, and by no means least the electric telegraph, at first exclusively a railway appendage'.[3] The impacts were profound: 'In most [country] areas for at least two full generations all important comings and goings were by train. The price of coal nearly always fell by a third with the opening of the local line, and every new piece of agricultural machinery also came on the freight . . . The pair of rails disappearing over the horizon stood for progress, disaster, the major changes in life: the route to Covent Garden and Ypres, the way one's fiancé paid his first visit to one's parents, one's children returned for deathbed leavetaking, the way summer visitors, touring theatricals, cattle buyers, inspectors, came.'[4]

Tourism was opened up by the railway, and Murray's *Handbook* for Scotland (1894) – as quoted by John Thomas and David Turnock in Volume 15 of *A Regional History of the Railways of Great Britain* – illustrates the ways in which trains gave a stimulus to tourism and brought about a transformation of towns and villages across the country: 'Callander . . . boasted "numerous villas and lodgings for visitors; [besides] it has of late years become of importance as the nearest railway station to the Trossachs, Lochs Vennachar, Achray and Katrine and the most beautiful scenery in this part of Scotland, so that it is animated and bustling enough in summer" . . . It is with such literature and contemporary editions of *Bradshaw* that one can sense the feelings of adventure and romance which urged countless numbers of Victorian and Edwardian travellers to contemplate journeys which their ancestors a century before would never have dreamt of undertaking.'[5]

The railway also facilitated regional specialisation of the production of goods, as well as centralisation (see below), so that many entirely new freight flows were created, rather than the same goods – linking the same origins and destinations – simply shifting mode from canal, road or sea to rail. Railways were at the heart of profound changes in both the economy and society. Thomas and Turnock provide an overview of some specific freight impacts across the north of Scotland: 'Thanks to the railway taking fat animals to market and bringing in the store cattle and the fertilisers, the [Grampian] region became one great beef factory,' and 'the fishermen also gained immeasurably. A lot of fish continued to be cured in the traditional manner and sent overseas but there was a herring boom at Peterhead in 1884 when "the catch was so tremendous that all the continental markets were glutted". However, the railway gave the option of sending more of the catch away in the form of fresh or kippered herrings and the same trend became evident as railway services were provided at other places on the Moray Firth.'[6]

Thomas and Turnock also consider the impact on the industrial sector: 'With the reduction in transport costs there was much greater competition to supply markets which had previously offered situations of near-monopoly for local manufacturers . . . Yet manufacturers in towns with railway communication had great opportunity to market traditional products more widely and to diversify into other profitable branches.'[7]

The changed patterns of development following the arrival of the railway and its easier, faster journeys, created both winners and losers. Thomas and Turnock reflect that 'the railway tended to encourage centralisation on the regional centres and other towns which could now be reached by many more people taking day trips than had ever been the case before. The larger places developed their industries and service functions at the expense of the weaker centres as people found themselves able to leapfrog the nearest market in favour of the more distant places if the latter were more competitive. Without exception the main regional centres grew rapidly during the railway age.'[8]

The same authors contrast Aberfeldy's population decline from 1801 through 1861 and 1921 to 1981 – despite the arrival of a branch line from Ballinluig in 1865 – with the growth of nearby Pitlochry, where 'the [main line] railway transformed the village in the late nineteenth century', its population almost doubling between 1861 and 1981. Meanwhile, the population of Crieff – one of a number of 'market towns on the mountain edge' which benefited considerably from tourism – more than doubled between 1801 and 1921 (to 6,445), then fell to 5,737 in 1981,[9] perhaps in part due to the loss of its last passenger railway in 1964 (of which, more later). More prosaically, it has been claimed that the railway age also 'inspired the beginning of the age of affordable glasses for all': 'Travellers had to be able to read station clocks, the small print in Bradshaw's railway guides and the narrow columns of *The Times* bought from WH Smith on the concourse.'[10]

Difficult finances

The private enterprise 'mania' of 19th-century railway building – with railway companies, landowners and local enterprises pressing, for financial, prestige or wider economic reasons, to get seemingly every last settlement of significance (and many of no significance) on the railway map – created a network larger than was needed, even in the age of rail's virtual monopoly of overland transport.

Competition led to some small towns such as Bonnybridge, Bothwell, Kilbirnie and Montrose briefly benefiting from a choice of stations operated by two different companies, but these would eventually be seen as wasteful duplication where a town's two stations both fell under the control of a single large company – either the London & North Eastern Railway (LNER) or the London, Midland & Scottish Railway (LMS), which between them absorbed Scotland's five largest 'pre-Grouping' railway companies in 1923. However, the biggest challenge to an over-large network would come from the emergence of modern road transport.

Until the Light Railways Act of 1896 (see page 9), all new railways required an Act of Parliament to permit their construction, and the Board of Trade regulated safety standards. However, unlike the situation in a number of continental countries, the absence of a strategic 'guiding hand' from government to help plan the development of the network led to a financial fragility within the system, storing up problems which would become rudely apparent with the rise of the bus, car and lorry.

6

New railways could prove to be significantly more expensive to construct than had been anticipated – through, for example, hitting tougher rock than previously identified. A number of Scottish branch lines and secondary routes involved major structures which had both capital and maintenance implications; these included the Connel Ferry bridge on the Ballachulish branch, the Cullen and Spey viaducts on the Moray 'Coast Line', Eyemouth viaduct on the branch from Burnmouth, North Water viaduct on the Inverbervie branch, and Tongland viaduct on the Kirkcudbright branch.[11] All had closed completely by 1968.

St John Thomas points out that many local lines found themselves unable to generate sufficient revenues to cover maintenance and operating costs, let alone provision for depreciation and emergencies, plus the substantial sums needed to service capital: 'Promoters usually over-estimated country traffic potentials [sic], as they seem to have under-estimated many urban ones.'[12] Consequently, as reported by David N. Clough in *Dr Beeching's Remedy*, returns to investors declined, and the ratio of running costs to receipts rose from 48% in 1870 to 62% in 1900.[13] St John Thomas concludes that this trend 'was partly due to rising wages, partly to Government control on fares and freight rates, factors not anticipated when companies were building up their capital debt. The whole system, like much of British industry then, was over-capitalised, perhaps the price we had to pay for being first in the field . . . But sooner or later it became clear to officials and directors of too many lines that the task was hopeless. The railway might have brought prosperity to their valley, but not to them.'[14]

Of the four largest pre-Grouping companies which met at or near the Scottish border, two (the London & North Western and the North Eastern) saw a decline in dividend as a percentage of 'share par values (moving average)' between 1872 and 1910, albeit that the 1910 figures, 6.3% and 5.9% respectively, were towards the upper end of performance by larger companies at that time. The Scottish companies (Caledonian and North British) experienced an increase in dividends, but only to 3.2% in the former case and a miserable 0.6% in the latter.[15]

Clough argues that the North British (NB) offers an example of a company 'with a balance in favour of country, as opposed to town', whereas the North Eastern (NE) was the opposite, to the advantage of its finances. David Prescott takes a rather different view, arguing that 'more than anything the NE was an efficient operator in a large area where it had a monopoly'.[16] Since parts of the NB 'ought to have been profitable,' Clough says, 'it is fair to conclude that country branch lines were uneconomic even then [in 1910].'[17] Rae Montgomery suggests that the NB is a prime example of a company which built some railways – such as Galashiels to Peebles – to keep their competitors (in this case their arch rivals, the Caledonian) out of 'their territory' rather than to make money.[18]

The longer-term consequences of the NB situation would not, as we shall see, become apparent until some 20 years later under the aegis of the LNER, and even, arguably, as late as the Beeching era under British Railways' control. Clough does, however, consider the opportunity the pre-Grouping railway companies had to tackle the branch line problem in the early years of the 20th century. He concludes that as 'there was no national network of metalled roads until the 1920s and 1930s, so the railways offered the only realistic form of communication. Government reaction to the problem, as expressed in the 1900s, was rationalisation by amalgamation. In other words, paper over the cracks and pretend the problem did not exist.'[19]

Wolmar advances two other reasons for the small number of early closures: 1) 'no legislative provision had been made to allow for their closure, so there was no legal way to close a railway', and 2) the longstanding difficulty of assessing the allocation of costs and revenue that would determine the profitability of (or losses from) operating and maintaining a branch line, a problem that would still be hotly debated in the Beeching era:

> . . . the kernel of the problem was to determine what proportion of that revenue would be permanently lost, as many people using a branch line travel on it at the start or end of a far longer journey. As regards maintenance too, determining the precise cost of keeping a small section of track in good fettle is more art than science, given how difficult it is to identify the costs attributed, for example, to a gang of trackworkers who spend only part of their time on the branch. Since most branch lines soon became incorporated into a large company's portfolio, such minutiae were of little concern. Was it worth antagonizing a local community, or possibly breaking the law, to save a few bob when it was impossible to know how much revenue the branch contributed to the main line network?[20]

Typically, a significant proportion of that branch revenue would come from freight traffic, whose handling had a major impact on the layout of country stations, as portrayed by St John Thomas:

There might be between four and ten tracks for public goods and coal, and except at the smallest stations a headshunt[21] to allow shunting to take place independently of the main running line. Additional sidings might serve the warehouse of grain or fodder merchants . . . a gas works, a council engineering depot, a milk depot, mill or brewery. Probably a quarter to a third of country stations, probably over half of the terminal ones, served some industry that may have preceded the railway's arrival or soon followed it. Not that the railway always spelt expansion, for some mills and breweries proved unable to withstand the competition from elsewhere. By the end of Victoria's reign there were thousands of mouldering factories and warehouses beside country stations – killed by the railway itself.[22]

A late development – which might have been more effective if it had been applied to new rural railways decades earlier – was the arrival of 'Light Railways' built to connect small towns and villages still isolated from the network. While exempting these new railways from the onerous requirement to secure an Act of Parliament, the Light Railways Act of 1896 did not actually define the nature of a light railway, but rather pressed a duty on the Light Railway Commissioners to 'carry this Act into effect, and to offer, so far as they are able, every facility for considering and maturing proposals to construct light railways'.[23]

The Act allowed companies to cut out much of the 'red tape' – as well as the expensive legislation – and facilitated cheaper construction and operation based on lower locomotive axleloads and train speeds (typically a maximum of 25mph), thereby requiring only modest earthworks, bridges and stations, with lightly-laid track spiked directly onto sleepers (i.e., without the usual metal 'chairs' to hold the rails in place). The Act also enabled avoidance of fencing and level crossing gates, minimal signalling, and, on shorter branches, the operation of 'One Engine in Steam' (i.e., with only one locomotive being allowed to work on the line at any given time).

In Scotland, the Act – sometimes aided by Treasury grant – led to the construction of 11 passenger branch lines over the following decade, including Elvanfoot–Wanlockhead, Fountainhall–Lauder, Fraserburgh–St Combs, Ormiston–Gifford, Strathord–Bankfoot, The Mound–Dornoch, Wick–Lybster and a unique narrow-gauge outlier from Campbeltown to Machrihanish. Many other proposed schemes never materialised, including the Cromarty & Dingwall Light Railway, where, by late 1916, earthworks had been completed over 12 miles, and rails laid along the first four miles from Cromarty (with a locomotive and works train operating over the line). Early 1917 saw an abrupt halt to construction when the permanent way material was commandeered and removed by the Ministry of Munitions for use in France.[24]

The relative failure of Light Railways – all the Scottish examples had closed by 1965 – can be ascribed not only to their appearing on the scene so late, serving very modest local populations, but also crucially to their arrival coinciding with the first appearance of cars and buses on Scottish roads. And, in some cases, established railway companies 'tended to revert to type by constructing them to conventional high standards'.[25] Conversely, might it not have been more useful if Light Railway legislation had been applicable to 'retro-fitting' *existing* (pre-1896) rural railways, allowing their costs to be sensibly trimmed, albeit in many cases only delaying the inevitable?

War intervenes – and 'the Grouping' follows

> The First World War and its demands were to transform the economy of Britain from one in which free-market competition was paramount to one that was closely regulated by the government. At its start the government commandeered the railway system. For over forty years the state had had powers to control the railways in time of war: they were put into effect on 4 August 1914.[26]

Thus does P.J.G. Ransom describe the beginning of the railway's massive war effort over the subsequent four years. Much of that effort – moving men, equipment and munitions – would focus on long-distance routes such as the Highland Main Line and Far North Line *en route* to the naval base at Scapa Flow in Orkney. But a more widespread impact was the loss of thousands of key staff to the military, with the government strangely having failed to decree that railways would be a 'reserved' occupation (as they would, however, be designated in the Second World War).

Passenger train services were thinned out in order to concentrate railway resources on freight and military personnel trains (such as the 'Jellicoe Expresses' from London to Thurso) which were contributing directly to the war effort. But line closures were few and far between in Scotland, a noteworthy exception being the Highland Railway branch from Keith to Buckie and Portessie, which was a duplicate route penetrating into Great North of

Scotland territory. The track was lifted as early as 1915 to help the war effort, and, although subsequently re-laid, the line was never officially re-opened.[27]

The unified railway proved its capabilities during the war, and it seemed unlikely that the system would revert to its former structure of nearly 200 separate companies. Also, as Ransom records, 'at the end of the First World War, railways were physically in a bad state'.[28] Various schemes were proposed for amalgamation on a large scale – short of nationalisation – and there was an early intention to set up a separate railway company for Scotland. However, this was opposed in Scotland because of concerns that the new national standard wage rate would raise the costs of a Scottish company disproportionately. If costs were to be raised to English levels, then the support of English traffic receipts would be needed through a financial link with the railways south of the border.[29]

In due course, the 1921 Railways Act provided for the Grouping of all Britain's railways into four companies, the largest of these being the LMS, incorporating the Highland, Caledonian and Glasgow & South Western within Scotland – with the North British and Great North of Scotland going to the LNER. At the time, in terms of paid-up capital, the LMS was the largest railway company in the world. The railways passed into the ownership of the 'Big Four' (LMS and LNER, plus the Great Western and Southern) in 1923. David St John Thomas relates a delightful story from the opposite end of the spectrum:

> While Victoria was still on the throne most locally-created lines sold out for between 40 and 60 per cent of their cost, and few were left to be amalgamated when all regular railways were compulsorily grouped into the Big Four in 1923. One such survival . . . was Killin's little village line, its sole purpose being to connect the lochside settlement with the Oban branch. It refused point-blank the first offer of £1 of LMSR stock for each £100 of its own; the secretary at first did not understand how the newly-formed LMSR came into the picture anyway, though he went on to negotiate and eventually obtained £8 per £100. When sending a copy of the accounts in handwriting he apologised: 'I am without a typist' but the Killin line never afforded anything as expensive as a typewriter.[30]

While the 16 pre-Second World War years of the LMS and LNER are often portrayed as a golden age of rail travel, exemplified by record-breaking

11

streamlined expresses on the West and East Coast Main Lines linking London with Glasgow and Edinburgh, the reality was far more mundane for the vast majority of services. The failure of the Government to adequately compensate the railways for their war effort put the Big Four at a disadvantage: 'They had to start rebuilding their railways, and could do so only slowly thanks to the lack of cash, rather than devoting all their energies to preparing the railways for the threat they faced from lorries and cars. That legacy of underinvestment was to hold them back for the next two decades until they faced a second world war that was to prove even more damaging.'[31]

Few branch line passengers would be contemplating such strategic financial considerations, but their fares were part of the lifeblood of railway operations. So, to use a modern term, who were 'the customers' and why were they travelling? 'Passengers represented the full cross-section of the community in a way not shared by expresses, which until after the 1939–45 war catered mainly for the select going on long journeys. Some used the country train as the first and last stage of a longer journey and came with conventional railway luggage – case upon case stowed in the van, hatbox and picnic hamper in the compartment. Most were on local journeys, about their everyday business; some never travelled on any train but that running through their own valley. Few would visit even half the places in the pictures hung under the luggage racks, even though all these were of places served by the same railway.'[32]

Branch lines also attracted tourists and day-trippers, with special excursion trains running to the most popular districts on holiday weekends. St John Thomas writes: 'Excursion trains arriving at small towns tended to have the same effect as modern cruise liners' calls at "unspoilt" Pacific islands, but every country station received a modest quota of discerning hikers and sightseers.'[33]

There was also a strong emotional attachment to the country station, perhaps best exemplified by John Betjeman's paeans of praise to the rural railway during the golden age of wireless broadcasting. Betjeman's descriptions were quintessentially English scenes, although he made the occasional foray to Scotland, and the atmosphere he conjures up could equally have applied to countless stations north of the border: 'one of the deeper pleasures of a country railway station [is] its silence, broken only by the crunching of a porter's feet on the gravel, the soft country accent of the stationmaster and the crash bang of a milk can somewhere at the back of the platform . . . if you want to see and feel the country, travel by train.'[34]

Unexpected connections – rural railways and the spirit of inquiry

In 2001, the Scottish author and journalist Kenneth Roy first wrote of something remarkable which happened at the railway backwater of Inveramsay (the junction for the Macduff branch) more than 70 years earlier.[35] This had been related from personal experience by the radical educationalist R.F. Mackenzie (whose father was stationmaster at Wartle, one stop along the branch from Inveramsay) in his seminal last book, *A Search for Scotland*.[36]

> If you were lucky, or unlucky, depending on your point of view, you would buy your ticket at Inveramsay from a singular man known as the railway clerk before being waved off in the general direction of Wartle. And if you were very lucky, or very unlucky, depending on your point of view, the train would be badly delayed and the railway clerk would usher you into a roughly assembled shack known locally as Utopia.

> I will describe Utopia. It consisted of two rooms. One half of it was partitioned off for sleeping. In the other half, there were two chairs, a table, a paraffin lamp, a paraffin stove, and scores of books gathered into shelves to form an informal library or study. It was, as Utopias go, rather Spartan.

> While passengers waited for trains, they became subject to inquiry; and the more important or self-important they were, the more challenging the inquiry tended to be . . . The ideas of people like Wells and Shaw, Bertrand Russell and John Stuart Mill, were discussed, dissected and disputed. Scripture was extensively quoted and examined. All this, when all the travelling public had paid for was a cheap day return to Macduff.

> Sometimes, after the last train of the day had gone, the railway clerk and his young friends would settle down in Utopia, light the lamp and talk long into the night about everything in heaven and earth; and the only sound, apart from the sound of their intense conversation, was the occasional glug glug of the stove.

Reflecting on that lost world of the spirit of independent inquiry and what is sometimes called 'the democratic intellect', Roy – who memorably and movingly described the approach of his death in *In Case of Any News: A*

Diary of Living and Dying – uses rural railways as a metaphor to explore the very point of our existence: 'Branch lines matter. They have all gone as physical artefacts – grassed over and eroded by rain and gravity as completely as any Roman road or earthworks. But they can still exist in our imagination. The main line proceeds at speed to a predictable and deadly terminus. On a mainline, the light at the end of the tunnel is that of the incoming train. Choose instead the gentle and meandering branch line of unorthodox thought and feeling.'[37]

Roy never found out the name of the railway clerk, but after the former's untimely death in 2018, his friend and colleague Barbara Millar discovered that he was Alan Gray Law, born in 1907 in rural Aberdeenshire. He was employed on the railway only from 1927 to 1930, then moved to London and ultimately worked in civil engineering across the world. Law died in 1979 – and never told his children about Utopia.

By a strange coincidence, my middle name is Law and my brother's is Gray – and our great-grandfather James Cruickshank Law (who died in 1952, three days after my birth) lived and worked in Banffshire only 30 miles from Inveramsay.[38]

Early competition – and closures

Railways – with their guided tracks of steel rail on a segregated and signalled right-of-way – are inherently expensive to build, maintain and operate. Light Railways helped to reduce costs, but they had come late and generally served corridors with very limited revenue potential – both passenger and freight – even in an era of only modest competition from road transport.

The first motor car to reach Scotland arrived at Leith Docks in 1895, and then an 1896 Act of Parliament permitted cars to travel faster than walking pace – and without being preceded by a man with a red flag.[39] Freed of these restrictions, car ownership multiplied quickly in the early years of the 20th century. In *The Motor Car and Politics*,[40] William Plowden records that when the first national registration figures were collected, in 1904, there were 8,500 cars in use in Britain. By the end of 1914 there were nearly 140,000 cars on British roads, and in 1925 – now that cars were being mass-produced for the middle classes, as opposed to only the wealthy – the figure reached a peak of 580,000, followed by some decline until 1932 due to the economic slump.

The more affluent who first acquired cars were a significant loss to the railways, having been key customers in terms of lucrative First Class ticket sales – but the big volume threat came from the bus (and the tram, within urban areas), not the car. Technological development, rising incomes and one-off events – like the return of surplus road vehicles and drivers from the First World War, and the 1926 General Strike, which shut down the railways for nine days – all played a part in the rise of this massive challenge to the hegemony of the railway as a passenger and freight carrier.

Prior to the Grouping, a Light Railways (Investigation) Committee had reported – in 1921 – to the Minister of Transport on the potential for bus–train transport integration, a perennial topic of unresolved policy discussion to this day. The report:

> . . . aimed 'at a solution of the problem by way of co-operation and co-ordination rather than of competition, between light railway enterprise and road-motor transport respectively.' This and most of the other sound advice was of course ignored. Britain indeed wasted every opportunity to develop basic, integrated country transport services at economic prices . . . Rarely was thought given to exploiting the advantages of both train and bus for different parts of a through journey . . . Inevitably, buses running from village centres to market squares at cheaper fares would cream off the best local traffic, leaving the railways to provide connection for long-distance passengers and to carry specific categories of people, such as mothers with prams – perambulators in railway parlance – and schoolchildren; the railways always had cheaper season-ticket rates.[41]

P.J.G. Ransom notes in *Iron Road* that 'motor bus services expanded greatly [in Scotland] during the 1920s. For short journeys, urban and rural alike, they offered flexibility and convenience that the railway could not match.'[42] The impact of new bus services on the railway was compounded by the world-wide economic repercussions of the Wall Street Crash of 1929, resulting in the LNER – financially the weakest of the Big Four – suffering a 50% reduction in income between 1929 and 1932.[43]

Prior to the Grouping there had been only just over a dozen passenger closures in Scotland (the majority being short branch lines), and 1930 was the first year in which more than a handful of closures was implemented – indeed, it was the fourth worst year for the number of passenger line closures in the country's entire railway history. A dozen routes lost their passenger trains that year, almost all of them in the industrial Central Belt, where bus competition was most intense: 'Falkirk had been a traffic centre in the canal age and the railway age. In the bus age it became the headquarters of Scotland's most enterprising road operator with sad results for the railway network of the Forth–Clyde Valley . . . [whose people] flocked to the new buses in thousands.'[44]

A startling nearby example of the collapse of rail traffic is at Clackmannan & Kennet station, which had booked an average close to 20,000 passengers in each half year in the early to mid 1920s, but bookings fell to only 1,092 passengers in the half year to December 1928.[45]

Bonnybridge (the last substantial settlement in the Forth–Clyde Valley to be reached by rail, in 1886) was perhaps the most unusual casualty of decline, losing two of its *three* stations in the 1930s. To some extent the closures came in company-specific swathes: in 1931 the cuts were largely LMS, while from 1932 to 1934 closure overwhelmingly befell LNER services. Across that decade, rural Scotland saw some 20 line closures to passengers: these were the delayed casualties of the financial weakness evident back in 1910. (A year-by-year list of passenger line closures from the Grouping to the present day can be found in the Appendix.)

Some of the nonsensical duplications resulting from inter-company competition in the 19th century were addressed fairly soon after the Grouping, including the closure by the LMS of former Caledonian routes in Ayrshire to Kilbirnie and Irvine in 1930, and to Kilwinning in 1932 – leaving the more logical ex-Glasgow & South Western routes to serve these settlements. More drastically, both the ex-Caledonian and ex-NB branches to industrial Morningside (Lanarkshire) lost their passenger trains in 1930.

If inter-company rivalry between the Highland and the NB had not intervened to block the progress of the railway any further up the Great Glen than Fort Augustus – leaving the expensively constructed branch from Spean Bridge (on the West Highland Line) with the most modest of traffic potential – then the former NB Fort Augustus station might well have survived beyond its 1933 closure to passenger services (freight in 1946) into the modern era, as the half-way point on a trunk line from Fort William to Inverness. Fort Augustus to Inverness was undoubtedly the biggest gap in the Scottish railway network at its zenith.

By the late 1930s, not helped by the downturn of the railways' core freight traffic during the Depression of 1929 to 1933, the financial position of the Big Four had deteriorated to the point where only the Great Western was paying a dividend. In 1938 the four companies jointly launched their 'Square Deal' campaign, seeking to be allowed to fix their own freight rates and services, instead of being subject to government regulation, including the 'common carrier' requirement, which obliged them to accept any freight traffic, unlike their road haulage rivals. They argued that the railways faced bankruptcy if they were not given the same commercial freedom. Whereas before the First World War there had been fewer than 100,000 vehicles on British roads, there were now 1.8 million cars and nearly half a million lorries. The road haulage industry, with all the wit of a Jeremy Clarkson, countered with the slogan "Give the railways a square wheel".'[46]

The arguments over railway finances, however, would have to be postponed in the face of the national emergency imposed on the rail system by another war.

Another war effort – and nationalisation beckons

The five and a half years of the Second World War – with the rail system, once again, as in the First World War, required to play a massive logistical role in the war effort – brought major traffic flows of men, equipment and munitions to key long-distance routes such as the Highland Main Line and the Far North Line. But branch lines also played a part, with armoured trains equipped with guns operating over a variety of routes along the east coast from 1940, their key roles being 'patrolling of coast rail-lines to locate enemy detachments and gain information; reinforcing threatened points with fire-power; dealing with tank attacks; and acting as an armoured roadblock or pillbox'.[47] The principal patrol routes included the branches to Fraserburgh and Peterhead, Inverbervie, Leuchars–St Andrews–Crail–Leven–Thornton and North Berwick.

The war effort also involved the construction of two new rural branch lines. The Faslane Military Railway was opened in 1941 to serve 'Military Port 1' (on the Gare Loch), providing alternative berthing and loading facilities in the event of Glasgow Docks being severely bombed. The 2½-mile branch line diverged north-westwards from the LNER's single-track West Highland Line north of Helensburgh, and, unusually for a British railway, right-hand running was operated over the double-track section of the branch, allowing military personnel to familiarise themselves with conditions likely to be encountered while serving in mainland Europe. An eminent passenger on the first train to use the platform for troop trains at the western end of

Faslane was Prime Minister Winston Churchill, at the start of a transatlantic voyage in 1943.[48] A similar railway (almost seven miles long) was built from Stranraer to Cairnryan – 'Military Port 2' – to cater for the eventuality of Liverpool Docks being badly damaged by enemy attacks.[49]

The passenger branch closure trend was partly interrupted by the war, with a few exceptions in the shape of generally short lines to small towns with no significant war role. Dalkeith was a notable loss in terms of size, as the county town of Midlothian, but it enjoyed frequent bus services to Edinburgh and ready access to the nearby Eskbank & Dalkeith station on the Waverley Route, thereby tempering the impact of closure. Of 16 Scottish route withdrawals[50] between 1939 and 1947, no fewer than 13 were in LMS territory.

Britain's railways came out of the war in a similarly exhausted state to that which they had experienced in 1919. After the hostilities ended in 1945, rail recovery was generally slow. However, the railways had again demonstrated the benefits of unified control and, following the landslide Labour victory in the 1945 General Election, it came as no surprise when the British rail system was fully nationalised. Ironically, the private railway companies got a better deal from a Labour government than their predecessors did from a Conservative government prior to the Grouping. The railway assets may have been in the poorest condition, but 'that did not stop the railway companies receiving over-generous compensation terms, a result of timid government and powerful lobbying from the companies and their City friends . . . The shareholders were given £900m (a remarkable £22.5bn in today's money) in government stock which guaranteed 3 per cent nationally . . . British Railways was burdened with annual interest payments of £27m (£675m today) to reward these stockholders, a handicap that was to hamper its ability to invest in the railways.'[51]

Looking back at 120 years of private-sector branch line operation

The first conventional railways in Scotland, with locomotive-hauled trains conveying passengers and freight, opened in the early 1830s. Today we would recognise initially isolated operations such as the Dundee & Newtyle, Edinburgh & Dalkeith and Garnkirk & Glasgow Railways as forerunners of the traditional branch line. The rail network then developed – sometimes in surges, at other times gradually – over the following seven decades, with inter-city lines linking all Scotland's regions and cross-border to England,

and scores of branch lines and cross-country routes providing the infill, ensuring that every settlement of significance would enjoy the benefits of this revolutionary form of transport.

No region of the country failed to attract branch line construction. Having said that, the Highland Railway, with only a handful of branches, was characterised by W.M. Acworth[52] as 'all mainline', its network of long straggling routes in many cases following the only geographically feasible corridor. In contrast, its neighbour to the east, the Great North of Scotland Railway – serving fertile, generally lowland terrain, with dispersed agricultural settlements and small market centres – earned the soubriquet 'all branch line'.

The presence of agriculture (or fisheries), industry, mining – and people – were the key stimuli to railway construction. In the Central Belt, Ayrshire and Fife, all four factors came strongly into play – and dense networks of main lines, secondary routes and branches resulted. But branch lines also flourished in the rich agricultural counties of Angus, the Borders, the North East and Perthshire.

The zenith of the network was short-lived: only 21 years between the 1909 opening of the Glenburnie Junction–St Fort line and 1930, the first year to witness a swathe of closures across Scotland. But branch lines were still playing a very significant part in Scottish economic and social life in the first few years after the Second World War, more than a century after the first arrivals – even if the direct financial benefits of many of them to the railway companies were by now dubious.

The early line closures – 48 between 1930 and 1947 – reflected a need to improve railway finances in the face of traffic lost to the roads. Branch line passenger services disappeared from all regions of Scotland, but the largest concentration of closures was in the Central Belt, where early bus competition was particularly fierce. The railway's varying responses to the challenge of the bus, car and lorry were to be a key feature of the nationalised era in Scotland.

2

Blowing hot and cold – the public sector era before the Beeching Report

At nationalisation in 1948, Scotland had a rail network of 3,625 route miles, including dozens of branch lines which still allowed trains to penetrate well beyond principal and secondary main lines to almost every mainland town of significance. However, political attitudes to the rail system were often negative. In their meticulously researched *Holding the Line: How Britain's Railways Were Saved*, retired senior railway managers Richard Faulkner and Chris Austin quote the Chancellor of the Exchequer, Hugh Dalton, addressing the House of Commons on 17 December 1946: 'This rail system of ours is a very poor bag of physical assets. The permanent way is badly worn. The rolling stock is in a state of great dilapidation. The railways are a disgrace to the country.'[1]

Although this may have been simply a frank critique of a situation delivered by the private sector (in large part reflecting a massive war effort on behalf of the country), underpinned by a determination to nationalise the railways to address the problem, Faulkner and Austin have a different take: 'This perception of a run-down and declining industry epitomised the views of the post-war Labour Government and those that followed. It led to the opinion that closure was a preferable outcome for much of the network rather than renewing the assets worn out over the previous six years, in which the railways had been an essential part of the defence of Britain.'

The British Transport Commission (BTC) was created by the post-war Labour government as part of its nationalisation programme, to oversee railways, canals and road freight transport in Great Britain. The brave new British Railways was owned by the BTC and managed by the Railway Executive. The radical change in ownership occurred on 1 January 1948, with a degree of devolved administrative control enshrined through the creation of six geographical regions, partly based on the territories of the old companies. Political pressures north of the border ensured that Scotland, however, became a separate region – Scottish Region – with its own Chief Regional Officer (CRO) and supporting headquarters structure based in Glasgow. The first CRO was Thomas Cameron, a career railwayman who, nevertheless, as noted by A.J. Mullay, had a 'curious insistence on retaining a flat in Edinburgh's [railway-owned] North British Hotel and commuting over daily by car to Glasgow'. Meantime the BTC had a totemic Scottish representative: 'Old Etonian Sir Ian Bolton, a Glasgow accountant with, needless to say, no operational railway experience. One area of expertise in which he excelled was in company liquidation, a point to remember as the Region's history unfolds [not least in the context of realising the value of redundant assets following line closures].'[2]

The new Railway Executive made a fundamental error in failing to recognise – despite the long-felt views of its member for mechanical and electrical engineering, Robert Riddles[3] – that the future lay not with steam traction, but with electrification for main lines and dieselisation for cross-country routes and branch lines, 'partly because its members felt that the continuous availability of coal was assured, whereas the steady supply of oil was, at the time, doubtful and had to be paid for by expensive dollars'.[4] But steam was labour-intensive, requiring large numbers of men to fuel, water, clean, maintain and operate the locos. By contrast, diesels required significantly less time and labour, with a much greater mileage range between refuelling.

As far back as the 1930s, the Great Western Railway (GWR) had introduced single-unit diesel 'railcars' with underfloor engines, and these would survive in regular use into the 1960s. They offered obvious branch line advantages: quick turn-rounds (a driving cab at each end of the train avoided the locomotive run-round), one man less in the train crew (there was no coal to shovel) and – being much lighter than locomotives – less wear and tear on the track. In the early 1950s, when thousands of similar trains were being introduced around the world, BR remained reluctant to follow suit, but 'there was really little excuse for the excruciatingly slow progress made in Britain where modern rail traction was concerned'.[5]

Another GWR innovation – which came much later to other parts of the rail system – had been the pioneering introduction in the 1900s of 'halts', which were typically unstaffed, simple stopping-points between orthodox stations, initially without platforms, with tickets bought on the train. The GWR system alone had several hundred halts in 1939, with examples on all but 27 of its 150-odd branches. Yet as late as 1960 the largest BR region, the London Midland, opposed having any unstaffed halts: 'where trains called at all, they had to be met by at least a porter'.[6]

Despite deep-seated underlying financial difficulties in a transport mode that was both labour and capital-intensive – in the face of rapidly growing competition from more flexible, and invariably cheaper, road transport – there were only a handful of rail closures in Scotland in the period between the end of the war and 1948. Among the most noteworthy were the withdrawal in 1946 of passenger services to Strathpeffer (an LMS branch which should have been on the through route to Kyle, but was not, due to 19th-century landowner resistance), and the complete closure in 1948, post-nationalisation, of the Ellon–Boddam branch (which should previously have been extended the three miles to Peterhead, creating a much more direct route from the latter to Aberdeen than that via Maud Junction).

There were no fewer than 36 withdrawals of passenger services in Scotland during the first five years of BR, 1948–52. In 1949 the new Railway Executive established a Branch Lines Committee, with its remit requiring 'an investigation of every branch line whose earning capacity may be in question'. During the four years up to June 1953, the committee considered 200 cases and recommended complete closure of some 500 route miles[7] – but not all of these were implemented, in part due to the intervention of the Transport Users Consultative Committees (TUCCs), which ran the appeal process for objectors to closure (see below).

Possibly hastened by the end of petrol rationing in 1950, the period from then to 1952 produced a host of cuts in Scotland. While swingeing Scottish closures are usually associated with the 'peak Beeching' years of 1964 and 1965, it was 1951 which saw the largest number of route service withdrawals (18) in a single year in Scotland's railway history. The county towns of Berwickshire (Duns) and Selkirkshire (Selkirk) both lost their passenger train services. The axe was wielded much less brutally in 1952 – the opportunities were diminishing – but, in a cruel blow, the town of Brechin lost both of its remaining passenger services, to Forfar and Montrose.

The role of the TUCCs

It is not widely known that TUCCs had been playing a role, albeit generally less visible than it would be post-1962, since the late 1940s. The 1947 Transport Act, which created BR, had set up the Central Transport

23

Consultative Committee (CTCC) and a network of regional TUCCs (including one for Scotland) as passenger representative bodies.

The TUCC for Scotland (TUCCS) held its inaugural meeting in September 1949. Much of the committee's work involved consideration of proposed closure of lines and stations and de-staffing of the latter – not only passenger, but also freight, as BR remained (until 1962) subject to a legal 'common carrier' requirement, which obliged it to carry any goods presented for transportation. The detailed nature of much of the workload is illustrated by the minutes of the 1 September 1961 meeting at the North British Hotel in Edinburgh.[8] No fewer than 18 cases of closure / destaffing were cited – either implementation dates for proposals previously approved by the committee or new proposals for consideration. The minutiae extended to the case of 'Inchture Station – Proposed Conversion to Unstaffed Public Siding (Summer Months)'.

Much of the work may have been prosaic, but what of the calibre and status of the committee tasked with this detailed consideration of the practical consequences of declining passenger and freight traffic across the network? Of the 17 members present there were two MBEs, two OBEs and a CBE – and an absent member had recently received a CBE. Was such an august body really needed to determine whether Inchture Public Siding should be de-staffed in the summer months?

On the more serious issue of determining the fate of passenger services, the system could be seen – in hindsight – as favouring the establishment: 'the TUCC system placed no particular emphasis on Scottish or Welsh rail closure proposals, where geographical isolation, and lack of alternative road services, might have been factors worthy of greater consideration . . . Another problem relating to the TUCC's remit was that they had no powers to recommend alternatives to closure; for example, they could not suggest allowing to run at a more manageable loss if it served a public need, nor could they make any suggestions for more economical operation.'[9]

In 1952, however, the BTC was becoming exercised over pressure from TUCCs to demonstrate the *actual* savings achieved by branch line passenger service withdrawals. In February of that year it wrote to the Railway Executive advising that 'the present shortened procedure for estimating economies' (which had been introduced in 1950) should continue, and – pointedly – that 'no undertaking should be given to Consultative Committees that, in future years after a closing, a special investigation will be made at the time of their enquiry to ascertain realised economies'.[10]

At its June 1952 meeting the Branch Lines Committee (BLC) approved a response to the BTC in which it advised that an 'estimated net annual economy' of £276,385 had been realised from closures in 1948–50, and that there were still over 100 branches across Britain to be considered, from whose closure the estimated economy was 'not less than £675,000'. Included in the list of those 'still under consideration' were 16 Scottish branches, of which four – Aberdeen–Ballater, Alloa–Kinross, Fraserburgh–St Combs and Maud–Peterhead – would survive for more than a decade. Together with another 11 Scottish branches, the Connel Ferry–Ballachulish line had been spared, since 'after investigation, there is no case at present for closing'. So, it was not all one-way traffic – but an underlying intent was evident in the BLC minutes: 'if necessary the question of carrying the [closures] policy further may be considered by the Commission'.[11]

Out of 919 line and station closures proposed across Britain by the BTC up to 1960, only 25 were rejected by the TUCCs.[12] One of these was the Gleneagles–Crieff / Comrie line in 1955, which is explored in some detail in Chapter 8, and another the same year would have involved withdrawal of passenger services from the Boat of Garten to Ballindalloch section of the Speyside Line to Craigellachie. The BTC – having been rebuffed on closure of the latter – changed tack, introducing 'railbuses' to replace steam in 1958 and opening four new low-cost halts in 1959. A similar approach was adopted in the case of the Crieff / Comrie line. The late 1950s would prove to be a brief period when accusations against BR / BTC of branch line rundown were difficult to sustain.

The make-up of the 1955 TUCCS makes for interesting reading: of 24 members only two were women, 'appointed by Minister of Transport'. Other than the chairman, Sir John Maxwell Erskine, CBE, DL, JP – a banker and businessman (and also a member of the North of Scotland Hydro-Electric Board) – the 21 members appointed within Scotland were variously 'representing Agriculture', 'Commerce and Industry', 'Shipping', 'Labour' (TGWU and NUR), 'Local Authorities' and 'British Transport Commission'. The latter was represented by four individuals, including Sir Ian Bolton (member of the BTC), James Ness (General Manager of BR Scottish Region) and two representatives from the road sector – since this remained part of the TUCC remit until 1962 – namely, the Scottish Divisional Manager of British Road Services (the state-owned road haulage company) and Mr James Amos, the Chairman of Scottish Omnibuses Ltd. Was it appropriate for BR to be on both sides of the fence? And where was the fairness in having Amos as a member, when the bus operator would be certain to benefit from passenger station closures? As we shall see in the case of the Peebles line, he made no effort to disguise his enthusiasm for withdrawal of rail services.

Concerns about rural bus services were a major element of the TUCCS annual report in 1957. A member of the committee representing agriculture had raised the issue of reduction of services 'and, in particular, those services which had been augmented to permit of the withdrawal of branch line train services'.[13] Scottish Omnibuses had undertaken 'a very full examination' of curtailments since the beginning of 1957 and found that 'only two services connected with the withdrawal of branch line trains were affected and that forty-two other rural services had been curtailed'. The financial problems of the bus industry evidently extended well beyond rural areas, as the annual report records: 'At the present time 45.59 per cent of the services operated by Scottish Omnibuses are unremunerative and the average loss per mile is 5½d. to 6d., giving an annual loss of approximately £450,000 [over £10 million in today's prices].' Buses to replace trains would, in due course, become a central concern of the TUCCs – which were to be, superficially, key players in the ultimate fate of threatened branch lines in the Beeching era.

Why Penicuik?

While many of the early 1950s' closures could be characterised as 'deep rural', one exception was the 4½-mile branch from Hawthornden Junction, just south of Rosewell & Hawthornden station on the Peebles line, to the town of Penicuik (then population 6,500), as shown in the map on page 104.[14] Known for its paper mills established along the River North Esk during the 18th century – and by 1959 no less than 80% of the town's employable population worked in the mills[15] – it developed as a residential centre for professional people working in Edinburgh following the opening of the railway in 1872.[16]

However, as early as the 1930s the Scottish Motor Traction Company (SMT) established an extensive bus network radiating from Edinburgh, with an at-least hourly service from Penicuik to the capital, supplemented by the regular bus service from Peebles to Edinburgh, which passed through Penicuik (unlike the Peebles train, which came no closer than Pomathorn station, half a mile up a steep hill to the south of the town). As Jeff Hurst notes in *The Glencorse Branch*, as well as this attractive frequency the bus had

26

the decided advantage over the train terminus at Waverley station of avoiding 'the traditional blustery exit via the Waverley steps to Princes Street'.[17] And John Yellowlees highlights the geographical difficulties south of Edinburgh: 'The topography of Midlothian cursed its railways with the gorges of the North and South Esk, so that Penicuik and its hinterland was actually served by three branch lines: Penicuik itself, Glencorse, and the Peebles line. And the lie of the land resulted in the railway being routed east of Arthur's Seat whereas buses could follow the more direct A702.'[18]

The final Scottish Region timetable featuring the Penicuik branch covers the period 18 June to 23 September 1951[19] and shows a poor service of only four trains a day from Edinburgh on Mondays to Fridays, with an additional two on Saturdays. The fastest Monday–Friday train – with six intermediate stops – did the journey in a reasonable 38 minutes, but the competitive pressure from a frequent (and doubtless cheaper) bus service, and growing car ownership, perhaps inevitably led to the withdrawal of passenger train services.

This was five years before modern Diesel Multiple Units (DMUs) entered service in Scotland, and while one can speculate that an earlier generation of railcar (as operated on the Great Western Railway) might have improved the service and cut costs, it is easy to see the rationale for closure. But A.J. Mullay reflects on the Penicuik line's fate in the wider context of lack of strategic perspective on the rail network: 'The short-sightedness of the management's closure activities was confirmed by the withdrawal of Penicuik branch passenger services in 1951, in an area where the population trebled in post-war times – making the town larger than, for example, Hawick . . . but where the Midlothian road system had seen almost as little investment as the railway. Perhaps Penicuik's example of negative thinking in the Lothians should have come as no surprise. The nearby burgh of Dalkeith had seen its passenger terminus closed by the LNER in 1942, yet the station site could not have been more central to the town, and was converted into a bus station as soon as BR put it on the market.'[20]

The early 1950s: a wasted opportunity

In almost every case of 1950s' passenger closure, freight services would linger on for up to a decade or more (largely sustained by domestic coal traffic), but an exception was the Comrie–Lochearnhead–Balquhidder cross-country route, closed completely in late 1951. The line had been expensively constructed by the Caledonian Railway (a characteristic of that company), including substantial viaducts at Comrie and Lochearnhead and elaborate station buildings, and was not opened throughout until 1905. It must be doubtful that it ever earned a surplus of revenue over costs during its 46-year life, however generous a formula for cost-allocation might have been applied.

Leaving aside such examples of lines which should never have been built, the failure of BR in its early years to invest in the replacement of steam haulage of branch passenger trains by lightweight DMUs – faster and cheaper to operate, and imposing less wear and tear on track – condemned too many useful services to premature withdrawal, saddled as they were with infrastructure and rolling stock little changed in the previous 50 years.

However, while dieselisation could and should have been pursued on at least some of these doomed services, the option of stripping back track and signalling to a minimalist 'basic railway' – as would belatedly happen from the late 1960s – was not readily available then, as freight services typically continued and generally did not succumb to withdrawal until the mid 1960s, once Dr Beeching had diagnosed the deep-seated problems of wagonload freight which the 1955 'Modernisation Plan' (see below) had failed to address. Nevertheless, some rationalisation could have been achieved by replacing signal boxes which controlled freight sidings with 'ground frames' – signal and point levers situated on the ground adjacent to the sidings, operated by the train guard.

More far-sighted and innovative management in the early years of the BTC, and the Railway Executive / BR would have intervened to tackle 'the rail problem' before it got out of hand. David N. Clough has an interesting perspective on this, in his analysis of the lead-up to the Beeching period: 'Clearly between 1948 and 1961 something had gone radically wrong with the mindset of railway managers because their pre-Nationalisation counterparts were certainly businessmen. This attitude is the sign of a peculiar malaise . . . both Robertson [General Sir Brian Robertson, BTC Chairman from 1953 to 1961] and Beeching had a low opinion of the railway managers who worked for them.'[21]

But poor personal performances – which seem in part to have been attributable to an unconducive organisational environment (see also page 34) – cannot explain away all the railway's ills at the time. David Prescott reflects on how organisational aims and structure can be fundamental to outcomes: 'Prior to the outbreak of World War Two, the Big Four had been run as businesses, albeit large and complex ones, but the war necessitated an "administrative" approach. This continued for most of BR's history until the introduction of "business management" for the different sectors of the railway – properly managing costs and revenue together – in the late 1980s. Privatisation brought about the administrative approach again, this time through regulation, in the shape of Railtrack – and this has continued with Network Rail because of the requirement for Government oversight and regulation of its monopoly.'[22]

As Charles Loft comments in his *Last Trains: Dr Beeching and the Death of Rural England*, the overall structure in the 1950s was cumbersome: 'the BTC typified the vast public corporations that ran much of Britain by the end of the 1940s.' And achieving the second guiding principle of the 1947 Transport Act (the first being public ownership) was more easily talked about – as it had been since the 1930s – than put into practice:

> The integration (or coordination) of transport is often treated – in particular by critics of Beeching – as being synonymous with better rail services and restrictions on road use. The most obvious form of integration by 1951, however, was to replace rural railways with bus and road freight services; or rather to close the rail services that had already lost most of their traffic to road. Progress was slow; the Commission was feeling its way and was wary of imposing a particular mode on its customers . . . A small body whose members were generally past the peak of their professional abilities, it oversaw a vast undertaking, the structure of which, divided into executives responsible for railways, docks and waterways, hotels, London Transport, road haulage and buses, was hardly conducive to either inter-modal coordination or central direction.[23]

BTC progress on closures may have been slow in England but, as we have seen, the same could not be said of Scotland. Unfortunately, it was not only the passenger routes closed in the early 1950s which paid the penalty for BR's 'excruciatingly slow progress' in introducing DMUs. As Wolmar points out, the failure to dieselise cross-country routes and branch lines across the board 'was a missed opportunity given that the resulting cost economies could have made these [surviving] lines far more resistant to the Beeching axe wielded in the 1960s'.[24]

At last, rural dieselisation

After the 1950–52 flurry of cuts, the years 1953 and 1954 saw the network north of the border left virtually unscathed. And, as 1955 approached, attention was turning to a possible new dawn for the rail system.

During 1952 – at a time when more than 3,000 diesel railcars were operating in Europe – a committee report to the Railway Executive had at last recommended the trialling of lightweight DMUs, with the aim of cutting the cost of equivalent steam services by over 50%.[25] It was suggested that DMUs could replace push-pull steam trains on 168 routes, and the first order was placed in November 1952 for 21 two-car sets, which were built at BR's Derby Works.[26]

In the meantime, in October 1951, only weeks after a swathe of service withdrawals in Scotland, the Labour government had been replaced by the Conservatives, led by Winston Churchill. There were changes in transport policy, but little to benefit the railways:

> Privatization of the railways was not on the agenda but the 1953 Transport Act denationalized road haulage [which had been nationalised by the Labour government], resulting in the sale of 24,000 lorries to small, mostly one-man companies which were far more adept at handling loads for short and medium distances efficiently. The Railway Executive was abolished and instead area railway boards were placed directly under the aegis of the BTC. This was the first of 'several defective solutions' to change the organizational structure of the industry during its fifty-year history of state ownership – all devised by outsiders with little understanding of the industry. Crucially, British Railways was not allowed to stand on its own but remained subsumed within the monolithic British Transport Commission until the latter's abolition a decade later.[27]

BR as a whole was profitable until 1955, but Scottish Region receipts only exceeded or equalled expenditure in 1948 and 1951. P.J.G. Ransom reflects, from his own recollections, on the traffic trends which produced this poor financial performance: 'By the mid-1950s passenger trains, so recently overcrowded, were running half-empty or worse. To look at the Scottish Region summer timetable for 1954 is to be struck not only by how extensive the system still was, but also how limited were the train services provided over so much of it . . . Between Aberdeen and Ballater there were three [trains a day], with one more during July. Between Ladybank and Perth there were only two, between Crieff and Comrie but one. Between Edinburgh and Galashiels via Peebles there were three: I recall seeing these go by on the last stage of their journey and thinking how empty they were.'[28]

As Ransom observes, these limited services had been reduced compared to earlier times – and would do little to attract passengers. If the BR strategy was to respond to declining traffic by withdrawing trains, then this was a vicious circle. And yet, intriguingly, he offers evidence that 'in 1956 Scottish Region management went on record with the opinion that it would be unrealistic to contemplate wholesale closure of branch lines, as railways had a social obligation to the communities served'. That opinion, however, would be drastically revised only seven years later.

Andrew O'Dell, the first Professor of Geography at Aberdeen University and author of the seminal *Railways and Geography*,[29] was one outside observer who clearly saw how threatening to the railway the rising challenge of road transport in the mid 1950s was. He had 'strong views on railway operation, based on his knowledge gained from practical railwaymen, with whom he had a happy rapport', including a conviction that the industry was grossly overmanned.[30] In 1957 he cited the local example of the Deeside Line – and in a foretaste of what consultants would argue seven years later in the face of closure – highlighted the staffing of no fewer than eight signal boxes to control only 10 trains daily, and suggested that just one or two boxes would suffice.[31] This was part of a wider critique that many Scottish railways could have remained viable if freed from the burden of Victorian railway legislation.

In the meantime, BR was demonstrating that the introduction of DMUs was seen as a key part of the answer to its financial problems – both costs and revenue. The 'Derby Lightweight' DMUs built from 1954 to 1955 were first introduced on services around the West Riding of Yorkshire from June 1954.[32] It was not until two years later that the first DMU reached Scotland for trials, but in this case the two-car unit came from the private Metropolitan Cammell Carriage and Wagon Company in Birmingham, whose 'Metro-Cammell' units (later known as Class 101) were to become Britain's most successful first-generation DMU, some lasting 45 years in traffic. The Borders and the Corstorphine branch in Edinburgh were early beneficiaries: on 11 July 1956, a regular – but trial – DMU service began on the Galashiels–Peebles–Edinburgh route and proved to be so successful that BR later introduced two extra trains a day to cope with the increased traffic.[33]

Clearly 'the public liked these new trains with their clean and bright interiors, particularly the view ahead from the forward compartment through the driver's windscreen'.[34] And immediate traffic growth was to prove a widespread phenomenon when DMUs were introduced on regular service – as opposed to trials – on Scottish branch lines from early 1958. Also introduced in this phase of dieselisation were smaller, two-axle railbuses, which in theory offered even lower operating costs suited to the most lightly trafficked routes – but in practice would famously fail to be saviours of the branch line.

The Modernisation Plan

In light of decades of underinvestment and the overworking of railway assets during the war, the Conservative government gave BR one last chance to prove its worth with an unprecedented modernisation programme set out in the *Modernisation and Re-equipment of British Railways* report published by the BTC in 1955. The Modernisation Plan, as it quickly became known, is now widely discredited, for reasons summarised in the *Railways Archive*:

> This report . . . was commissioned as part of an attempt to stem the losses being incurred by BR due to competition from road and air traffic. Among the recommendations taken up were massive spending – £1.2bn – on the replacement of all steam traction with diesel and electric, and construction of vast marshalling yards using automated shunting.

> The failure of the plan was that nothing was done to address pre-war working practises [sic], or the 'common carrier' requirements which meant road haulage firms could cherry-pick the lucrative freight traffic and leave BR with the rest. The diesel traction was poorly procured, with some types scrapped only 10 years after their introduction.

> The failure of the plan led directly to the Beeching reports and closures 10 years later, and was seen by government as a squandering of a once-in-a-generation spending plan; the failure soured the relationship between railway and government for decades after.[35]

It is fair to criticise the plan's failure to take on board the nature of growing road competition by investing more selectively in the traffic and technologies of the future. However, the large-scale production of a multiplicity of different types of untested diesel locomotive was, in fact, a consequence of the BTC being panicked – by mounting BR losses in the late 1950s, after its first annual loss in 1955 – into swift and wholesale replacement of steam without trialling diesel prototypes, as advocated by the Modernisation Plan.[36]

The Modernisation Plan report may have been short – only 36 pages, compared to the 148 pages (plus maps) of the Beeching Report eight years later – but it was not lacking in strategic insight: 'The aim must be to exploit the great natural advantages of railways as bulk transporters of passengers and goods and to revolutionise the character of the services provided for both – not only by the full utilisation of a modern equipment but also by a purposeful concentration on those functions which the railways can be made to perform more efficiently than other forms of transport, whether by road, air or water.'[37]

This perspective bears strong comparison with Beeching's analysis of the essential rail problem, and a later paragraph reinforces the point: 'It would . . . be useless, or worse than useless, to limit the Plan so that the investment incurred would do no more than enable the railway services to continue in more or less their present shape and form . . . . In a world which has seen the technical revolution of the last few decades and widespread changes in the social and industrial structure, the railways cannot hope to survive unless the transport services they provide keep pace with the demands of a changing environment.'[38]

The plan had a strategy for extensive use of DMUs in three distinct markets: 'City-to-city express services, Secondary and cross-country routes, Branch lines' – with deployment of about 4,600 vehicles envisaged (including 300 then in use or on order). However, there was clearly no assumption that all branch line services would continue – and the scope for de-staffing stations was also flagged up:

> . . . certain stopping and branch-line steam services are carried on at a heavy loss. For the most part the carriages employed on these services are of the non-corridor compartment type. Broadly speaking, it must be accepted that these services will either be replaced by diesel multiple-unit trains (which will normally be the case where

there is a reasonable prospect of stimulating sufficient additional traffic), or by appropriate road services.[39]

... Apart from the benefit obtained by reducing the mileage of such services, the major economic improvement effected under the Plan lies in the reduction of the direct costs of train movement, chiefly as a result of the changes to be made in motive power and, consequently, in methods of operation. Some improvement is also to be expected from the modernisation of important stations, and through the closing of little-used wayside stations or their conversion to halts.

... If the volume of slow and stopping train services is reduced, it should be possible to eliminate a number of passenger stations, to develop others and to turn yet others into halts [i.e., de-staffing].[40]

These quotations demonstrate a willingness to rationalise and move out of increasingly inappropriate markets, which is rarely attributed to the Modernisation Plan, but as David Prescott points out: 'The change in method of operation was often only the traction, not the different service pattern opportunities which the new diesels offered. So the railway carried on doing what it had always done, although at less cost with the more efficient traction.'[41]

The grand hopes of the plan – not least the elimination of BR's operating losses – were not to be realised, however. Organisational structures did not help – there was no 'champion' for recasting services – and Loft notes that the abolition of the Railway Executive under the 1953 Transport Act was followed by 15 months of an interim organisation: 'This was superseded in January 1955 by a new organisation which Gourvish[42] describes as "a great semi-military bureaucratic edifice", which lacked a clear chain of command, confusing and demoralising railway managers. The fact that the *Modernisation Plan* was produced during this disruptive double re-organisation of 1953–55 contributed to its shortcomings.'[43]

The Modernisation Plan's specific failure to face up to the underlying weakness of much wagonload / rural freight saddled many branch lines with the ongoing cost of the extra infrastructure (run-round loops, sidings, signal boxes, etc.) partly or wholly necessitated by freight. Track rationalisation in the mid to late 1950s – together with earlier introduction of DMUs – would have presented Dr Beeching with a rather different rural picture to that which confronted him in 1961–62. It would not have been enough to save many of the least-used passenger routes, but it would have given a fighting chance to dozens of secondary routes and significant branch lines across Britain which were needlessly lost in the mid to late 1960s. As David Prescott reflected in 2019: 'The 1955 Modernisation Plan suddenly pushed the railway into lots of big schemes – ill-conceived or otherwise. I wonder whether it sapped the energy to find more cost-effective working methods for doing small schemes such as level crossing automation, signalling rationalisation – for example, intermediate block signals[44] to replace individual signal boxes – as well as the cost-saving from the big centrally-driven schemes. A bit like HS2 dominating everything in the industry at the moment and no-one looking at all the small changes that will make a quick and real difference.'[45]

Charles Loft rightly comments in his concluding thoughts on this unhappy chapter of British railway history, that 'the failure to address the underlying causes [of BR's financial crisis], meant that the submission of the *Modernisation Plan*, like the passing of the 1953 Act, was a missed opportunity to ask what sort of railway was required and how much it would cost'.[46] And, following further deterioration in BR's finances, that missed opportunity was to have profound consequences for the rail network less than a decade later.

Even in the year of publication of the Modernisation Plan, the closure axe was being sharpened again in Scotland. 1955 saw the withdrawal of passenger services from the two remaining cross-country lines linking the Dundee–Kinnaber Junction section of the East Coast Main Line (ECML) with the inland Strathmore Route from Perth to Kinnaber Junction, plus several other branch lines across Scotland. 1956 was relatively quiet for line closures but included the Edinburgh to Glasgow via Bathgate cross-country service (eventually re-opened in two stages, 30 and 55 years later) and passenger services over the 42-mile Border Counties line from Riccarton Junction to Hexham. BR Scottish Region's tough line on loss-making services was exemplified by that year's closure of no fewer than 26 intermediate stations on the Glasgow–Aberdeen main line, including eight over the 44½ miles of the Strathmore Route between Stanley Junction and Kinnaber Junction. However, few of the communities which lost their trains were left more than 10 miles from the nearest railhead.

Meanwhile, another false dawn was rising for rural railways . . .

'You've never had it so good' – but only briefly on Scottish branch lines

On 20 July 1957, Prime Minister Harold Macmillan delivered his classic paean to the success of the post-war consumer society in the often misquoted phrase, 'most of our people have never had it so good'. That rise in affluence and the associated growth in car ownership lay at the heart of the problem the railway faced as its annual losses mounted in the late 1950s.

However, the years 1957, 1958 and 1959 in Scotland briefly fulfilled the Modernisation Plan's vision that the introduction of regular DMU services would have a transformative impact – on both costs and revenues – on a wide variety of types of rail route. The nine services converted to DMU, battery railcar (see Chapters 8 and 12) or railbus operation in 1957 and 1958 north of the border – encompassing inter-city, suburban, rural cross-country and rural branches – *all* exhibited a distinctive pattern of market response, in which the first year of diesel operation saw substantial increases in revenue (from 23% in the case of the Edinburgh Suburban Outer Circle & Rosewell service to an astonishing 158% on the Crieff / Comrie branch), as shown in the table below derived from a 1960 BR 'Report on the progress of diesel schemes in the Scottish Region'.[47]

Table 1: Scottish Region passenger services dieselised in 1957–58

Date	Service	Diesel Type	Revenue improvement	
			1st year % v. steam	2nd year % v. 1st year*
7.1.57	Glasgow (Q St)–Edinburgh (Wav)	126	28.7	5.1
3.2.58	Corstorphine–North Berwick	100	65.8	9.5
17.2.58	Edinburgh (Wav)–Peebles– Galashiels	100	111.5	4.3
21.4.58	Aberdeen–Ballater	Battery railcar	64.9	11.5
5.5.58	Edinburgh (Princes St)–Leith (North)	100	41.9	-18.7
9.6.58	Edinburgh Sub Outer Circle & Rosewell	100	22.7	15.2
9.6.58	Edinburgh–Musselburgh & Sub Inner Circle	100	30.2	11.5
15.9.58	Gleneagles–Crieff–Comrie	Railbus	158.1	-29.5
3.11.58	Aviemore–Elgin	Railbus	88.5	-19.1

* In all cases, except Glasgow–Edinburgh, the '2nd Year' column shows the increase or decrease in 1959 over the corresponding number of (less than 12) months of diesel operation in 1958

As Rae Montgomery has rightly commented,[48] the *absolute*, as well as the *relative*, numbers are important – and the 'steam' receipts for the three routes in the table which are examined in Part Two of this book show an enormous variation: from allegedly only £277 (£5,442 in today's terms) in the case of Crieff / Comrie, through £7,894 (£155,512) for the Peebles line, to £9,383 (£183,364) in the case of the Ballater service. The Crieff / Comrie figure is simply not credible, as it equates to around £1.25 revenue in today's money *per train*; its value at the time (1s 3d) may be compared with ticket prices quoted only five years later during the closure process: *one* Cheap Day Return from Crieff to Gleneagles cost 2s 10d.[49] Yet on the basis of such dubious figures the fate of many rural branch lines was decided.

In any event, in every case the second year of diesel / battery railcar operation saw the rate of increase in revenue slacken or even decrease – perhaps inevitably, when the novelty effect wore off – compared to the major improvements versus steam in the first year of diesel operation. In three cases, revenue in the second year actually dropped back in absolute terms from first-year levels.

An explanation for this positive-to-negative trend may well lie – in the case of the Crieff / Comrie and Aviemore–Elgin lines – at least partly with the unreliability of the two-axled railbus technology, as memorably described in the headline 'Too little, too light and too late' in the January 1968 *Railway Magazine*.

An interim report, 'Review of diesel railbus operation in Scotland', was submitted by BR to the TUCCS at its 2 December 1960 meeting in the North British Hotel, Edinburgh.[50] While BR looked on the project 'as an important contribution to the problem of rural transport' (was that a Freudian slip?), it acknowledged that Scottish Region management 'have not yet been able to develop the experiment to the full', citing four reasons:

- limited deployment potential due to unreliability in activating track circuits
- 'teething troubles' with four different makes of vehicle
- negotiations with the trade unions to secure agreement to guards issuing and collecting tickets
- 'the fact that the use of wayside halts has not been fully exploited' – this is not explained, but suggests that BR wanted to introduce even more new halts (as distinct from converting staffed stations to unstaffed halts).

The paper noted that, in consequence, detailed movement costings were not yet available. Operating costs had been 'greatly reduced, although not yet to the full extent possible because of the need to "revert to steam" rather frequently during the initial "teething" period'. Receipts had increased and station working costs had been saved through ticket-issuing on trains (evidently some negotiations had succeeded). Overall, to date 'the operation of the railbuses has only reduced the gap between movement expenditure and receipts', and '[the experiment] has some way to go before conclusions can be reached'. And the conclusions would not be good for railbuses or branch lines.

The real successes of dieselisation came later when the new DMUs were combined with a revamped regular-interval service of faster and more frequent trains – as in the Edinburgh–Dunfermline–Kirkcaldy timetable, switched from steam to DMU in 1960, which saw year-on-year increases in patronage until the opening of the Forth Road Bridge in 1964. Sadly, the bold 1957–58 dieselisation initiative across Scotland would prove to be a failure on branch lines, A.J. Mullay noting that 'no fewer than seven [of the above nine routes] would close completely, and one partially (Corstorphine–North Berwick], within eight years'.[51]

However, BR had shown imagination (but again too late, and in most cases misconceived) when it complemented dieselisation with eight new halts designed to attract additional traffic: on the Ballater branch (Dee Street); Gleneagles–Crieff (Pittenzie and Strageath); the Speyside Line from Aviemore to Craigellachie (see below); and the Peebles line (Rosslynlee Hospital Halt). These involved minimal cost, often being little more than slabbed ground the length of the railbus door width, with a single set of portable / retractable steps used to mount the railbus. But, in truth, the likes of the delightfully named Ballifurth Farm Halt, Dalvey Farm Halt, Gilbey's Cottages Halt and Imperial Cottages Halt (on the Speyside Line) served tiny populations and had no future, as household incomes rose and rural car ownership grew. They also extended journey times between more important centres – Gilbey's Cottages Halt, for example, was only a quarter of a mile from Knockando Station – an evident contradiction to the thinking of the Modernisation Plan, which had referred to 'the closing of little-used wayside stations' and a reduction in the volume of 'slow and stopping train services'. All eight halts had closed by 1966.

The pace of passenger route closures slowed markedly in the years 1957 to 1961 as DMUs drastically cut movement costs – by around two-thirds compared to steam[52] – and initially boosted revenue (typically by 30% or more), thereby 'raising doubts about the closure policy in the minds of railway managers'.[53] Indeed, no Scottish routes were closed to passengers in 1957 or 1958 and only a handful in 1959. 1960 brought the end of the Dornoch branch, together with 20 of the 41 stations on the Far North Line (although five have subsequently re-opened). There were no passenger route closures in 1961, but 1962 would be a very different matter . . .

The financial crunch

On the wider front, as noted by retired senior railway manager R.H.N. Hardy in *Beeching: Champion of the Railway?*, BR's financial problems were mounting: 'Before the advent of severe road competition, a railway could make large profits on some part of the service and then cross-subsidise. But by 1960 the large profits had disappeared and the retention of loss-making services was driving the railway into further deficit.'[54]

BR's working deficit in 1959 actually represented a modest improvement on the 1958 performance, but as Transport Minister Ernest Marples told the House of Commons: 'the true deficit for the railways in 1959 [is] £110 million, made up of £42 million working deficit, £42 million central charges and £26 million further interest charges. This is a very formidable total.'[55] The 'further interest charges' were presumably a legacy from the Big Four shares, David Prescott suggesting that 'it is like a company bidder buying the company then landing it with the costs of buying it'.[56] £110 million equates to £2.6 billion today, or around two-thirds of the cost to the taxpayer of supporting the pre-Covid privatised rail system. However, Harold Macmillan's Conservative government was alarmed, and on 10 March 1960 the Prime Minister, speaking in the House on the rail problem, said: 'First the industry must be of a size and pattern suited to modern conditions and prospects. In particular, the railway system must be remodelled to meet current needs, and the modernisation plan must be adapted to this new shape.'

Marples – appointed as the new Minister of Transport in 1959 after the Conservatives' third successive General Election victory – was a politician who could be expected to be very much open to the idea of a reshaped (i.e., reduced) rail network. The road construction business Marples Ridgway, of which he had been Managing Director, was involved in a number of major road-building contracts, including the Chiswick and Hammersmith flyovers in London. Simon Bradley describes him as an 'able and slippery self-publicist whose reputation never quite escaped the taint of shady deal-ing'.[57] And Charles Loft reports that Marples's 'cunning' kept his name out of Lord Denning's report into the security implications of the Profumo affair, even though he was almost certainly the 'important minister whose liaison with a prostitute involved practices that put him at risk of blackmail'.[58]

It is chastening to ponder that had this disreputable character been named in Lord Denning's report, the programme of rail closures might have lost momentum. However, as Christian Wolmar reminds us in *Fire & Steam*, both Conservative and Labour administrations at Westminster through the 1950s and 1960s were strongly influenced by 'the feeling within government that cheap fuel for motoring was a permanent fixture and there-fore the demand for travel by railway would inevitably fall over time'. And that feeling was echoed at the grassroots within the railway itself, as Rae Montgomery remembers: 'Who could have thought then other than that the railways were on their way out? I recall that when I joined BR as a temporary Summer Class 4 clerk in the Yardmaster's Office at Leith South being asked: "Why are you joining the railways, son? The railways are finished." And that was from Yard Inspectors who had known "the railways" when they were at their height.'[59]

Taken together with political panic about BR's mounting losses, this widespread perception put the 'branch line problem' centre-stage, with profound consequences: 'It led to the largest disinvestment in transport infrastructure ever seen in Britain, the consequences of which remain with us today in terms of miles of abandoned earthworks and thousands of redun-dant viaducts, bridges and tunnels, as well as communities denied access to a sustainable transport system.'[60]

The start of that process of disinvestment can perhaps be traced to April 1960, when Marples created the Special Advisory Group (or Stedeford Committee, named after its chairman, the industrialist Sir Ivan Stedeford) to advise him on the appropriate size and structure of organisation to secure a profitable British railway system. One member of the group was Dr Richard Beeching, Technical Director of the chemicals giant ICI. He came with an enviable reputation for thorough and clinical analyses of business problems, and he was appointed Chairman of the BTC in June 1961. The Special Advisory Group's deliberations led to the 1962 Transport Act and the asso-ciated abolition of the BTC, and Beeching then became the first Chairman of the new British Railways Board (BRB) in January 1963. BR was charged with breaking even over a five-year cycle.

In July 1960, the House of Commons Select Committee on Nationalised Industries had published its report on BR finances, suggesting that most of the £42 million loss in 1959 had been incurred on passenger traffic, particularly on branches and lightly-used services – although it is not clear how they were able to reach this conclusion, given that BR's detailed studies of the finances of different types of traffic (see below) had yet to begin. And only four years later the Beeching Report would describe both wagonload freight and less-than-wagonload sundries traffic as 'a bad loss maker'.[61] But passenger network change was definitely in the air: 'The Committee was highly critical of the Modernization Plan, whose costs had risen to £1.5bn [around £35 billion in today's prices], arguing that the return on the investment was likely to be far lower than expected. The notion of investing out of the crisis was quickly being replaced by the idea that salvation lay in reducing the size of the network and cutting back on services.'[62]

Beeching's work on reshaping the railway began in late 1960, with intensive studies started on traffic flows, costs and suitability of rail. As P.J.G. Ransom records: 'Nothing so searching and widespread had ever been attempted before.'[63] A week's comprehensive traffic surveys were undertaken nationwide by BR in April 1961, and the data which these generated provided much of the raw material on the different traffic types and methods of rail conveyance which underpinned the analysis by Beeching and his team leading up to the March 1963 publication of his infamous report.

Gearing up to fight Beeching

The prospect of an accelerating programme of cuts under Beeching was well understood, and in April 1962 a campaigning group, the Scottish Railway Development Association (SRDA), was formed as an advance response to the emerging threat to Scotland's rail network, arguing that strategic economic and social considerations demanded a different solution.

The first SRDA publications did not specifically mention environmental issues but did call for wider appreciation of moves away from conventional economic evaluation. While environmental awareness – and the big differences between the impact of rail and road – would not break significantly into public consciousness until the 1970s, the arguments were beginning to be understood by deeper thinkers a decade earlier, in part inspired by Rachel Carson's seminal *Silent Spring*, published in 1962 and soon to be, as noted by Charles Loft, a global catalyst for the environmental movement. He records that a correspondent for *The Times* linked Beeching's work to environmental destruction, 'as we move into the era of the coach crawl and (if Miss Rachel Carson's warning is not heeded) the silent spring'.[64]

My father, Frank Spaven, was a founding member of the SRDA, which took the line that the optimum level of closures had almost been reached already (the map on page 94 shows the broad extent of the network in early 1962) and that the emphasis should be on continued improvements.[65] But the SRDA's fears were soon confirmed when, on 13 July, under the headline 'Beeching axe draws nearer', *The Scotsman* reported that a map of freight carryings on BR, issued by the BTC the previous day as the initial outcome of Dr Beeching's traffic surveys, indicated that all railways north of Perth (except those linking Aberdeen with Edinburgh and Glasgow) were 'hopelessly uneconomic . . . This map is openly described by B.T.C. officials as a "softening-up" for the master hatchet plan which Dr Beeching will produce at the end of the year.' On 20 July, under the headline 'Cartographic requiem', *The Scotsman* published the next BTC map, of passenger traffic densities. The newspaper reported: 'It would seem that more than a third of the network will be recommended for closure.' The BTC's own press release commented that '[the freight and passenger maps] show how much of the railway is seriously under-employed. The freight map shows that 50% of BR is used for 95% of the freight traffic and the passenger study likewise reveals that 50% of it is used for 96% of the passenger travel.'

Seemingly not spotted at the time was the fact that any analysis of usage of the national *road* network would probably show similar patterns. Beeching was implicitly to make this very point two years later when he suggested that he should undertake a road system study to complement that which he had done for rail. This was not a suggestion which went down well with the 1964–66 Labour government.

In any event, in mid 1962 it did not take the Scottish media long to digest the implications of Beeching's maps. And, after the line closure lull lasting from 1957 to 1961, the year 1962 – in anticipation of the following year's Beeching Report – saw the beginning of the closure storm. Four of the nine pioneering dieselised services from 1957–58 were axed in 1962: Leith North, Rosewell, Peebles and the Edinburgh Suburban Circle (but with the associated Musselburgh branch surviving until 1964). The stage was now set for perhaps the most infamous year in British railway history.

D34 No. 62489 *Glen Dessary* shunts at Inveramsay on 13 August 1954. Alan Gray Law's 'Utopia' had been on the island platform, but was destroyed by a lightning-strike fire in 1932. *Neville Stead collection / Transport Treasury*

Driver and Fireman take a break from train engine No. 55221 on 9 October 1958 at Lossiemouth. The five and three-quarter mile branch from Elgin closed in 1964. *Stuart Sellar*

An eastbound mixed freight and passenger train also conveying fish vans has just cleared Cullen Viaduct on 29 August 1961, headed by one of the 20 new NBL Type 2 locos allocated to north-east Scotland. *Frank Spaven*

A BR 'Derby Sulzer' Type 2 breasts Dava Summit – the fourth highest on Scotland's main lines – with a northbound passenger train in the early 1960s. *Peter Oliver (David Spaven Collection)*

'The Scottish Rambler' railtour, hauled by English Electric (EE) Type 1 D8028, waits to depart from the classic rural terminus at Edzell on 22 April 1962. *WAC Smith / Transport Treasury*

An 'Orange Walk Special' en route from Glasgow to Greenock battles north of Kilmacolm on 6 July 1963, hauled by a Standard Class 4 and a Standard Class 4 tank. *WAC Smith / Transport Treasury*

A Coast Line DMU for Aberdeen approaches Tillynaught Junction in September 1963, while just visible on the right is the steam-hauled branch train for Banff. *Norman Turnbull*

The branch to Banff, seen here in September 1963 with a BR Standard Class 2, was the last in north-east Scotland to be wholly steam-operated. *Norman Turnbull*

By 16 May 1964 Balquhidder station may have been neglected, but not so the appearance of the immaculately-dressed Guard checking a ticket on the platform, as seen from a Glasgow–Oban train. *Norman Turnbull*

The ubiquitous Royal Mail van stands out against the distinctive Callander & Oban Railway wooden building at the single-platform Crianlarich (Lower) station on 16 May 1964. *Norman Turnbull*

The Signalman at lonely Inches and the Driver of a Muirkirk–Lanark DMU exchange a few words in September 1964, just weeks before the complete closure of this section of the line. *Frank Spaven*

The use of 1,160hp locos – here a 'Birmingham' Type 2 at Grandtully on 27 March 1965 – to haul one coach was a commercial nonsense, and the Aberfeldy branch closed five weeks later. *Norman Turnbull*

BR Standard Class 4MT (2-6-4 tank) No. 80093 sits at Killin station on 7 August 1965, just seven weeks before the closure of the branch from Killin Junction (an exchange station with no road access). *Norman Turnbull*

The Throsk Signalman hands over the single-line token to cross the 'Second Forth Bridge' to the Driver of the last northbound Larbert–Alloa train to have called at Throsk station, on 18 April 1966. *Frank Spaven*

Dr Beeching's father had yet to be born when the passenger station closed here, in 1868! North British Locomotive Company 0-4-0 D2747 shunts coal wagons at Scotland Street goods yard in Edinburgh in mid-1966, a year before its final closure. *David Spaven*

Side by side at Balmenach Distillery in October 1966, one mode of transport will extinguish the other just two years later. Two Speyside Line distilleries latterly still had their own steam 'pug' locomotives. *Frank Spaven*

In December 1966, with the diminutive signal box to the left, a track-lifting train does its dismal work at Glenoglehead Crossing on the Callander & Oban line. *Frank Spaven*

Seen here on 1 March 1967, a month before the last freight train departed, the railway estate at Penicuik had changed little since 1951 passenger closure, with paper mill traffic and coal wagons dominant. *Norman Turnbull*

The 10.10 Speyside Line freight trip from Aviemore exchanges single-line tokens with the Grantown-on-Spey (East) Signalman on 11 April 1968, six months before complete closure. *Frank Spaven*

The Grantown-on-Spey (East) Signalman, James Telfer, exchanges some final thoughts with the Driver and Secondman of the last westbound Speyside Line train (a passenger special from Aberdeen) on 2 November 1968. *David Spaven*

The end is nigh. The statutory notice seen here (on the right) at Buckie station on Thursday 2 May 1968 lists the 32 North East stations to be closed the following Monday. To the left is notice of the concurrent withdrawal of freight services. *David Spaven*

At Buckie on Thursday 2 May 1968, D5335 is shunting coal wagons on the penultimate daily freight trip from Aberdeen. This loco is now preserved on the heritage Caledonian Railway at Brechin. *David Spaven*

What might have been the beginning of a through coastal route to Oban did extend, as a headshunt, a few hundred yards south of Fort William's station, seen here in 1971. *Frank Spaven*

Conclusion: 15 years of BR – but no consistent strategy for the branch line

Given the transfer of the rail network from private to public ownership in 1948, it was perhaps inevitable that the vagaries of politics – with General Elections at least every five years – would foster inconsistent approaches to the direction of the industry. But changes of railway direction came much more frequently than the one change of government, from Labour to Conservative in 1951.

The battered state of Britain's economy – epitomised by petrol rationing, which did not end until 1950 – meant that limited funds were available for re-equipping the railways after their massive war effort. The early failure to plan for replacement of steam traction by diesel (and electric for main lines and commuter networks) did no favours to branch lines and cross-country routes, saddling them with old rolling stock and expensive-to-operate loco-motives. Financial imperatives, hastened by the rise in road competition, then brought a flurry of closures in the early 1950s – with 1951 being the worst year for passenger route closures across Scotland's entire railway history – but the scope for dieselisation was belatedly recognised in 1952. By the time that DMUs had reached Scotland in 1956, BR's major Modernisation Plan was already a year old – the last, eventually forlorn, attempt to modernise the railway largely as it was, rather than as it should be in an era of fast-growing road competition for passengers and freight.

Nevertheless, a brief period of optimism for branch lines and cross-country lines saw – initially – substantial growth in patronage following the introduction of DMUs and railbuses in regular service in 1958–59, sup-ported in some cases by the opening of new low-cost halts. However, as car ownership rapidly grew in the era of 'never had it so good', so the renewed decline in rail business and finances, locally and nationally, soon brought full focus on the fundamentals of the railway system. The 1961 arrival in the industry of Beeching – a clear-eyed businessman – meant that branch lines over-equipped with infrastructure (in part for freight traffic, which was haemorrhaging to road haulage) and over-staffed for their core service needs, were brutally exposed to the winds of change which he would bring.

3

Dr Beeching's prescription –
'conservative with regard to closures'

The Reshaping of British Railways – the Beeching Report – was published on 27 March 1963. For branch lines, the die was apparently cast by two powerful statistics in the early pages of the report: one-third of the rail system carried 1% of the passenger traffic, and half the system carried 4% of the passenger traffic (and the picture was very similar for freight).[1]

There was widespread expectation that Beeching would propose many service withdrawals, but the sheer scale of his proposals came as a shock. Passenger services were to be withdrawn from 5,000 route miles across Britain (one-third of the network), and 2,363 stations would be closed (more than half). The pessimists had been proved right. Yet – astonishingly – the report describes his prescription as 'conservative with regard to closures'.[2]

However, there was logic underpinning the new strategy aimed at creating a profitable railway. This would largely be based on bulk and container freight innovations and inter-city passenger trains to meet the challenge of road transport. The third chapter of the report – 'Analysis of the problem' – succinctly sums up the basic characteristics of railways and the circumstances which were likely to make them 'the best available form of transport':

> Railways are distinguished by the provision and maintenance of a specialised route system for their own exclusive use. This gives rise to high fixed costs. On the other hand, the benefits which can be derived from possession of this high cost route system are very great.

> Firstly, it permits the running of high capacity trains, which themselves have very low movement costs per unit carried. Secondly, it

permits dense flows of traffic and, provided the flows are dense, the fixed costs per unit moved are also low. Thirdly it permits safe, reliable, scheduled movements at high speed.

In a national system of transport we should, therefore, expect to find railways concentrating upon those parts of the traffic pattern which enable them to derive sufficient benefit from these three advantages to offset their unavoidable burden of high system cost. In other words, we should expect the provision of railways to be limited to routes over which it is possible to develop dense flows of traffic, of the kinds which lend themselves to movement in trainload quantities and which, in part at least, benefit from the speed and reliability which the railways are capable of achieving.[3]

This was a sound analysis, albeit that 'high system cost' – track and signalling, and stations – is not fixed, but can be changed over time. However, the Beeching Report was not subtle in its presentation of the closures element of the prescription, which inevitably attracted the headlines. Coming from a business background, Dr Beeching was perhaps naive in not foreseeing the political storm that such a transparent announcement of drastic surgery would cause. Part of the transparency was a fascinating portfolio of 13 detailed maps, with Map 3 of 'Passenger traffic station receipts' (see after page 74) revealing that the vast majority of stations on branch lines and secondary cross-country routes in Scotland fell into the lowest revenue category (less than £5,000 per annum).

This grim statistic led on, inexorably, to the most notorious of his maps, Map 9, 'Proposed withdrawal of passenger train services' (see after page 74), which featured prominently on the front page of *The Scotsman* on 28 March under the headline: 'The lines that stay and the ones that may go'. The paper reported that 6,720 Scottish jobs were to be lost, and that the rail route network would be cut by 41% to 1,350 miles.

Interestingly, not every branch line was slated for closure – a point to which we will return – but the overall impression was one of savage butchery. Passenger services were to be cut across large swathes of Scotland: everything north and west of Inverness; everything in the North East other than the Aberdeen–Inverness main line; the Strathmore Route through Forfar; everything in Galloway; the entire Waverley Route through the Borders; and many branch lines and secondary routes in a list totalling no fewer than 51 service withdrawals (eight of them local stopping services on passenger routes which would be retained).

It would be wrong to suggest that there was anything new about railway closures, as the media – perhaps unwittingly – may have implied. Prior to the Beeching Report there had been more than 130 passenger route closures in Scotland, while after 1963 there would 'only' be some 50 – but the latter were largely concentrated in six hectic years from 1964 to 1969, whereas the former were implemented over a century or more, albeit mostly over the three decades from 1930. The furore over Beeching was inevitable.

A conspiracy to run down the railway?

It is still not fashionable to say so, but in some ways Beeching has had an unfair press. His promotion of fast inter-city services, 'merry-go-round' coal trains from colliery to power station, and the pioneering Freightliner intermodal (container-carrying) concept took the railway in the right direction, all proving their worth in subsequent decades and continuing to do so today. And indeed, of 13 cost-reduction or revenue-enhancement measures set out in the Beeching Report, only 12–16% (£18 million annually) of the consequent financial benefits were forecast to come from passenger service withdrawals and station closures alone, although 'subsequent closure of lines', reduction of other lines to freight-only maintenance standards and freight withdrawals / closures would contribute another 14–16% (£16 million–£23 million annually).[4] And as noted by Charles Loft, 'much of the rest of [the financial] improvement depended on indirect savings which would emerge as the cumulative effect of groups of closures'.[5] Whether closures would actually save such sums *in practice* was an altogether different question, and one which does not seem to have been answered. Based on long experience of managing costs on the modern railway, David Prescott comments: 'Removing management overheads is a much bigger challenge and it is highly likely that the busier routes and more complex engineering of the busy parts of the network were what generated most of the overhead costs at that time.'[6]

It was the closures – not intangible concepts, but threats to the life of places where people lived, worked or holidayed – which defined Beeching's image in the public mind. As Loft reflects: 'Even when opposition was based on an arguably outdated attachment to the railway as a symbol of an area's continuing significance, this itself reflected a fear of being left behind while the rest of Britain was modernised . . . The withdrawal of a local facility, whether rail, hospital or post office, is almost always opposed.'[7]

It is Beeching's approach to branch lines, and the consequent closures in Scotland, which concern us here. The debate was heated in the 1960s, and people of a certain age still express regret, and even anger, over 'the Beeching Axe'. The scale of destruction, and the unseemly haste with which it was perpetrated, led the public to question the motives of government and BR managers. The claimed scale of financial savings from closure was routinely challenged, and it is perhaps little wonder that conspiracy theories began to emerge. This is addressed head-on by Richard Faulkner and Chris Austin: 'There was no single conspiracy to destroy the railways, but individuals from various parts of the political spectrum were drawn to the supposed holy grail of a much smaller network and a profitable "core". They included right-wing free-market ideologues opposed to the concept of public transport, well-meaning but misguided social democrats who saw rail subsidies as regressive, beneficial only to the middle classes, and a variety of lobbying interests who would benefit from the expansion of road building, car ownership and road haulage – including trade unionists opposed to the development of rail freight services.'[8]

John Yellowlees comments on that reference to misguided social democrats: 'Being seen to preserve public transport as the residual haunt of the working classes would conflict with the notion of Anthony Crosland MP – a leading Labour intellectual – and others that the ladder of opportunity by which the middle class had climbed to affluence should be left in place for the working class to follow. Which meant things like car ownership. Crosland also favoured removing subsidy from rail which he saw as elitist, and the legacy is that his Grimsby constituency today has no through trains to and from London.'[9]

To the list of those drawn to the holy grail of a smaller network and profitable 'core' can be added some, but not all, railway managers, who saw implementation of closures as their key immediate management task in order to survive in a down-sizing railway. Gerry Fiennes memorably characterises (some of) them as 'a bandwagon of nihilists . . . For a while not only no traffic but no piece of railway was safe from them.'

Rae Montgomery's personal experience provides a valuable insight: 'There seemed to be rivalry between the three Scottish Region Divisions – based in Glasgow, Edinburgh and Inverness – as to the number and pace of closures which might be completed, a sort of closures league-table. I remember the Northern Division manager, Miles Herbert – who had a slight speech impediment – telling us to go for the "wipe pwums".'[10]

Montgomery concludes that to be seen not to support the closure programme could blight a career, and that there were significant cultural barriers to making economies as an alternative to closure: 'Whereas experienced railwaymen, Station Masters, Signalmen, long-served station staff and District Inspectors would know perfectly well that there was a surfeit of staff, there would be a reluctance to declare the fact and to offer suggestions for rationalisation, (a) because they were comfortable with the status quo, (b) they wouldn't want to make men whom they had known (and their family circumstances) redundant, and (c) if they did propose redundancies their own posts would be at risk and they might be obliged to uproot their wives and families and move elsewhere on a railway system that was beginning to show signs of instability countrywide.'

But, as we shall see, experienced railwaymen (perhaps by exception) *did* suggest rationalisation as an alternative to closure, a strategy which would cause much less redundancy and upheaval, as well as protecting an important public service.

On the 'conspiracy to close' front, a related perception was that services were deliberately run down to help justify closure, as reported in Mayer Hillman and Anne Whalley's study of *The Social Consequences of Rail Closures* (see Chapter 4), in which they note that 'supporting evidence can be cited from several areas where the level of service was reduced in the years leading to the [TUCC] Inquiry'.[11] On the other hand: 'For its part British Rail could argue that it was bad commercial practice to invest in improving the quality and thereby encouraging use of services that it had satisfied itself were wholly uneconomic to maintain. Indeed, it could be argued that to promote use in these circumstances could be construed as being counter-productive in that it might generate additional inconvenience and hardship in the future for some new users who in all likelihood would then have to make further adaptation to the pattern of their travel if and when the line closed.'

Hillman and Whalley studied the rail patronage figures on five of the lines investigated against figures for 'five fairly well matched extant lines' over a number of years prior to the closures, and concluded that allegations that BR deliberately ran down services and discouraged use on routes that it wished to close were not reflected in the figures. Analysis showed that although there was generally a decline in use in the years prior to closure, the rate of decline was less than the rate of decline on lines that remained open.[12]

The surveys for their study also did not support the proposition that, by the time of the TUCC inquiries, the quality of rail travel on the branch lines was in a 'parlous' state. Far from former rail users having a jaundiced view of the attractiveness of their service prior to closure, 92% ('perhaps informed with hindsight') expressed satisfaction with it, including two-thirds who said they were 'very satisfied'.

Of course, these findings did not address the views of *potential* rail users, and nor do they preclude the conclusion, as Hillman and Whalley report from discussions with stakeholders, that 'more aggressive marketing and more imaginative and economical management could have significantly altered the income and expenditure accounts for several of the lines'. The analysis of a dozen individual Scottish closures in Part Two of this book clearly points to substantial cost-saving *and* improved services being feasible on the majority of the lines examined. While the absence of sensible economies in order to avoid closures is striking, *inappropriate* cost-cutting on some routes prior to closure was a recurring feature, as Faulkner and Austin explore in some depth: 'The [British Transport] Commission cut train mileage to save costs, reflecting low levels of demand on some of the routes, but in most cases these cuts made using the services for business trips or commuting impractical, and it seemed very much like sabotage . . . some of BR's economies simply had the effect of destroying demand and added fuel to a conspiracy theory that implied managers were running down services to a point at which closures would become inevitable.'[13]

Railways costs – a complex calculation

The underlying financial machinations may have been much more complex than generally acknowledged at the time, but the Beeching Report sums up the rationale for its list of proposed withdrawals in the category of 'Stopping-Train Services' very briefly: 'So far as the services themselves are concerned, closure proposals have been determined by the inability of the services to produce revenue sufficient to cover the direct cost of operating them.'

It all sounded so simple, yet since the early 20th century railway management had been wrestling with the problem of assessing the allocation of costs and revenue associated with operating and maintaining branch lines. Faulkner and Austin pointedly note Beeching's failure to address the *actual* costs which would be saved by a specific line closure and how long it would take to achieve such savings: 'Instead Beeching used average costs for track maintenance, train operations and staffing, along with an assessment of the renewals of structures and earthworks required to maintain services over the ensuing five years. The latter figure was also potentially misleading, as the maintenance of track and structures was not determined by a preset formula but expertly assessed by experienced engineers used to making accurate judgements about when a structure or length of track required renewal, given the traffic passing over it . . . Inevitably, if a five-year forecast had to be made, renewals would be included that might, in practice, have been deferred or undertaken more cheaply.'[14]

To build up his argument for the withdrawal of lightly-loaded passenger services, Beeching takes the example of 'a single track route with small stations at intervals of 2½ miles carrying a stopping passenger service of one train per hour in each direction from 7.0 a.m. to 10.0 p.m.'[15] Track and signalling costs of £3,000 per mile per annum are flagged up – but there is no indication of how many crossing loops are assumed and to what extent this would match the actual capacity needs of the trains running (as opposed to the typical over-provision of loops on threatened lines at the time); nor can we glean whether there is an assumption of automated or staffed level crossings, and traditional or modern / simpler signalling methods. The report is deafeningly silent on all of this. And in any case, how many single-track routes actually had a service anything like as frequent as hourly? Very few.[16]

The feasibility of earlier implementation of mechanised track maintenance as a potential cost-saving measure for threatened branch lines is arguable. 'On-Track-Mechanised-Maintenance' (OTMM)[17] was introduced on some BR divisions as early as 1963 and was adopted as a general policy in 1964.[18] Indeed, BR had started to invest in track machines in the early 1950s, but, as noted by retired railway civil engineer Bob Gardiner (whose railway career from 1974 to 2011 involved working in a wide variety of roles throughout Scotland), these would normally have been used for track renewal work, which would be predominantly on main lines rather than branches:

Where was the incentive or opportunity for Divisional Engineers to call for investment which would enable OTMM on the threatened branch lines and secondary routes? After all, payback would only be achieved over a period measured in many years. It would not be a 'quick win'.

1964 was not a good time in the context of the general demoralis-
ation and loss of job security among Permanent Way staff when a
large proportion of the track mileage was under imminent threat
of closure. Railway communities were about to be destroyed, and
families uprooted and scattered. Implementing the changed working practices for track maintenance at this time would have been
a major task for Divisional Engineers, both from the training and
up-skilling needed as well as being able to manage the Industrial
Relations aspect of an overall 'downsizing' of P. Way staff. There
would have been little energy or appetite to try anything else,
unless so directed by the Chief Civil Engineer on the instructions
of the BR Board.[19]

Gardiner also points out that more efficient maintenance methods did, in
due course, become a key aspect of the sustained operation of routes which
had survived the immediate Beeching threat, such as Ayr–Stranraer and the
West Highland Line.

Having set out a rigid formula for the maintenance/operating costs of
track and signalling – which at that time represented around one third of the
total running costs of a typical 'stopping passenger service'[20] – the Beeching
Report's financial analysis of lightly loaded passenger services then assumes
an annual 'terminals' cost of £2,500 per station. But what would be the
impact of de-staffing the stations? Beeching has nothing to say on the scope
for such economies anywhere in his report, instead simply referring (on page
17) to stopping passenger services (and, by implication, branch line services)
'necessitating the provision and manning of small stations'. Was this a men-
tal block or a deliberate evasion? David Prescott describes it as 'a complete
failure of management to address a key issue'.[21]

Lastly, the report assumes a DMU 'movement' cost of '4s 0d – 6s 0d per
train-mile according to density of traffic', yet a table of 10 case studies (one
being steam-operated, costing 7s 7d) later in the document[22] shows five of
the nine non-steam (DMU / diesel loco / diesel railbus / battery railcar)
examples as costing *less* than 4s 0d per train-mile.

Searching for the viable railway

Based on these cost assumptions, Beeching then proceeds, in a table setting
out 'Margins of Revenue over Costs for Low Density Passenger Flows', to

show that where the 'whole system cost [is] charged assuming passenger traffic only on the route' then 'routes carrying up to 17,000 passengers per week may barely pay their way'.[23]

Taken at face value, this was a grim prognosis for Scotland, as the report's Map 1 (see after page 74) showed that other than key Strathclyde commuter routes, the Glasgow–Edinburgh main line, the three principal Anglo–Scottish routes and Glasgow / Edinburgh–Dundee / Aberdeen, virtually every other line in Scotland carried 10,000 or fewer passengers per week. Most of the latter routes still carried freight, sharing infrastructure costs, which brought down the theoretical break-even point to around 10,000 passengers, assuming 'profitable freight' (although there was no guarantee that freight was profitable either). Loft notes that setting the bar at 10,000 was 'widely regarded as too high and too dependent on the assumption that track and signalling costs could not be reduced'.[24]

The Beeching Report spelt out that the track and signalling costs allocated to passenger services in its various examples and case studies represented 'the additional expenses incurred in providing track and signalling to passenger train standards for the services concerned'. In other words, where a freight service still operated (and was expected to continue), the assumption was that it would bear the basic infrastructure costs necessary for that service to operate, with the passenger service only bearing the cost of track and signalling provision required over and above that level. This was to prove an assumption of grandiose but misguided proportions as the 1960s wore on and rail freight increasingly haemorrhaged away to road haulage – the *raison d'être* of many secondary and branch lines becoming overwhelmingly the passenger market. Beeching said that 'without freight the main railway network could not exist', but the situation since the 1970s has been that without *passenger* traffic, itself often heavily subsidised, most of the main railway network could not exist.

Beeching sought to answer some questions posed by the public in response to a rail service not paying, including: 'Why not substitute rail buses for trains and decrease the cost of the service?' This he rejected, on the basis that the suggestion 'ignores the high cost of providing the route itself, and also ignores the fact that rail buses are more expensive vehicles than road buses'.[25] Beeching was on strong ground when highlighting the contrasting costs of road-based and rail-based services for *some* corridors. As Charles Loft points out: 'The decisive advantage of the bus [over lightly used branches] was convenience, because it could pick up passengers nearer their home; but it also won on cost, being available for a third of the price of a railcar and not requiring dedicated track and signalling, all of which was nearly as expensive to maintain for one train a day as for twenty.'[26]

But this was not an argument which had the same weight for secondary routes and better-used branch lines. And one wonders why Beeching referred specifically to railbuses. Their reliability and comfort levels were poor compared to standard DMUs, and their very limited capacity – only 46 to 56 seated passengers, depending on the model, compared to up to 130-plus in a two-car DMU – could not cope with significant increases in patronage, nor with much in the way of parcels and luggage. Neither could railbuses run in coupled formation or have other vehicles (e.g., parcels vans) attached to them. And the (theoretical) operational cost saving through using railbuses rather than DMUs was not necessarily huge, given their much lower carrying capacity: the Beeching Report suggests a movement cost of 3s per mile for a railbus, compared to 4s–6s per mile ('according to density of traffic') for a DMU.[27] Also, as David Prescott points out, in practice the small fleets of railbuses, scattered in penny numbers around the network, had inherent inefficiencies for maintenance and operations.[28]

Appropriate rationalisation and cost-effective service improvements would not have been enough in most cases to achieve 'profitability' – in terms of covering all attributable costs – but they would have allowed substantial reductions in losses, to a level more commensurate with the wider economic, environmental and social benefits of a continuing rail service. These kinds of external benefits of the railway were not measured at that time, but it is interesting to note that – in contrast – support for the case for road building was provided by the pioneering 1960 cost-benefit study of the first section of the M1. It would be several years before such an approach was taken for a rail scheme, and that was for the construction of the high-density underground Victoria Line in London – light years away from the circumstances of justifying the wider benefits of retaining branch lines. The Beeching Report does refer to 'social benefit' – buried in a short sub-section on 'Other factors influencing the future role of the railways' – but curtly concludes that 'only in the case of suburban services around some of the larger cities is there clear likelihood that a purely commercial decision within the existing framework of judgment would conflict with a decision based upon total social benefit'.

In fairness, rigorous cost-benefit analysis was still a developing science at the time, and in its absence – for practical reasons – from the consideration of individual closures within the Ministry of Transport (MoT): 'it was left to civil servants to weigh up in each case the figures that the railways offered against the factors that made almost every case a special case – the holiday traffic, the hardship, the bad road, the particular likely investment or development put at risk, the undesirability of leaving a really large area devoid of any railway. This was the minefield Beeching had entered.'[29]

Beeching's blind spot

Back on the supply side, Beeching – strangely – seems to have regarded 'the high cost of providing the route itself' (page 18 of his report) as immutable. In practice, track rationalisation (singling, removing superfluous crossing loops, etc.) could readily deliver savings on what he saw as 'fixed costs', particularly if unprofitable freight services were withdrawn – as he implies should happen, only a few sentences later! And to take just one Scottish route example of significant pre-Beeching Report rationalisation, in the 1950s and early 1960s six crossing loops were removed from the southern half of the Far North Line[30] – and 20 of the route's 41 stations were axed in 1960.

In his 1973 critique of BR's 'chronic financial failures', Stewart Joy, a former Chief Economist of the BRB, is scathing about the so-called 'fixed' costs: 'Although this categorical assertion of the fixedness of track and signalling costs remained the official line of the BTC's and the BRB's costing experts [until 1967], it was completely wrong. Constant reiteration of this assertion led to its adoption as a foundation of BR policy, with distressing results . . . but I have never met a railway civil engineer or signal engineer who did not accept that if you run fewer (or slower) trains, the track and signalling cost can be reduced.'[31]

Ingenuity would be demonstrated by railway managers in the late 1960s, creating 'basic railways' to improve the economics of reprieved rural services – but Beeching failed to take the lead in this critical aspect of branch line economics. Yet it was not as if the concept of sensibly rationalising the infrastructure and cutting the costs of other aspects of rail operation was particularly revolutionary: the GWR had pioneered the introduction of unstaffed halts in the early 1900s; in 1952, the Branch Lines Committee of the BTC – set up to close the least-used branch lines – was considering whether lightly used railways might be converted to lower-cost tramways;[32] that same year the BTC 'asked the [Railway] Executive to consider cost-cutting measures and improved services before recommending a line for closure';[33] and the 1955 Modernisation Plan advocated the conversion of little-used wayside stations to halts.

It is clear – even without hindsight – that the assumptions made about costs (and the failure to address how economies could be made, short of closure) were instrumental in the conclusions reached by Beeching on which services should be withdrawn. In essence, he had concluded that large swathes of the network were *inherently* unprofitable, a view challenged by Gerry Fiennes, based on his long career as an insightful railway manager: 'In 1962 the Marples / Beeching axis began to define their territorial ambitions about rural railways. They laid it down in general that rural railways did not pay, which was true; and could never pay, which was false. They did not, therefore, require more than the most elementary arithmetic on the losses either in general or in particular.'[34]

However, another former BR senior manager, R.H.N. Hardy, rejects the view that Beeching should have devoted more attention to finding the scope for economies, short of closure:

> But how would any findings which favoured retention be put to immediate use? Could there be an alternative to closure in 1963 and sadly, the answer must be 'no'. A year or two hence, it might possibly have been different but, in 1963, however enthusiastic the intentions of one or two very wide-awake young managers, BR management had not shown itself to be committed to a policy of cutting costs in a way imaginative enough to be worthy of consideration . . . To simplify and then run a railway in basic form cannot be done overnight, but it would eventually be done when ministerial interventions had prevented closure, and once the political mind had been made up . . . It needed time and it was in any case a denial of the remit given to Beeching by Marples.[35]

For me, Hardy's arguments are unconvincing. Beeching's whole thrust was about changing outdated attitudes and practices, as well as ensuring that management were committed to change. Admittedly, lack of time to make economies – because of political pressure to quickly reduce the BR deficit – has been cited elsewhere as a reason for Beeching concentrating on the simpler option of closure.[36] But closures often took several years anyway: nearly 2½ years between closure proposal and actual closure in the case of the Ballachulish branch and the Waverley Route, for example.

There was nothing technically difficult in many of the suggested economies: de-staffing stations was only complex in terms of industrial relations; singling double-track railways was a straight-forward engineering and signalling task; the first automated level crossing with barriers had been introduced in 1961 at Spath (near Uttoxeter in Staffordshire), and the first automatic open crossing – cheaper, and suitable for quieter railways and roads – in 1963 (at Yafforth in North Yorkshire).[37] And Marples's remit to Beeching was to undertake measures to ensure that BR broke even over a five-year cycle (an impossible target, as it proved), with no suggestion that this could or should be achieved only by closures, the Beeching Report noting categorically (on page 2) that 'it must be clearly stated that the proposals now made are not directed to achieving that result by the simple and unsatisfactory method of rejecting all those parts of the system which do not pay already or which cannot be made to pay easily'.

The Waverley Route is thought to be the sole example of BR introducing into the public domain projected costings for a 'basic railway' as an alternative to closure. But by the time that the BR projections reached the public domain – where they could be challenged in conditions of open scrutiny – the closure consent had already been given![38]

Nowhere in the Beeching Report is there *any* mention of infrastructure rationalisation, yet only a few years later civil servants working on the new Transport Bill were developing ideas to incentivise BR to reduce surplus track capacity. The 1968 Transport Act included provision (in Section 40) for a 'surplus capacity' grant payable to BR to cover its temporary maintenance costs pending removal of track (from reprieved and other routes where there was scope for rationalisation) within five years. If such an arrangement had been in place at the time of the Beeching Report, BR could have been grant-funded – to maintain the surplus second track and / or crossing loops until singled – on a significantly larger tranche of reprieved routes, thus reducing their operational costs during the transitional years.

Beeching – rather than acknowledging an important middle ground where there were choices to be made in order to improve BR's finances – polarised the options (on page 58 of his report) between, on the one hand, the plan 'to build up traffic on the well-loaded routes' and, on the other hand, 'to close down routes which are so lightly loaded as to have no chance of paying their way'. As David Prescott reflected in 2019: 'Given that Beeching was a physicist, perhaps it is not surprising that he had no shades of grey – physics is absolute!'

Yet more questionable assumptions

There were flaws in Beeching's approach not only to costs, but also to revenue: 'No attempt was made to consider the scope for developing new business, even though the experience of introducing diesel railcars had resulted in very significant traffic increases and reductions in costs.'[39] And there was another fundamental weakness, in that the financial snapshot used by Beeching was a one-week traffic survey in April 1961: 'While this was a reasonably represent- ative period, it was a mistake to base momentous decisions on a single week and to ignore the summer traffic that was such a feature of many routes.'[40]

The extent to which tickets bought by branch line passengers on longer-distance journeys contributed to the revenue of main lines – and how much of that would be lost if the branch lines shut – was always controver- sial. Optimistic assumptions that passengers would simply jump in their car, or on a bus, to the nearest railhead seem to have been generally wide of the mark, with a majority preferring a seamless through journey rather than the inconvenience and uncertainty of having to change modes, as explored in Chapter 4. And in some cases, the nearest railhead might no longer be at the former junction of the branch and the main line. Andrew Boyd notes that:

> Often the issue was not necessarily the withdrawal of the rail- way service *per se* but rather the failure to provide an integrated system linking bus services into convenient railheads to provide assured connections for longer-distance traffic. For example, when Aberfeldy closed in 1965 railway passengers could have been pro- vided with a connecting bus from Ballinluig but that station was also closed. Aberfeldy still has an hourly through bus to Dunkeld and Perth, via a turning point in Ballinluig village where smart connections in both directions are available each hour to and from Pitlochry. This is all fine, but the result is a slow tedious journey for passengers to and from Perth or further afield, most of whom will now be lost to the railway.[41]

Doubts about the way that Beeching and his team went about their analysis and decision-making were shared by even one of his most loyal lieutenants, R.H.N. Hardy: 'there were innumerable critics who said, not without some justification, that our figures were suspect, that we based everything on one single week's traffic – which was true – that we closed on crude statistics

– they had a point – and that both our staff and the public were bulldozed into submission.'[42] As Loft records: 'The figures used in individual cases were generally worked up in the months following the report's publication. The ministry was told that annual earnings figures for individual lines were calculated by multiplying the results of surveys carried out over one or two weeks, a process hardly beyond question. In fact a variety of methods was used, none without its failings, and often the work was slipshod . . . these figures were in some cases vague calculations in support of a general principle that rural railways did not pay.'[43]

Rae Montgomery recollects a classic example of slipshod (or rather, imaginary) figures which he encountered in 1965 when undertaking traffic surveys in BR's Edinburgh Division, as part of a programme of rationalisation of freight facilities. Down at Reston station in Berwickshire, watched by the stationmaster, he was digging through a stack of consignment notes for livestock forwarded and received at the local auction mart when he began to realise that something was seriously amiss. Turning to the stationmaster, Montgomery said: 'These don't bear any relationship to the figures we received from you at the Divisional Office.' To which came the response: 'Well, they asked for figures, so I sent them some figures.'[44]

Despite widespread suspicions, the cost and revenue figures for threatened passenger services were difficult to challenge for those outside BR senior management or Beeching's implementation team in London. The most rudimentary of financial data – typically only 'Estimated Receipts' and 'Estimated Direct Costs' – were circulated in the public domain in BR's 'Heads of Information' supporting each closure proposal (these documents set out the details of the service proposed for withdrawal, the level of patronage of trains, the planned replacement bus services, comparisons of rail and bus fares and journey times etc.). They were not conducive to forensic analysis and questioning, although the TUCCs did receive additional financial information on a confidential basis, providing a breakdown – as in the 10 case studies in the Beeching Report – of receipts into 'Net Earnings' and 'Contributory Value' to the rest of the network, and direct costs into three constituent components, namely 'Movement', 'Terminals' and 'Track and Signalling' costs.

How far this information enabled TUCCs (in theory) to challenge BR's financial case is unclear – and such a challenge was not even within their remit, which was restricted post-1962 to reporting on hardship and how it might be alleviated. Research for this book has yielded no evidence that the TUCC for Scotland made practical use of the additional data. In any event, the accuracy and relevance of official financial statistics would be a recurring source of distrust among objectors and campaigners against line closures.

The railway trade unions would, on occasion, challenge the figures provided by management to justify closures, but the pattern of intervention was patchy. The future direction of the rail network was of course primarily determined by politicians and senior railway management, but BR was also a heavily unionised industry where the workforce was potentially very influential. There was less opposition nationally to the Beeching cuts than one might have expected, and it has been suggested that the unions' priority was, above all, to protect the terms and conditions of established grades and the heavy concentration of jobs in the major conurbations. As David Prescott points out, from a government / management perspective there should have been an understanding that it was not only the rural branches which were the key drivers of the overall scale of BR losses.

Philip Bagwell, in his history of the NUR, writes that 'the campaign against the Beeching closures was ineffective and lacking in a strong, central direction. It must be conceded that very few closures were stopped as a result of union pressure.'[45] His analysis of the reasons for this lack of success comes up with a blunt conclusion: 'That strike action by the railway unions was limited to the one-day stoppage on 3 October 1962 [against the closure of workshops] was largely due to Dr Beeching's willingness to lean over backwards to make concessions on redundancy payments, provided his main objective of a drastic slimming of the railway industry remained unimpaired, and to [NUR General Secretary] Sidney Greene's belief that the union's main objective in the negotiations was to obtain more generous compensation for those members of staff who lost their jobs.'[46]

David Prescott, who began his career in the industry in 1974, concludes: 'I get the feeling that Scottish Region management in the late '60s, into the '70s, were hell-bent on closures, possibly because it was easier with the unions. Rationalisation, as opposed to closure, required them to negotiate the cost reductions – whereas closure would have been simple consultation. It may also have suited the unions not to negotiate staff reductions on rural routes, which might have had wider implications elsewhere on staff numbers.'[47]

The TUCCs and 'hardship'

The TUCCs had been created by the 1947 Transport Act, but the 1962 Act brought important changes to their role. By the time Beeching took charge of the BTC in 1961, a closure programme was firmly on the agenda behind the scenes, and 'officials were already working to ensure that the Transport Bill would reduce the role of the consultative committees in order to speed things up and quieten them down'.[48] The Beeching Report (on page 52) couches this in slightly more diplomatic terms: 'Hitherto, station closures, withdrawals of passenger services and curtailments of freight facilities, have been pursued at a rate which was very largely governed by the management's capacity to investigate, document and present a succession of individual cases to both Transport Users Consultative Committees and Staff representatives. As a consequence, it has taken 12 years to withdraw unprofitable passenger or freight services from 4,236 route miles. *Effective implementation of the plan will depend on a speedier realisation of intentions than has been found possible in the past.* [emphasis added]'

As Charles Loft notes, ironically, the reform of the closure procedure 'took place just as objectors' criticism of the procedure reached a crescendo, and just at the point where the closure programme began to deal with services and encounter issues that really did deserve the sort of in-depth analysis objectors called for. The sad irony of the Beeching years is that having struggled with a closure procedure that made mountains out of molehills, the government abandoned it just as it got to the mountains.'[49]

The 1962 Act had finally relieved BR of its 'common carrier' obligation, so TUCCs no longer had any statutory right to comment on proposed freight withdrawals. Members were appointed on a voluntary basis, usually for a three-year term of office, and the character of the membership – compared to the pre-Transport Act situation – had changed in one small, but possibly revelatory, way: the 1963 TUCCS annual report[50] reveals that the committee could now boast only one CBE and one MBE.

Of the 26-strong membership, no fewer than 11 were from agriculture / industry / business backgrounds, eight from local authorities and six from unions (of which three were from the National Farmers' Union of Scotland) – supplemented by an 'Ex-Chairman' of the Scottish Committee of the National Union of Townswomen's Guilds. Interestingly, farmers were among the key protagonists in the successful 1963–64 campaign to oppose rail closures north of Inverness,[51] but it would not be many years before the connection between agriculture and the railway was largely severed, as a consequence of BR's steady withdrawal from wagonload freight services in the face of ever-increasing competition from road haulage.

The 1962 Transport Act introduced a new procedure for the withdrawal of railway passenger services: Section 56(7) required BR to give at least six weeks' notice of its intention to close a line to passenger services and to publish this proposal in two local newspapers and to post notices at the stations affected during two successive weeks. The notice would give the proposed closure dates and details of alternative transport services, and would invite objections to the regional TUCC, which would then report to the Minister of Transport on the individual user 'hardship' which it considered would be caused, making recommendations which could include enhanced replacement bus services or, if the 'essential needs' of rail users could not be met more cheaply by the bus (funded by the taxpayer), that the rail service should not be withdrawn. Defining 'essential needs' was, as noted by Loft, 'an inexact process', but the MoT definition which emerged 'can be summed up as being able to get to work or school without an absurdly long journey and not being completely cut off otherwise'.[52] This was a desperately narrow criterion, ignoring the importance of shopping and leisure trips for a civilised existence in towns and villages the length and breadth of the country.

Unlike the pre-1962 situation, the final decision on a threatened service now lay with the minister, bringing rail closures firmly into the political arena. Although he was not obliged to accept TUCC recommendations, he could choose to make consent to closure subject to certain conditions (such as improved bus frequencies). He could also reprieve the service – as in the case of nine Scottish lines and more than 30 in England and Wales. But in the overwhelming majority of proposed closures he (and it was always 'he' until the arrival of Barbara Castle in 1965) proceeded with consent to closure. Between 1959 and 1969 there were no fewer than five Ministers of Transport, the longest-serving – by far – unfortunately being Ernest Marples and his five tumultuous years. And although it was Castle who would eventually institutionalise (through the 1968 Transport Act, see page 74) a very different approach to railways, she was by no means always a dove when it came to closures: for example, arguing strongly for the closure of the entire Waverley Route, in order to contain public spending.[53] The 'closure culture' was a long time dying.

In a tiny number of cases, no objections were lodged against closure, and BR could proceed without recourse to the TUCCS or the MoT. Within a TUCCS-compiled list of 91 routes / local services on main lines / individual stations proposed for closure between 1963 and 1975,[54] only five proposals (for individual stations) attracted no objections: Stranraer Town in 1965;[55]

Throsk Halt in 1966 (I was the last passenger at this lonely stop between Alloa and Larbert); Easter Road Park Halt in Edinburgh in 1967;[56] Lanark Race Course Halt in 1967;[57] and Fort William in 1970 (closure of the original Victorian station, attractively located beside Loch Linnhe, to make way for a 'relief' road – and replaced in 1975 by a grimly utilitarian structure half a mile to the north).

The 'social benefit' and 'hardship' to which the Beeching Report briefly referred was – insofar as TUCC consideration of closure proposals was concerned – narrowly drawn in terms of individual hardship, and it was made clear that this issue (and any wider social considerations) was the responsibility of government rather than BR. This was set out explicitly in a letter from Prime Minister Harold MacMillan to Ernest Marples in September 1962: 'If the Government decides that on social grounds a railway from Inverness to Wick is necessary then . . . Dr Beeching will quote a price . . . for keeping the line open . . . the government will pay this, if it decides to do so, as a social service, but the management of the railway will not be accused of inefficiency or an increase in their deficit made a subject of attack on them on this account.'[58]

On paper, replacement buses could look almost more attractive than the threatened rail service, if one measured this purely on the frequency / regularity of the timetable. This was the case on the northern section of the Waverley Route – where 95 buses a week replaced 44 trains[59] – although the buses would take almost twice as long to reach Edinburgh from Hawick as did the train. And where was the evaluation of a service with – in contrast to the train – no toilets, no non-smoking areas, little or no room for luggage, none for prams, no on-board refreshment facility, and no opportunity to get up and stretch your legs? A.J. Mullay reflects on a key failure of the statutory process which determined the fate of the Waverley Route: 'Closure was concluded just before the new [1968] Transport Act reached the statute book, requiring TUCCs to be more stringent in their assessment of replacement public services' – in other words, the *quality* as well as quantity of replacement buses.[60]

Beeching drafted *The Reshaping of British Railways* report himself, and his otherwise objective and unemotional style of writing deserts him in the opening phrase of the section entitled 'Hardship': 'It would be folly to suggest that widespread closure of stopping train services will cause no hardship anywhere or to anybody.' Despite protesting too much, he then seeks to minimise the scale of hardship:

With the exception of northern Scotland, and parts of central Wales, most areas of the country are already served by a network of bus services more dense than the network of rail services which will be withdrawn, and in the majority of cases these buses already carry the major proportion of local traffic. With minor exceptions, these bus services cater for the same traffic flows as the railways, on routes which are roughly parallel. Taken as a whole, they have enough spare capacity to absorb the traffic which will be displaced from the railways, which will do no more than replace the bus traffic which has been lost over the last decade, and which will provide a very welcome addition to the revenue of the bus operators.

Beeching's concern for bus operators was touching, but the cost of subsidising additional bus services to replace trains was not normally part of the financial equation presented to the public. In the case of the Waverley Route, for example, a confidential April 1967 Scottish Office memo estimated the cost of the replacement bus services at £73,356 per annum, compared to BR's 1968 estimate of £220,000 to operate a 'basic railway' between Hawick and Edinburgh.[61] What was entirely absent from Beeching's four-paragraph analysis of hardship was any acknowledgement that, in most circumstances, the quality of the bus service – not just the cost of running it – would be far lower than the train service.

Although TUCCs would sometimes step outside their allocated role of assessing personal hardship and comment on wider economic and social hardship in the settlements and communities affected, it seems doubtful that governments attached any weight to this. The TUCCS 1966 report on the Waverley Route, for example, records objectors' views on the regional development issue, flagging up an indirect impact which was to become a repeated theme later in the campaign against closure: 'Without a rail service the area would be less attractive to industrialists, and difficulty would also be experienced in arresting the flow of people leaving the four Border counties which, in the period 1951–1961, lost 20% of the working population in the 20–45 age group. The psychological impact would, in all probability, exacerbate the problem of depopulation in this area.'[62]

Beeching and the Scottish Office

While Beeching had no remit beyond the narrow (albeit enormous) task of trying to make BR break even, the wider economic and social implications of the Beeching Report were a serious concern for a number of government ministries. The Minister of Transport was required to consult other departments and the regional economic planning councils on the strategic impacts of closure proposals, as well as the TUCCs on personal hardship to travellers. As Marples told the House of Commons: 'I shall . . . consider all closure proposals against the background of future economic and population trends, taking fully into account the possible economic and social consequences, including road congestion.' This was a pious statement of supposed intent, which meant little in practice – the key missing adjective before the word 'consequences' being 'political'.

Any nationwide reshaping of the railway would have significant implications for Scotland, as evidenced by the copious Scottish Office files of the time now held at the National Records of Scotland, many of these dealing with the wider implications of the threatened closure of individual routes, as explored in later chapters.

Early file references indicate that the initial Scottish Office position on rail closures – before the economic and political ramifications became clearer – was more amenable to cuts than would later be the case. In response to a request from the Secretary of State for Scotland for 'an assessment of the desirable pattern for a Scottish railways system', a confidential memo on 28 March 1962 from Mr J.B. Fleming of the Scottish Development Department (SDD – part of the Scottish Office) summarised a meeting at St Andrew's House. This memo stated that a note to the Secretary of State should say – having consulted colleagues in the Scottish Home Department, and the Department of Agriculture & Fisheries for Scotland – that 'the abandonment of all lines north and west of Inverness would be accepted but the [British] Transport Commission's wish to close the Perth–Inverness line would be opposed'. The same memo suggested acquiescing in the closure of all lines north and west of Aberdeen.[63]

A fundamental lack of appreciation of the extent of likely opposition to closures was revealed in a throwaway comment in a 'Draft Joint Submission to [Scottish] Ministers' (undated and unattributed, but likely to have been written around the same time) titled 'Future of Scottish Railways': 'In the Borders as with the far north closures would probably be accepted after initial protests.' Fortunately for the Far North Line, and the swathe of other important routes which were being virtually conceded for closure before proper survey of their economic value, this kind of defeatist thinking had effectively disappeared from the Scottish Office 18 months later.[64]

The civil service attitude changed partly in response to a wide variety of commentaries on closures by my father, Frank Spaven, whose planning officer role at the SDD encompassed analysis of the regional development implications of the Beeching Report. His first recorded rail memorandum, handwritten on 6 April 1962 to colleagues Messrs Jenkins and Sheldrake, comments: 'You may care to glance at the attached reports by the people who are usually regarded as Mr Marples' nominees to rubber stamp BTC proposals. Did you notice in yesterday's papers that the loss and misuse of tarpaulins in Scottish Region of BR is now costing them more than they will save from branch line closures?'[65]

This would not be the last time that my father – and others – would draw attention to alternative options for rail cost-saving, short of wholesale route closures, and his (presumed) criticism of the TUCC would also find an echo elsewhere. And bodies with interests in regional economic development would sometimes intervene strongly – behind the scenes – to oppose closures. In November 1965 the Scottish Economic Planning Council (SEPC), advised by the Scottish Economic Planning Board (SEPB), comprising mainly Scottish Office officials, including my father, confidentially asked the Minister of Transport to oppose publication 'at this time' of BRB's Waverley Route closure proposal, in view of 'the nature, size and importance of the area served by this line and . . . the need to avoid a move that would be judged inconsistent with the aim of developing the Borders'.[66]

On 28 January 1964 the *Inverness Courier* reported that a meeting at 10 Downing Street between a deputation of more than 20 Scottish interests, led by the Scottish Council, Development and Industry (SCDI),[67] and Prime Minister Alec Douglas-Home (with Michael Noble, the Secretary of State for Scotland, and Ernest Marples), had lasted almost two hours. A joint statement had been issued, and the PM 'had assured the deputation that the implications for the future economic development of different regions of Scotland would be fully taken into account before decisions were taken'.

A day later, the SCDI circulated a paper to its members, welcoming the government's change of position from one where it was not prepared to discuss 'matters other than hardship . . . with any outside bodies including Local Authorities' to a new position in which 'the Secretary of State for Scotland will discuss with outside bodies, and particularly the Scottish Council, the economic implications of proposed rail closures'. In practice, the SCDI is not thought to have brought much pressure to bear in respect of branch lines, as opposed to threatened secondary routes and main lines. In the aftermath of the Downing Street deputation, at a 29 January meeting of the Scottish Vigilantes (campaigning under the slogan 'MacPuff' against closure of the lines north and west of Inverness)[68] it was reported that 'the Prime Minister had said that he would prefer to use the existing machinery, but that both the Scottish Council and the North of Scotland Transport Conference would have access to the Secretary of State for Scotland on social and economic grounds for resisting closures. Mr. Noble would take the decisions with the Minister of Transport and would have just as big a say, and the primary decision would usually be made *on grounds other than personal hardship* [emphasis added].'[69]

It seems remarkable that the prime minister had suggested that the one statutory ground for objection to rail closures – personal hardship – would not normally be the main consideration in the decisions made. But of course *politics* would be central to many of the ministerial decisions, albeit never working to the benefit of a threatened rural branch line in Scotland – even, as we shall see, in the PM's own constituency.

The limits to Scottish influence

The underlying tensions between the Scottish Office, the MoT and BR are evident in the minutes of the Scottish Economic Planning Board's 29 April 1965 meeting at St Andrew's House in Edinburgh.[70] What must have been a tricky meeting for J.H. McGuinness of the Scottish Office to chair had no fewer than 33 attendees, representing the Scottish Office, the SDD (including my father), Scottish Information Office, Scottish Education Department, Department of Agriculture for Scotland, Board of Trade, British Rail (the brand name changed from British Railways that year), Department of Economic Affairs, Ministry of Aviation, Ministry of Labour, Ministry of Technology, the MoT, Post Office and Registrar General.

The meeting opened with an explanation of the two-stage opportunities which planning boards and councils would have to comment on proposed closures, by D.G. Fagan of the MoT, who, three years later, would sign off the official closure notice for the Waverley Route. John Yellowlees was a fellow civil servant when Fagan retired from the International Transport Division in 1978, and he recalls Fagan commenting on the Borders closure on his last day at work: 'Of course we'd never do it now, but it seemed the right thing then.' At the St Andrew's House meeting, Fagan was clearly keen to expedite the closure process: 'He hoped that, in order to minimise delay, it might be possible for the Council to clear some of the early sift cases out of the way altogether and, in all cases, to deal only with the broad planning implications of the proposed closures.'

Gordon Stewart, the Assistant General Manager of BR Scottish Region – who was an implacable champion of line closures – was quick to follow this with a hard-line view: '[He] was opposed to any extension of the Planning Council's discussion into matters which had clearly no direct connection with economic planning; the Council's views, together with those of the S.T.U.C.C. [TUCCS] on hardship and any other considerations which were relevant, would be taken into account by the Minister in reaching his final decision.'

The minutes strongly imply that the majority of those in attendance did not agree, and I like to think I can detect my father's breadth of vision in the collective opinion recorded:

> On the other hand, the view was expressed that discussion of rail closure cases on the Council must be expected to proceed on a frank and uninhibited basis. While it was appreciated that it was on the planning implications that the Minister of Transport would be seeking the Council's views, it was unrealistic to think that members would ignore other aspects of the proposals. They might wish to know about, e.g., the operating financial losses, the position as regards freight services, S.T.U.C.C. views, and any projected improvements in the services or facilities. In practice, it might be difficult to draw a line between the hardship and the purely economic issues and it would be unreasonable – and clearly impolitic – to try to deny the Council such information as was available on these matters.

This firm rebuttal of the BR / MoT hard-line stance would lead to the SEPB / SEPC considering a wide range of aspects of proposed closures. But, inevitably, branch lines were less likely to figure in a strategic planning perspective than cross-country routes or main lines – and even SEPB support for the retention of threatened strategic routes was far from a guarantee of reprieve. The final decision rested solely with the Minister of Transport.

The pattern of Beeching cuts and reprieves: an overview

Of the 40 or so routes[71] slated by Beeching for passenger closure in Scotland, only nine were reprieved, most notably Inverness to Kyle, Inverness to Wick/Thurso, Glasgow to Edinburgh via Shotts (serving declining coalfield communities) and Ayr to Stranraer Harbour (linking to the Northern Ireland ferry).

Commuter / urban branches from Glasgow to Kilmarnock (via Barrhead), East Kilbride and Kilmacolm, and from Ayr to Kilmarnock (but only until 1967) also survived, as did the 335-yard branch from Harbour Junction to Stranraer Town (but only until 1966). Also reprieved were 'stopping' services on the Fort William–Mallaig line and a handful of intermediate stations on lines not proposed for closure, such as Bishopbriggs, Carrbridge, Croy, Dalwhinnie, Insch, Inverurie, Kirkconnel and Springfield (Fife).

But main lines and / or cross-country routes disappeared in virtually every region of the country, notably:

- the former Highland Main Line from Aviemore to Forres via Grantown-on-Spey and Dava Summit
- the Speyside Line, the Moray 'Coast Line' and the Keith- Dufftown-Elgin 'Glen Line' in the North East
- the prestigious double-track Strathmore Route, where Glasgow–Aberdeen expresses traversed the fastest stretch of railway in Scotland
- the East of Fife railway from Leven to St Andrews
- the Dunblane–Crianlarich section of the line to Oban
- the 'Port Road' from Dumfries to Stranraer
- the double-track Waverley Route through the Borders

More than 20 branch lines (mostly rural) were lost, and this affected every region, including the last branch in the Highlands, to Ballachulish (the surviving Georgemas Junction–Thurso branch being effectively part of the 'main line').

Overall, the regions which suffered worst from closures of all types of line were the North East (everything closed except the Aberdeen–Inverness main line) and the Borders (everything closed except the ECML, which no longer had any stations within the Borders). Ironically, the region which suffered least was the Highlands, which had the lowest population – key reasons for the contrasting outcome to other regions being political sensitivities and the fervour of campaigners, as explored in my *Highland Survivor* and *Waverley Route*. Essayist Iain Mackenzie, reflecting on a 1997 car journey through the North East, comments: 'That was a massacre about which as usual we grumbled, but in which as usual we were overcome. Owing to the north-east being deficient in approved scenery and retired generals, it was the region hardest hit.[72] The latter sentence may have been couched in humorous terms, but there was a degree of truth underlying the wry sentiment.

A *Press and Journal* (*P&J*) story on 3 March 1964 hinted at the behind-the-scenes manoeuvring which would result in very different treatment of, on the one hand the North Highlands, and on the other hand North East Scotland and two lines at the southern margins of the Highlands:

> There have been reports of a clash in the Government between Mr Marples and Mr Noble [Secretary of State for Scotland] over the Beeching proposals for Scotland. It is known that the Scottish Secretary feels strongly against many of the Scottish proposals.
>
> The [14 out of 42][73] lines which have been considered by the TUCC and upon which recommendations have been submitted to the Minister and upon which he may be making announcements today include: Aberdeen to Fraserburgh, Maud to Peterhead, Elgin to Lossiemouth, Fraserburgh to St Combs, Craigendoran to Arrochar, Gleneagles to Comrie.
>
> Scottish M.P.s said last night it was a fair guess that Mr Noble would be prepared to give way on these services so that he could get his own way later in retaining the much more important lines in the Highlands.[74]

These six services outwith the Highlands proper were all sacrificed (but three of them by the next Labour government) and Noble did get his own way in April 1964 with the reprieves north and west of Inverness.

In Scotland there were – ironically – no closures in the year of the Beeching Report, 1963, although 284 route miles were closed to passengers across Britain as a whole.[75] However, four passenger services listed for closure in the report had already been axed (in 1962) by the time of its publication: the Beith branch in Ayrshire, the Edinburgh South Suburban Circle, Hamilton–Motherwell–Holytown–Coatbridge–Glasgow Buchanan Street local services and the short-lived Rosewell stub of the Peebles line.

In October 1964 Labour came to power after what it described as '13 wasted years' of Conservative control. Given Labour's high-profile criticism of the Beeching Report while in opposition, rail campaigners had hopes of some easing of the closure programme. Addressing the House of Commons in a 30 April 1963 debate on the Beeching Report, the Labour leader Harold Wilson had commented:

> Dr. Beeching was given a job of surgery to do, and he has done it, deep, incisive, antiseptic, amputative surgery on the grand scale, although many railwaymen and railway users in Lincolnshire and many other parts of the country might prefer the word 'butchery' to 'surgery'. But this was not Dr. Beeching's fault. He was told to apply surgery in a situation where surgery was not the main or relevant answer, and, as was made clear from the Minister's speech yesterday, the surgery has preceded the diagnosis.
>
> . . . I want to put this plain challenge to the Minister, and if, as he intends, this ever-tolerant and long-suffering House gives him leave to reply tonight, I hope that he will reply to it. I want him to answer this question: suppose the Minister had given Dr. Beeching these terms of reference, namely, to survey the whole of inland transport, having regard to alternative services, to economic development, to social needs, to distribution of industry policy and to real cost, as apposed [sic] to narrow bookkeeping considerations. Does he think that we would have had the same Report? Of course we should not, or the same proposals for closures. So I hope that the right hon. Gentleman will answer that question frankly tonight.[76]

But Wilson was careful to caveat: 'This is not to say that some closures will not be necessary. We have never claimed otherwise' – and his reference to surveying the whole of inland transport proved to be breathtaking hypocrisy: two years later Beeching left BR in part because of Labour's refusal to commission such a survey.

Campaigners against rail closures were to be grievously disappointed by Labour's performance in power. 1964 was the peak closure year across Britain (961 miles), while in Scotland the length of lines cut peaked in 1965. The new regime's first Minister of Transport was the Scottish MP Tom Fraser, during whose short tenure (until December 1965) no fewer than 1,071 miles of railway were closed. Indeed, he went further than Beeching had suggested, notoriously authorising the closure of the Oxford to Cambridge line.[77] Fraser could not, however, be accused of favouritism, as he gave the green light for closure of the Coalburn and Strathaven branch lines in his own constituency.

1964 was an exceptionally busy year for the TUCCS, which held 10 public hearings and submitted seven reports to the minister on closure proposals. It must have been a depressing experience for those committee members who questioned the sheer extent of network retrenchment, particularly in those cases (the majority) where its views on greater degrees of hardship were not enough to convince the minister.

However, of 14 passenger route withdrawals that year, six were short rural branches where – in most cases – closure could be more easily justified, as replacement bus services were readily available: Banff, Crieff / Comrie, Dalmellington, Darvel, Langholm and Lossiemouth. The 20-mile branch from Lanark to the declining coalfield town of Muirkirk in Ayrshire also succumbed that year. Only in the case of the short branch from Lenzie to Kirkintilloch, which was part of the Glasgow commuter network, had the committee expressed a strong view: 'General hardship to present substantial number of users.'[78]

Of the two cross-country routes closed in 1964 – the Devon Valley line from Alloa via Dollar to Kinross, and the St Boswells–Kelso–Berwick route – the first served a modest population and had only *one* end-to-end train daily, while the second also suffered from a sparse train service. The most significant loss was in urban Scotland where the Glasgow Central Low Level and associated lines succumbed – although the main section of the former would re-open, as the electrified Argyle Line, 15 years later.

In response to the accelerating closure programme, in mid 1964 the Scottish Railway Development Association issued its 'Scottish Railways – the next five years' briefing, incorporating two lists of routes facing closure which should be reconsidered. Fourteen mainly long-distance or commuter services were 'urged for retention or improvement', including the Aberdeen–Fraserburgh, Maud–Peterhead (freight only) and Dunblane–Callander routes dissected in Part Two of this book. A further three of the latter (Ballater, Leven–Crail and Crieff) were among nine routes 'not to be closed without investigation of improved working results if modernised'.[79]

Scotland's worst railway year?

In terms of route mileage, 1965 was the worst year for cuts in Scotland, although the actual number of passenger service route withdrawals – at 14

– was the same as the previous year (and we should remember – in fairness to Beeching – that it was 1951 which saw the largest number of route withdrawals in a single year in Scotland's railway history). But some of the lengthiest closures were implemented in 1965, five of the 12 routes outwith Scottish cities being cross-country or main lines longer than 25 miles:

- Aviemore–Boat of Garten–Grantown–Forres
- Boat of Garten–Craigellachie (the Speyside Line)
- Dumfries–Stranraer (the longest, at 65 miles)
- Dunblane–Callander–Crianlarich
- Leven–Crail–St Andrews

Grantown-on-Spey lost both its stations – West on the original Highland Main Line, and East (a mile from the town centre) on the Speyside Line – but neither route had a strong case for retention. Grantown was not a big town, and there was nowhere else of any size on the lonely route over Dava Moor, which essentially duplicated the direct route from Aviemore to Inverness via Carr Bridge. The only other significant settlement on the Speyside Line was Aberlour, just a few miles from the (temporarily) surviving Keith–Dufftown–Elgin railway at Craigellachie. Replacement buses – and, increasingly, the car – could cater adequately for the displaced passengers, albeit with much less comfort in the case of the bus. Perhaps the 'correctness' of closure is confirmed by noting that, while there is still today a bus service from Grantown via Boat of Garten to Aviemore, there are no longer any bus services from Grantown to Forres or Aberlour. But for those without cars that is obviously no consolation.

1965 also saw the loss of the 18-mile branch line to the declining coalfield town of Coalburn in Lanarkshire (plus a further branch to Strathaven). The North East lost Fraserburgh, Peterhead and Scotland's only surviving Light Railway, to St Combs. The final passenger train ran along the Aberfeldy branch in Perthshire that year, while Killin to Killin Junction (an exchange station with no road access) could not survive the demise of the 'main line' from Dunblane to Crianlarich. In total over 300 miles of passenger railway closed in Scotland that year, compared to less than 150 in 1964.

(Almost) the last of the Beeching cuts

Only eight of Beeching's services listed for closure in Scotland – other than those already reprieved – were still surviving by the beginning of 1966. All would be gone by 1969, the majority in controversial circumstances. Most were cross-country services or main lines, with only two threatened branches: Ballachulish and Ballater. Both of these closed in 1966 – to be explored in later chapters – as did the Edinburgh–Lanark direct train service and its four lonely intermediate stations between Midcalder and Carstairs.

The passenger route mileage closed annually across Britain dropped each year from the 1964 peak to 1966, but the trend for total route mileage closed (i.e., including freight) went in the opposite direction, peaking at 1,127 miles in 1966, as Beeching's conclusions on wagonload freight – and growing competition from road haulage, plus continuing decline in traditional bulk industries – worked their way through on the ground. No fewer than 408 miles of freight-only route were lost that year.[80]

It had been a busy few years for the TUCCS: its 1966 annual report noting that since October 1963, 67 public hearings on closures had been held in 33 different centres throughout Scotland.[81]

Outwith Edinburgh and Glasgow there was only one passenger line closure in Scotland in 1967 – but it was a big one. On 4 September of that year, the entire Strathmore Route, from Stanley Junction to Kinnaber Junction, closed: 44½ miles of double-track main line, which had boasted Scotland's fastest point-to-point rail timings on the 'race track' through Coupar Angus, Alyth Junction, Forfar and Bridge of Dun. Glasgow–Aberdeen expresses were diverted via Dundee.

Back in late 1965, according to Charles Loft, Prime Minister Harold Wilson had 'begged' Barbara Castle to take the job of transport minister: 'Wilson's overriding transport policy objective was to make sure transport policy was not a problem and it was Castle's job to deliver that objective.'[82] Loft reckons that 'Castle's significance is not as great as has sometimes appeared', but her 1967 'Network for Development' document (see page 170) did bring a degree of stabilisation to the network (albeit not without some further closures) and her 1968 Transport Act was certainly ground-breaking – a key turning point in modern transport policy.

The Act relieved BR of the impossible task of breaking even and acknowledged that it needed financial support from the government – with a clear distinction between commercial services, which should pay for themselves, and 'social' ones, which needed subsidy. Section 39 of the Act introduced the first government subsidies for railways which were loss-making but deemed socially necessary. Grants could be paid where three conditions

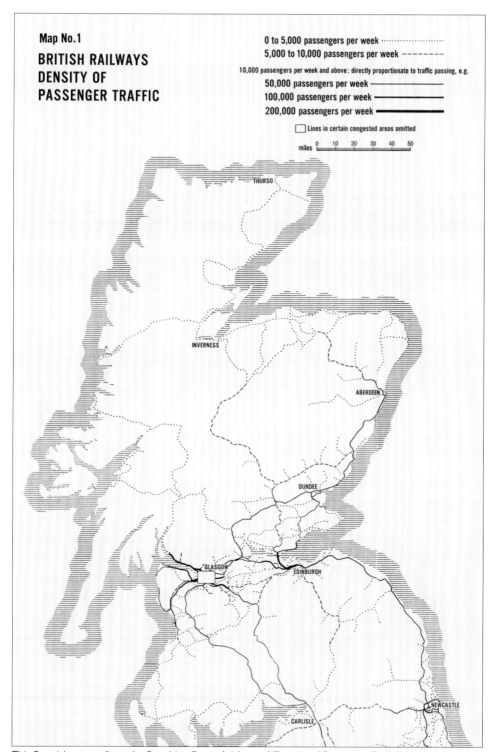

Map No.1

BRITISH RAILWAYS DENSITY OF PASSENGER TRAFFIC

0 to 5,000 passengers per week ....
5,000 to 10,000 passengers per week ---------
10,000 passengers per week and above: directly proportional to traffic passing, e.g.
50,000 passengers per week —————
100,000 passengers per week —————
200,000 passengers per week ━━━━━

☐ Lines in certain congested areas omitted

miles 0 10 20 30 40 50

THURSO

INVERNESS

ABERDEEN

DUNDEE

GLASGOW

EDINBURGH

CARLISLE

NEWCASTLE

This Scottish extract from the Beeching Report's Map 1 of 'Density of Passenger Traffic' shows that all the branch lines closed post-1962 as featured in Part Two of the book fell into the lowest density category, with the exception of Leuchars to St Andrews. *British Railways Board / HMSO*

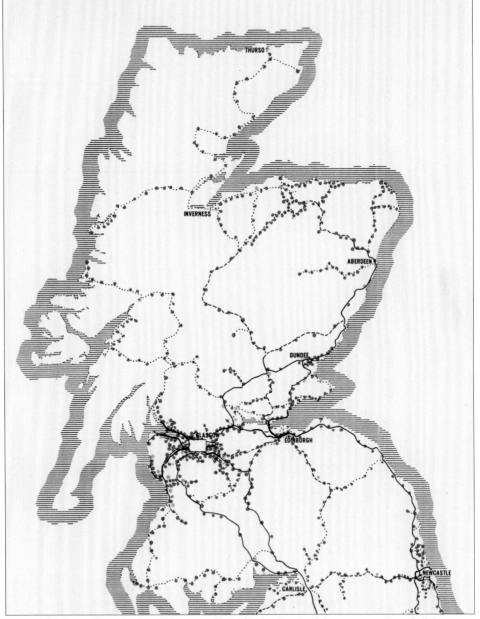

Map No.3

BRITISH RAILWAYS
DISTRIBUTION OF
PASSENGER TRAFFIC
STATION RECEIPTS

Red ● £0 to 5,000 per annum
Blue ● £5,000 to 25,000 per annum
Green ● £25,000 and over per annum
Stations in certain congested areas are omitted

THURSO

INVERNESS

ABERDEEN

DUNDEE

GLASGOW

EDINBURGH

CARLISLE

NEWCASTLE

Beeching's Map 3 of 'Distribution of Passenger Traffic Station Receipts' demonstrates that of all the post-1962 branch lines featured in Part Two of the book, only one – St Andrews – had a station in the highest revenue category. *British Railways Board / HMSO*

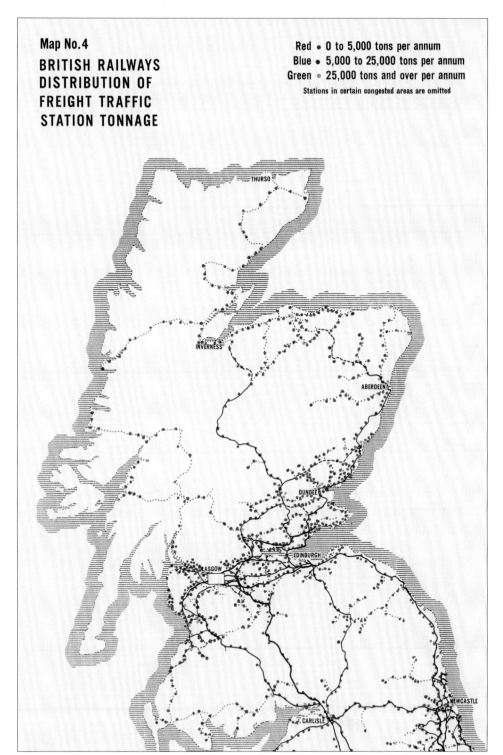

In Map 4 of the Beeching Report – 'Distribution of Freight Traffic Station Tonnage' – only two of this book's featured post-1962 closures had stations in the highest tonnage category (Fraserburgh and Peterhead), the rest falling into the lowest (predominantly) and medium categories.
British Railways Board / HMSO

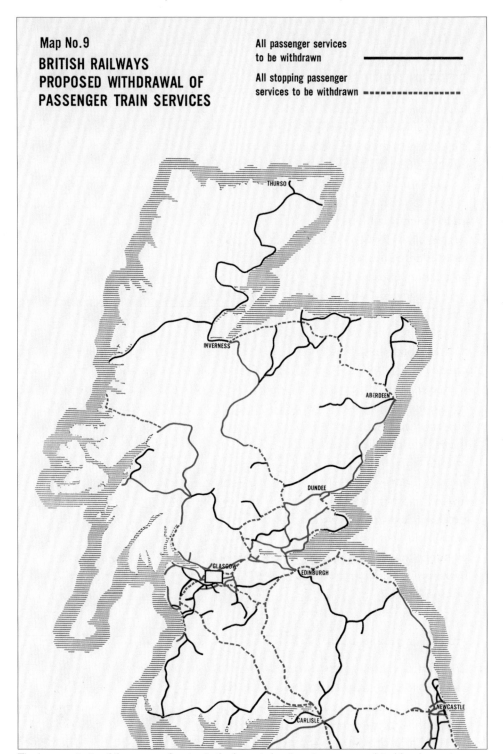

Map No.9
**BRITISH RAILWAYS
PROPOSED WITHDRAWAL OF
PASSENGER TRAIN SERVICES**

All passenger services
to be withdrawn ━━━━━━━

All stopping passenger
services to be withdrawn ▬▬▬▬▬▬▬▬▬

The large majority of the scores of routes in the lowest-density category were slated for closure in Beeching's Map 9 – 'Proposed Withdrawal of Passenger Train Services'. Among the dozen or so exceptions were Aviemore and Keith to Inverness, the core West Highland lines (saved by the new Corpach pulp mill) and freight-dominated routes radiating from Alloa. *British Railways Board / HMSO* were met: (i) the line was unremunerative, (ii) it was desirable for social or economic reasons for the passenger services to continue, and (iii) it was financially unreasonable to expect BR to provide those services without a grant. But none of this would prevent continuing closure of branch lines and cross-country routes in Fife, along the Forth estuary and in the North East during 1968 and 1969.

The two former Great North of Scotland cross-country routes from Huntly / Keith to Elgin closed in 1968, once difficult bus replacement arrangements had finally been put in place. The Glen Line via Craigellachie served relatively modest settlements (but would remain open for freight as far as Dufftown until 1985), while the Coast Line had a bigger catchment population, in particular at the town of Buckie. However, some of the route's stations suffered from the railway following an alignment at the top of the coastal escarpment, not always convenient for the town and village centres closer to the sea-shore – in contrast to the flexibility of the bus.

The replacement bus from Buckie to Keith station, along the B9016, actually offered a better line-of-route journey to Aberdeen than the local rail service skirting to the east via Cullen and Portsoy, but, unforgivably, the bus service no longer exists – yet another testament to the lack of guaranteed bus–train integration in Britain. As John Edser recalls: 'In about 60–70% of the rail closures, very few of the replacement buses lasted more than three to four years.'[83] This was quite a contrast to the glib assumptions encouraged by BR and the MoT at the time of rail closures, but perhaps Beeching himself had revealed his underlying defeatism in a short paragraph in the Beeching Report: 'Today, rail stopping services and bus services serve the same basic purpose. Buses carry the greater part of the passengers moving by public transport in rural areas, and, as well as competing with each other, both forms of public transport are fighting a losing battle against private transport.'[84]

How influential was the TUCCS?

The TUCCS attributed varying degrees of hardship to 42 of 91 routes / local services on main lines / individual stations on main lines in Scotland proposed for passenger closure between 1963 and 1975.[85] But, as we have seen, only nine routes were reprieved.

The TUCCS typically submitted its reports to the minister within a few weeks of the public hearings held to consider objections, but ministerial decisions inevitably took rather longer. Of the nine main post-1962 Transport Act route closures considered in greatest detail later in this book, the longest period which elapsed between TUCCS submission and announcement of the ministerial decision was 15 months (Ballachulish), while the shortest was five months (Crieff / Comrie and Leven). The former was unsurprising, as we shall see, given the need to arrange an entirely new bus service and undertake road improvements. Other than the Ballachulish extreme, no underlying relationship between degree of severity of hardship and time taken to reach a ministerial decision is immediately apparent: the remaining six took between seven and 10 months.

TUCCS assessments of hardship were, perhaps inevitably, qualitative in nature; over the period 1963–75 greater degrees of assessed hardship were variously described by no fewer than six adjectives: 'considerable', 'extreme', 'serious', 'severe', 'substantial' and 'widespread'. Fourteen of the 50+ proposed service withdrawals (40 or so routes and around a dozen stopping services on main lines)[86] attracted such verdicts, yet only six were reprieved,[87] demonstrating the limits of TUCCS influence – albeit that in some cases provision of additional alternative bus services and / or road improvements were deemed by the TUCCS / MoT to alleviate the degree of hardship.

Few rural branches were judged to involve these greater degrees of hardship, virtually the only examples being the Ballachulish and Coalburn / Strathaven lines, both assessed to involve 'considerable hardship' resulting from closure – albeit to be alleviated by road improvements and additional alternative bus services, respectively. Perhaps if the local MP, Tom Fraser, had *not* been the Minister of Transport charged with choosing between closure or reprieve for Coalburn / Strathaven, then – in the absence of any accusation of favouritism – part at least of these lines might have survived? Fortunately, the first four miles – from Hamilton to Larkhall – would re-open as an electrified commuter railway 40 years later.

As regards the influence of the TUCC, the officials who had been working behind the scenes in 1961 – when Beeching took charge of the BTC – 'to ensure that the Transport Bill would reduce the role of the consultative committees in order to speed things up and quieten them down', had clearly succeeded. Former railway manager Alick Arnold, whose final post after a 39-year career in the industry was Outdoor Superintendent (East) for Scottish Region, recollects how he was involved in producing 'endless' closure consultation memoranda for BR, 'but it was a waste of time, because the decisions had effectively already been made'.

The 'post-Beeching' closure surge

Other than the two former Great North of Scotland cross-country routes from Huntly / Keith to Elgin, every rail service withdrawal in Scotland in 1968 was part of a wider phenomenon of 'post-Beeching' closures, namely lines which the Beeching Report had *not* proposed for closure, but which were axed by the Labour governments of 1964–70, concerned about railway finances continuing to deteriorate despite the implementation of much of the Beeching closure programme. The pattern of these closures was far from evenly spread across Britain, with one of the most notable concentrations being in Fife and along the Forth estuary. Indeed, for anyone living in an area west of Edinburgh's Haymarket station, and bounded elsewhere by Falkirk, Stirling, Perth and Dundee, the outcome of Beeching's vision would have been considerably better than what actually happened.

Alloa had long been a major (passenger and freight) railway centre, and until 1964 it had enjoyed cross-country passenger services in four differ-ent directions: to Kinross over the Devon Valley line (a Beeching cut), Dunfermline, Larbert (via 'the other Forth Bridge') and Stirling. By the end of 1968, all its passenger services had gone, and would not return until the re-opening of the Stirling–Alloa line in 2008. Also axed in 1968 was the short branch line from Falkirk to Grangemouth, whose station was not well placed in relation to the main residential areas of this admittedly sizeable town (around 20,000 residents at the time). It also had the misfortune to be partly served by the unreliable railbus technology.

The other post-Beeching cut of that year was the short branch line from Ayr to the Butlin's holiday camp at Heads of Ayr. The train service only operated on summer Saturdays, and in some ways it is surprising that it had survived Beeching's scrutiny of summer holiday and public holiday peak traffics (with rolling stock lying idle for much of the year) in his 1963 report.

1969 saw the last – and worst – Beeching closure in Scotland: the 98¼-mile Waverley Route, whose loss left Galashiels and Hawick further from the rail network than any other towns of their size in Britain. Ayr to Kilmarnock lost its passenger service only five years after being reprieved by Marples – although a rudimentary service was subsequently reinstated in 1975 when the sleeper train from Stranraer to London was diverted from its former route via Annbank and Mauchline. The other post-Beeching closures in 1969 were the remaining branch-line stubs of the railway around the East Neuk of Fife: to Leven, Newport-on-Tay and St Andrews.

Leven and St Andrews are discussed in Chapter 10; arguably the fate of the latter – plus Newport-on-Tay – was sealed by the opening of the Tay Road Bridge in 1966. Works for the bridge had precipitated the closure of the Newport–Tayport railway, and the remaining short-distance commuter railway to Dundee perhaps had little chance of survival against bus and car competition once the Tay Road Bridge had opened, not least due to the associated inner-city road construction which helped to disconnect Dundee's station from its city centre.

1969 was, however, also notable for a rare railway reprieve: the four-mile North Berwick branch and its through train service from Edinburgh Waverley. A spirited campaign learnt lessons from previous closures and mobilised widespread public and political support locally. The campaigners made the tactical concession that a reduced level of service could be introduced as long as the line remained open, and then ensured a substantial turn-out at the TUCCS hearing: more than 400 people to support the formal written objections.[88]

The TUCCS verdict was 'substantial hardship', and the line was reprieved on the basis of a much-reduced service (down from more than a dozen trains daily to only three). The combination of a text-book campaign, with plenty of 'movers and shakers' involved, the short length of track which needed to be maintained to carry branch services, and the scope to make significant economies, ensured that North Berwick survived where so many other Scottish branches did not. Subsequently the line went from strength to strength and is now electrified with an hourly service frequency, prompting thoughts of how many other lines might have benefited from this kind of treatment, rather than closure.

1970 was the first year without any Beeching-inspired passenger withdrawals in Scotland, but it featured by far the worst of the post-Beeching closures. To facilitate the construction of the M90 motorway through Glenfarg, the 22-mile double-track main line from Cowdenbeath via Kinross to Bridge of Earn was closed completely, and all Edinburgh–Perth–Inverness trains were diverted via Stirling. This turned a 48-mile rail journey from Edinburgh to Perth into one of 69½ miles, increasing journey times (although Transport Minister Barbara Castle had claimed, before Scottish Office road engineers got wind of the opportunity, that operating Perth–Edinburgh trains via Stirling would be cheaper), and – once the M90 had opened – facing severe competition from a road journey of only 43 miles, over motorway and dual carriageway. It is hard to avoid the conclusion that this was one of the most egregious railway policy decisions perpetrated in Scotland in the latter half of the 20th century.

After 1970 there were only a few intermittent line closures: the ¾-mile Fairlie Pier branch in 1971; in 1973, the potentially strategic Dalry to Kilmarnock double-track, cross-country route which had carried London sleeper trains (with a call at Paisley) and freight traffic, having lost local services in 1965; the Bridgeton Central branch in Glasgow on the re-opening of the Argyle Line (with a new Bridgeton station) in 1979; in 1983, the Kilmacolm branch; in 1985, Errol station (between Perth and Dundee), which was a mile distant from the village it served; and finally in 1986, the SPTE-driven cut-back of the Balloch Pier branch (by Loch Lomond) to Balloch Central, in order to save the cost of a level crossing.

For many towns and villages across Scotland, the widespread implementation of Beeching's vision and subsequent cuts had come as a rude shock. These were political decisions which not only led to a loss of local transport connectivity provided by a familiar institution, but also had profound social and economic implications, as we shall see in the next chapter.

4

The aftermath

Predictions of dire consequences – economic and social, as well as personal travel hardship – often followed announcements of line closure proposals and subsequent ministerial consents. Not untypical was the reaction to impending closure reported in *The St Andrews Citizen* in December 1969: 'The general opinion is that it will be a disaster for St Andrews.'[1] Yet two anecdotes illustrate that the consequences – in terms of individual transport arrangements for *some* former rail users – could be relatively mild.

Part of the explanation for the failure to save the Waverley Route was, perhaps unwittingly, confirmed by one of the key campaigners against closure, the Reverend Brydon Maben, when asked in 1993 to comment on his feelings in the weeks after the January 1969 closure: 'Well, naturally, sad. As I say, it didn't terribly affect me personally because we nearly all had cars . . .'[2]

In late 1967, retired engineer Duncan Kennedy revisited the scene of his working from 1898 to 1903 on the construction of the Ballachulish branch, 'to see what effect the change had made in the lives of the scattered folk the line had served'. Reviewing the opinions given by a wide variety of individuals, he was struck by the extent to which the various views were in accord:

> There was general agreement that the change from train to bus made no very great difference to the local travelling public. Most people now had cars of their own, and latterly few passengers had been using the railway . . . Whatever strong feelings had earlier been aroused, they spoke of it now with quiet resignation, as of the passing of an old friend . . . In regard to the closing of the railway I found on my journey no happy man, no happy woman. If they are to be found I did not meet them. Perhaps the general feeling was best put into words by a thoughtful businessman in Ballachulish:

'When the train came in, you met people. The line was a link with the outside world and kept us alive. Now the contact is broken and the place is dead.'[3]

As well as these partly psychological impacts, there were particular inconveniences for folk without cars. Some 170 miles to the south, life without the Waverley Route was a bitter pill to swallow for non-car-owners. Campaigner Madge Elliot wrote to the *Hawick News* on 22 May 1970: 'I have a friend who became so chilled while travelling from Edinburgh to Hawick [on the bus] that she developed pneumonia. There is no need to wonder why passenger numbers are dropping. One only undertakes such a journey by bus if it is absolutely necessary. I know pensioners who have had to keep medical appointments in Edinburgh which only lasted 10 minutes. Five hours travelling for a 10-minute appointment.'

This heartfelt plea encapsulated the real hardship that was being experienced by so many people in towns deprived of their train services.

A seminal study: *The Social Consequences of Rail Closures*

Academic endorsement for the view that non-car-owners were particularly affected by rural line closures came in 1980, with a unique 137-page report commissioned by BR to reach conclusions on the impact of rural rail closures. *The Social Consequences of Rail Closures*, written by Mayer Hillman and Anne Whalley of the Policy Studies Institute, found that the substitution of bus services had resulted in a marked diminution in the quality of public transport and in the activities and opportunities of the communities from which the services had been withdrawn.[4]

Hillman and Whalley's report examined 10 case studies in England, Scotland and Wales – chosen from a list of 47 rural lines closed since 1968 – selected to ensure that they were broadly representative of the different characteristics of rural railways. Eight were branch lines and two were cross-country routes: the two Scottish case studies focused on impacts in the commuter village of Wormit (on the former Newport-on-Tay branch) and the small town of Newtown St Boswells (whose station on the former Waverley Route was called 'St Boswells'). While impacts varied from route to route, reflecting their different characteristics, the authors were able to reach a number of robust overall conclusions.

Given that these lines were closed as a result of low patronage, Hillman and Whalley were surprised to find that use of the train services had been widespread, extending, on average, to around half of the population who had been living in the survey areas at the time, albeit that a high proportion used the rail service irregularly and infrequently, and for a variety of disparate purposes (in particular non-food shopping and personal business). As a consequence 'it is possible that this is not well understood when decisions are made because, in the search for evidence of hardship, the emphasis at TUCC inquiries has been on the frequent users, such as people going to work or school'.[5]

Although 'all social and age groups used the lines and there was little variation in how often they did so', former users were on the whole more likely to be women, and to be over rather than under the age of 55. Almost as many respondents to the study survey travelled on the branch lines in order to reach destinations on the main line rail network as travelled solely to destinations on the lines themselves, indicating that the branch lines had more than a local travel significance. And so the car and bus journeys which replaced rail travel on the branches would have ramifications for rail travel on the surviving network.

Having examined patterns of travel prior to closure, Hillman and Whalley then assessed the various impacts of closure, summarised in an opening paragraph as follows:

> Ideally, it would be hoped that railway closures would not affect people's levels of activity, the destinations of their journeys or the purposes of their travel, for care is taken to provide an adequate alternative public transport so that their lives and behaviour can continue as before. What actually happened, however, to the people in our survey was that the closures resulted not only in the obligatory change of travel method but also a change in lifestyle; many people travelled less after closure and some former activities were curtailed altogether ... Over two-thirds of the survey respondents reported some reduction, curtailment or reorientation of their former rail journeys – and about half these people were by no means easily reconciled to their changed behaviour, stating that they were very upset about the adjustments made.[6]

John G. Williamson, who hails from Fraserburgh and travelled on the branch to St Combs with his grandmother when he was three or four (in the early

1960s), has first-hand experience of upset at rail closures being a long-lasting phenomenon: 'Locals I have talked to over the years about the line have all said it was well patronised, and folk from Inverallochy, Cairnbulg and St Combs to this day resent its closure, in part due to the fact the cost of building it was funded in no small part by the villagers themselves.'[7]

The geographical pattern of travel in Hillman and Whalley's study areas was strongly affected, in that nearly a quarter of the types of destination previously reached by train were no longer visited. Of those whose activities reduced or stopped as a result of rail closures, 64% of respondents aged over 65 felt 'very upset' over the change in social visits, as did 72% of people in socio-economic group DE.[8]

One of the key findings of the survey was that 'the elimination of local rail travel leads to a very significant reduction in long distance rail travel and hence has a debilitating effect on the "health" of the rest of the railway network'.[9] More than two-thirds of the respondents who continued to make their long-distance journeys did not usually travel by rail after closure. In the period 1967–77, rail passengers nationally fell by 16%, but the survey showed that rail travel by respondents dropped by 68%, so the closures contributed to a substantial loss of patronage and revenue on the surviving rail network.[10]

Hillman and Walley's report chapter on the 'Adequacy of alternative bus services', was written – like the rest of the report – in a measured, academic tone. But it was undoubtedly a devastating rebuttal of Beeching's blithe endorsement of the ability of the bus to provide an adequate alternative to the train without imposing significant hardship on travellers. Across the 10 surveyed areas, only 46% of former rail users transferred to the bus – and this included 13% who used the bus before closure anyway.[11] This lack of enthusiasm for the replacement bus reflected respondents' perceptions of the practical quality of bus travel compared to rail across various surveyed attributes such as comfort, convenient timings, reliability, etc.

A majority of respondents considered the train better than the bus in every attribute other than frequency (50%) and getting to the bus stop as opposed to the railway station (18%), the location of the latter often being less convenient for the settlement served than the equivalent bus stop(s). The distinction between train and bus was most marked in the case of comfort and ease of using the service (78%), and this view was held by the great majority of respondents (in all but two of the 10 survey areas), most strikingly in Newtown St Boswells, where 94% of respondents rated the train better than the bus for comfort and ease.[12]

Even the sole attribute of the bus regarded as superior to the train – ease of access to a boarding point – was swamped by the substantially longer journey times for bus journeys compared to train. Perhaps the worst change of fortunes befell former rail users wishing to travel by bus from Newtown St Boswells to Hawick (then the largest town in the Borders): a train journey of 13–19 minutes became a bus endurance test of 55–68 minutes, with 44 direct trains a week being slashed to *five* direct buses. It was little wonder that those with a car switched to that mode and those without had to curtail activities and/or re-orientate their journeys to different destinations.[13] The loss of the railway certainly helped to precipitate the decline of Hawick, with Galashiels (now the largest town in the region) being significantly closer to Edinburgh – and reconnected to it by rail since 2015.

Of course, for many former rail users the most attractive alternative was the car. The view that 'most people have got a car now' was commonly expressed. However, analysis of the 1971 Census data in fact showed that in that year about 40% of households were without a car in the districts of which the survey areas formed part – and this proportion was similar to a comparable mix of small urban and rural districts for the country as a whole.[14] And it was much less easy to adjust to the loss of the train if you did not have a car.[15]

Hillman and Whalley did not find evidence to support some of the wilder predictions about the broader impacts of closure, such as depopulation, reduced economic activity, road congestion, etc., but: 'Young people seem to be affected, some who seek further education, wider job prospects or, to them a more stimulating social life, can no longer make the round trip to adjacent larger towns or cities in which these options are available unless they have a car, and so leave home.'[16]

Thirty years later, the mirror image of this pattern was invoked as a key reason to re-open a third of the old Waverley Route, as the Borders Railway, from Edinburgh to Galashiels and Tweedbank. And 'getting back on the map' was an important psychological driver for the Borders (and in 1986 for the re-opening of the Edinburgh–Bathgate line following the closure of the British Leyland truck factory at the latter) – the inverse of the 1980 study's regular encountering of the 'cut off' description used by respondents to describe the perceived isolation of the area after closure.

As reported in *The Social Consequences of Rail Closures*, attitudes to, and acceptance of, closure resulted not only from the real or perceived consequences, but also from a range of issues connected with the processes involved in making the decision about closure: 'Many discussants saw the closures as being inevitable not only because of the financial loss on the lines but also because it was strongly thought that policy had been determined years before the actual decisions were announced. The public discussion and related procedures are seen as being cosmetic, a "whitewash", and a sop to public feelings. Thus many people feel that a proposal to close a line is tantamount to a decision for closure.'[17]

Turning to the future of the remaining rural railways across Britain, Hillman and Whalley argued that a change of approach was required, not just to any future closure proposals – of which there would be fortunately very few, in part as a result of their report – but also to the way these railways were run by BR: 'Perhaps trains which mainly serve rural communities should be considered as a mode of transport in their own right, with financial, managerial and operational standards which are not necessarily those of the primary network.[18]

This was a prescient suggestion, perhaps an idea ahead of its time, preceding as it did – by more than a decade – the innovative concept of 'community railways' pioneered and promoted by Paul Salveson and the Association of Community Rail Partnerships from the 1990s onwards. The tragedy for dozens of closed branch lines and cross-country routes in England, Scotland and Wales was that BR had commissioned *The Social Consequences of Rail Closures* in 1978 rather than 1964.

While BR pursued no further significant official closure proposals after receiving the Hillman and Whalley report (other than March–Spalding in Cambridgeshire / Lincolnshire and the special case of the Settle & Carlisle line), this did not reflect complete acceptance that closing secondary routes was a thing of the past. In her *British Rail: The Nation's Railway*, Tanya Jackson records that 'the main lesson BR took from [the report], according to *Modern Railways*, was that replacement bus services needed to be more integrated in future, BR saying that "they need to be run, and seen to be run, as part of the railway system".'[19]

Given Hillman and Whalley's conclusive findings, Faulkner and Austin, in their exposé of *How Britain's Railways Were Saved*, express astonishment that both the Department of Transport and the BRB continued to pursue the scope for 'bustitution' on selected routes, their researches identifying that bus substitution studies were undertaken as late as the mid 1980s for the Kyle, Mallaig and Stranraer lines.[20] One might have expected that the widespread discrediting in 1983 of the government's Serpell Report[21] – which envisaged substantial network cuts – would have finally consigned 'the closure solution' to the dustbin of history, but in practice it was passenger traffic growth through the mid and late 1980s which ensured that by 1990 the emphasis had switched to extension of the network of routes and stations rather than retrenchment, for the first time in many generations.

The economic and employment consequences of the Beeching cuts

The impact of rail closures was not restricted to social consequences. The more extreme predictions of local economic Armageddon were certainly proved wrong in the vast majority of cases, but – while there has been long-running debate over the consequences of closures for the British economy, particularly in rural areas – there does not seem to have been any systematic assessment of the effects until recently. Evidence that areas deprived of rail services suffered economically finally secured academic endorsement in a 2018 discussion paper produced for the Centre for Economic Performance (CEP) at the London School of Economics, which found that 'the cuts in rail infrastructure caused falls in population in affected areas relative to less affected areas, loss of educated and skilled workers, and an ageing population. A 10% reduction in rail access over the 1950–1980 period (measured by a network centrality index) was associated with a 3% fall in population by 1981 (relative to unaffected areas). Put another way, the 1 in 5 places in Britain that were most exposed to the rail network cuts saw 24 percentage points less growth in population than the 1 in 5 places that were least exposed.'[22]

Usually forgotten in the public furore over passenger hardship were the railwaymen and women who lost their jobs and/or had to relocate away from their former place of employment. But a number of surviving sources help to give us a sense of the dislocation and financial consequences involved.

Only weeks after the Galashiels–Peebles–Hawthornden Junction line had been closed completely in February 1962, BR management responded to a request from the NUR for a statement as to what became of operating staff on the line.[23] The list of 31 staff members (which excluded clerical and management employees, represented by the Transport Salaried Staffs' Association, and engineering staff) showed that 17 fell into the category of 'Options not suitable and service terminated', nine had a new BR 'Post allocated', while four were 'Retired: Over-age'; and one person had resigned. The BR letter noted: 'The men whose services were terminated were dealt with under the Redundancy Arrangements and offered alternative posts, but they preferred to have their services terminated rather than transfer.'

Of the 14 crossing keepers (13 'Mrs' and a solitary 'Miss'), nine had been offered 'Carriage Servicewomens' posts in Edinburgh, but all had declined. This may have been due not only to the travel difficulties created by closure, but possibly also to the contrast between what had been home-based, rural jobs and the prospect of working in large urban teams (often on night shifts), an environment which could be intimidating – certainly in my experience in Inverness in the mid 1970s – for those unused to rumbustious behaviour! BR also advised the NUR that seven of the women 'have indicated that they wish to be considered for Crossing Keeper's positions that may arise in the future within a reasonable vicinity' – but that must have been a forlorn hope in 1962's contracting (and increasingly automating) railway.

Those men who were allocated to other railway posts inevitably found themselves some distance away from their former places of employment: transfers included Peebles to Eskbank, and Joppa and Pinkhill in Edinburgh, and Walkerburn to St Boswells; but one lucky porter guard in Galashiels found himself promoted to a motor driver post in the same town. Only one crossing keeper was allocated to a similar post: a Mrs Brock, who had operated the Venture Fair crossing at Leadburn, accepted a crossing keeper's post at distant Auldbar Road in Angus, possibly accompanying a Mr Brock who may have been made redundant as a permanent-way ganger (his name was not on the list of redundant operational staff) – but the railway in Angus (the Strathmore Route) would close completely just five years later.

The fate of the 200 redundant railway employees along the Waverley Route was recorded for posterity in an MBA dissertation (at Glasgow University, sponsored by BR) – *Redundancy and Manpower Policy on British Rail*. This was undertaken in 1970 by Douglas Paul, who had spent eight formative weeks of BR management training on the line in 1965–66. In an article in the North British Railway Study Group Journal of December 2010,[24] Paul recalls that the drawn-out closure process for the Waverley Route came at the price of employee uncertainty lasting for more than five years – and 'most people who worked on the line stayed in their jobs until the bitter end in the hope that the line would be reprieved'. Some 60% of the railway's staff were in their 40s or 50s, 'railway folk born and bred . . . and for most of them, their once valued skills were of no use outside the railways'.

From a total of 200 people who were made redundant, the actual number who had to find alternative jobs was 158, most of the remainder opting for retirement. Twenty-three of the 158 chose to remain with BR – most moving away, but with a few able still to live in the Borders and work on the railway, like the signalman who transferred to Elvanfoot in Lanarkshire, driving there by car each day from home in Canonbie. Only five years later even that job would disappear too, as power signalling centres at Carlisle and Motherwell eliminated all the manual signal boxes on the WCML. Redundancy was chasing railway staff round the country.

Some 135 ex-railway employees were therefore left to find jobs locally, and although their uncertain future was cushioned by BR's enlightened redundancy scheme and by the local textile industry's desperate shortage of labour, this came at a price, as Paul records: 'The type of work offered by the mills was an unattractive proposition for many railway employees. Typically it was unskilled and low paid work and represented a drop in status particularly for those who had progressed up the career ladder in their railway jobs.'

Paul quotes the example of a 59-year-old supervisor who was earning £27 a week with BR. While he was receiving unemployment benefit and continuing weekly payments, he was taking home £18 a week. He remained unemployed for the full 42 weeks of his entitlement to weekly payments before taking employment as a labourer in a mill and a wage of £13 a week: 'His wife then had to start working to make ends meet. He regarded mill life as 'just an existence' with none of the social rapport among employees which he had enjoyed on the railways. He wished he had been younger so that he could have moved on to another railway job.

So why didn't more people move to railway jobs elsewhere? Paul cites the age of much of the railway workforce and local family ties, plus their awareness that the railways in the late 1960s remained an insecure environment for employees – with a lingering threat of more line closures, replacement of manual signal boxes by centralised power boxes, and labour-intensive goods yards giving way to more capital-intensive container train operations. Paul notes that many people, torn between the option of a satisfying railway job elsewhere or staying put in the Borders, decided to opt for the latter.

A new era – re-openings on the national network, and the growing heritage sector

The late 1980s saw the peaking of a process of line and station re-openings throughout Britain which had begun gathering pace in the late 1970s. Road congestion, environmental concerns and population changes had demonstrated that road transport was not the panacea too often assumed in the Beeching period.

Line re-openings in Scotland have been heavily concentrated in the populous Central Belt, and in particular in the Greater Glasgow conurbation, which enjoys the largest commuter rail network outside London. The network elsewhere has seen many station re-openings, but very few on re-opened lines. The freight-only Ladybank–Hilton Junction–Perth line saw passenger service resumed in 1975 and at the time of writing was the route for almost all Edinburgh–Perth–Inverness trains. Hamilton–Larkhall was re-opened (and electrified) in 2005, as part of the Strathclyde commuter network. The seven-mile re-opening from Stirling to Alloa in 2008 in effect created a new branch line, but as all Alloa's trains run through to Glasgow or Edinburgh it is really an extension of the former's commuter network rather than being a 'rural' branch. The new Borders Railway (opened in 2015) is part of the Edinburgh regional commuter network.

The West Highland Line, North Highland lines and Ayr–Stranraer route are all too long to be described as branches, which therefore leaves us with only two rural lines in this category within Scotland: the Drem–North Berwick branch, but its electric trains operate through from Edinburgh and are part of the commuter network; and Georgemas Junction to Thurso, which is now really the 'main line', with trains from Inverness calling there first, prior to continuing to Wick.

We can therefore reasonably state that Scotland's rail network has lost all its traditional rural branch lines. However, due credit should be paid to some remarkable 'off-network' survivors. Rural branch lines *do* still exist in Scotland, but these are all within what is now known as the 'heritage' sector. 'Preserved' standard-gauge steam railways have been created by volunteer enthusiasts the length and breadth of Britain since line closures started biting in the 1960s.

Scotland has six standard-gauge heritage railways offering (pre-Covid) regular summer-season services – only two more than Wales (which also has many preserved narrow-gauge railways) and dwarfed by some 70 in England. All are 'branch lines' in rural or semi-rural areas of Scotland. Four are physically isolated from the national network: the Caledonian Railway from Brechin to Bridge of Dun (four miles in length); the Doon Valley Railway in Ayrshire (one mile); the Keith and Dufftown Railway (an 11-mile, diesel-only operation); and the Royal Deeside Railway at Milton of Crathes (one mile). The Bo'ness and Kinneil Railway (five miles) has a direct track connection to the national network, while the Strathspey Railway from Aviemore to Broomhill (10 miles) has both direct track connection and cross-platform passenger interchange with the national network.

These independent railways have been lovingly restored to their former glory – typically in inter-war or early BR guise – although some would argue that sparklingly clean coaches and immaculately maintained stations give a somewhat false impression of the railway as it really was in those years of decline!

Conclusion: a fateful decade for Scotland's branch lines

The first decade of Dr Beeching's profound influence on the British railway system was to have a dramatic effect on branch lines and cross-country routes throughout Scotland, removing almost all of them from the national network. And, without question, his 'vigorous axe-work has left deep scars in the collective memory'.[25] Yet, for all the revisionist arguments that too many of the folk who bemoaned the loss of their railway rarely or never used the train, it is not difficult to conclude that Beeching had a blind spot in his approach to loss-making lines, eschewing the scope for sensible economies short of closure in the headlong rush to deliver a turn-round in BR's financial performance.

However, not every Beeching cut was wrong – far from it, in an era when the more flexible bus, car and lorry were bound to be more realistic options for most smaller towns and villages – nevertheless we can still deplore the unnecessary loss of a significant number of useful secondary railways (and, indeed, some main lines) in most regions of Scotland.

But the many good things which Beeching did for the long-term prosperity of the rail industry as a whole should not be forgotten – and we should recognise that he was a businessman saddled with an unreasonable remit which he had to fulfil in a highly political environment. As Christian Wolmar concludes: 'It was not all Beeching's fault. His terms of reference had been too narrow; he was only supposed to find a way of returning the industry to profitability as soon as possible rather than consider the overall social and wider economic value of the railway or examine the economics of other modes of transport . . . The Beeching report had been commissioned in order to demonstrate that minor railway lines were fundamentally uneconomic and it was hardly surprising that this was its conclusion. He was searching for that Holy Grail, the myth of the profitable railway.'[26]

We also need to remember that the societal circumstances in the early 1960s were very different from today. Notwithstanding the strong opposition to *individual line closures*, the public might have taken a lot of persuading to demand a halt to the Marples-Beeching *national policies*, as Philip Bagwell argues in the context of a demonstrably half-hearted NUR response to the programme of cuts: 'With car ownership spreading rapidly, petrol selling at less than six shillings a gallon and blithe optimism that the era of cheap fuel would continue indefinitely, the growing body of motorists were not overconcerned at the disappearance of a large part of Britain's railway system. If the union had more success in resisting rail closures in the 1970s than it did in the 1960s, this was not only because it was better organised to meet the challenge, but also because the public had had its confidence shaken through the consequences of the Arab-Israel conflict of 1967 and of OPEC's determination to force up the price of oil.'[27]

But none of this is to argue that Beeching could not have developed a programme for rationalisation and more efficient operation of the 'best of the branch lines' which were closed, as Part Two of this book will demonstrate.

PART TWO

A dozen closures dissected

Alan Young's map shows the broad extent of the Scottish passenger rail network in January 1962, when every county north of the Border was still served by rail. Those lines studied in most detail in Part Two of the book are marked in bold. Not all lines open to passenger traffic are shown, particularly in the Central Belt.

5

Introduction

Part One set out the key events and trends in the life and death of Scotland's branch lines as a whole. Part Two begins with a short 'taster' of two very different railways: briefly examining the factors which sealed the fate of the rural line to Kelso in 1964, the first Beeching closure proposal north of the border; and then reviewing the changing fortunes of the commuter route to Kilmacolm, threatened twice with closure, surviving the Beeching axe, but abandoned in 1983 by Strathclyde Passenger Transport Executive, as the last significant rail closure in Scotland. These vignettes of two contrasting cases illustrate the bigger picture, and together they book-end the classic era of modern rail closures.

The choice of 10 lines for more detailed dissection reflects in part my view that the majority of these routes – which in some instances were only a section of what was a cross-country railway – should not have lost their passenger train services in the 1960s. And in some cases there now seems to be a case for re-opening (wholly or partially), due to changing population geography, road congestion, regional economic objectives or strategic environmental aims – aided by developments and innovations in railway engineering and operating practice.

In one case – Ballachulish – I suggest that a line extension should have been constructed prior to closure, transforming this inevitably threatened branch into a strategic through route.

The two main Buchan termini (Fraserburgh and Peterhead) have been incorporated within a single chapter, since they merged at a junction (Maud) less than halfway to the point where the main line was reached, and the operation of these two branches was an integrated arrangement focused on the key destination at Aberdeen.

In another case, three towns which were originally on the same railway

(Leven, Crail and St Andrews) saw the first and last survive as short stubs only until 1969. Given their history and inter-linked operation, all three services are explored in a single chapter.

The 10 most detailed case studies are taken in order of closure date (except where lines are grouped together, as above) so that the reader can relate these cases to the broader trends outlined in Part One. The first (Peebles) is a 'pre-Beeching' closure, followed by seven services withdrawn as a result of his 1963 report, then concluding with two 'post-Beeching' closures which demonstrate that – contrary to popular opinion – the great and good doctor should not be blamed for everything.

Kelso and Kilmacolm – book-ending the classic closure era

Kelso: a railway of mis-matched halves

The 33¾-mile cross-country route from St Boswells (on the Waverley Route) via Kelso to Tweedmouth (just south of Berwick on the ECML) had its origins in two separate branch lines built by the North British Railway and the York, Newcastle and Berwick Railway. Split management would survive the Grouping and nationalisation, and arguably contribute significantly to the line's demise.

One short period in which it was utilised as a strategic – indeed main line – railway was following the calamitous 1948 floods which closed the ECML between Berwick and Dunbar. The capabilities of the line through Kelso and the Waverley Route north of St Boswells were demonstrated to a wider public by handling up to 11 additional Anglo–Scottish trains in each direction daily during the 11 weeks the ECML was closed. These included on 17 recorded occasions the successful passage – without a stop – of *The Flying Scotsman* non-stop service between Edinburgh and Kings Cross, despite the longer route and the absence of water troughs[1] between Edinburgh and Tweedmouth.

That brief heyday could not however hide the underlying decline caused by bus and car competition – with, for example, the number of tickets issued at Coldstream declining from 22,341 in 1911 to only 1,366 in 1951.[2] Reduction in service frequency was both a response to decline and a contributor to further decline, the line's final (1963–64) timetable being a miserable offering, with only two trains a day linking St Boswells and Berwick, and two further 'short workings' between St Boswells and Kelso. One of the through trains was timetabled to stand at Kelso for 24 minutes (perhaps a reflection of the split between Scottish and North Eastern Region control of the route), giving a highly uncompetitive journey time of 1 hour 42 minutes for the 35-mile journey, with seven intermediate stops.

For such an infrequent train service – and modest freight traffic – the line was seriously over-burdened with infrastructure: three block posts / crossing loops over the 11½-mile St Boswells–Kelso section alone. Bizarrely, the 22¼ miles from Kelso to Tweedmouth, despite carrying even less traffic, remained double-track until the end – and paradoxically the LNER had singled the busier St Boswells–Kelso section in the 1930s. Alan Young – who has researched the line's history for the *Disused Stations* website[3] – comments: 'Perhaps the Scottish and Northern English districts of the LNER didn't communicate with each other; the continued insistence of the BR North

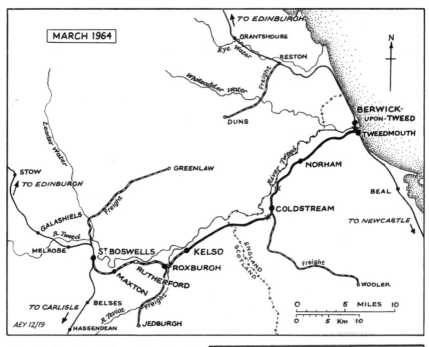

The York, Newcastle and Berwick Railway (in due course part of the North Eastern Railway) began operations from Tweedmouth to Sprouston (two miles east of Kelso) as early as 1849, and an end-on junction with the North British Railway's branch from St Boswells was established west of Sprouston in 1851. (Alan Young)

LEGEND FOR ALL BRANCH LINE MAPS

━━━ Single Track Railway
━━━ Multiple Track Railway
o   Single Track Station
•   Crossing Loop or Multiple Track at Station
X   Crossing Loop not at a Station

Eastern Region timetable in omitting the service west of Kelso, whilst BR Scottish Region included the whole route, possibly tells us something about fragmentation of thinking.'[4]

Unsurprisingly, closure of the line was already under consideration prior to the formulation of the Beeching Report, and the latter supported the proposed withdrawal in accordance with the provisions of the 1962 Transport Act. It was the first of the Beeching closure proposals in Scotland to be published – in June 1963. That the line was little loved (or rather, little needed in its then sub-optimal form) is evidenced by the fact that the TUCCS received only *six* objections to closure: three from individuals in Coldstream, Kelso and St Boswells, and institutional objections from the town clerk of Berwick, the town clerk of Edinburgh, and the county clerk of Roxburgh – but nothing from Kelso Town Council.[5]

Given the poor service provided, it is little wonder that patronage was extremely low. As the BR Heads of Information summarised: 'In winter, the service as a whole is used each weekday by 20 / 35 passengers in each direction and, in summer, by 30 / 50, the bulk of the patronage being between St. Boswells and Kelso.' The level of staffing was out of all proportion to the number of passengers, a BR North Eastern Region memo noting that Coldstream station (in England, although the town itself is across the River Tweed in Scotland) had 11 operating staff positions, albeit around half dealing with freight traffic.[6] A sensibly rationalised railway would have had only a couple of staff (signalmen) at Coldstream.

The TUCCS public hearing was held on 11 October 1963 in Kelso, with the committee thereafter concluding that (a) there would be no hardship to users in Coldstream, Norham and Tweedmouth, and (b) hardship would be experienced by users in the villages of Maxton, Rutherford and Roxburgh, there being no alternative public transport available other than on Saturdays.[7] The TUCCS submitted its report to the Minister of Transport in October 1963, and consent to closure was announced in February 1964. With 'Estimated Receipts' of £2,260 (plus 'Contributory Value' of only £520) and 'Estimated Direct Costs' of £58,920,[8] it is little wonder that only four months were needed to reach a decision, although additional alternative bus services on Mondays to Fridays were made a condition of closure. Passenger trains were withdrawn on 15 June 1964.

The strategic diversionary capability of the route (and its tourist potential) should have given pause for thought about the complete closure – which inevitably would (and did) follow passenger service withdrawal – but

Beeching's perspective was quite different: this was a 'duplicate route', acting as a drain on BR finances.

Kilmacolm escapes the axe – but only once

If the Kelso closure was swift – and barely noticed by the local community – the two separate proposals to withdraw Kilmacolm's trains provoked a very different reaction, stirring up considerable anger and taking a full 20 years to reach an unhappy conclusion.

In 1963 the Beeching Report slated for closure the entire 15 miles of the former Glasgow & South Western Railway route from Greenock Princes Pier via Port Glasgow and Kilmacolm to Elderslie (on the Ayr–Paisley Gilmour Street–Glasgow Central / St Enoch main line), together with the loop line from Elderslie via Paisley Canal towards Glasgow Central / St Enoch. Although the douce dormitory village of Kilmacolm lay in rural surroundings, this was far from a classic country branch line. East of Kilmacolm, the railway was double-track and enjoyed a Glasgow service of 16 trains a day in each direction on Mondays to Fridays. Patronage was as high: 1,500–1,600 passengers daily in each direction in winter, with slightly fewer in summer. As many as 96 passengers joined the 7.55 a.m. train to Glasgow at Kilmacolm, together with a similar number at Bridge of Weir.

However, the financial details (a rather generous description of two figures), as set out in the BR Heads of Information[9] which accompanied the closure proposal, did not make encouraging reading for campaigners: 'Estimated Receipts' of £31,050 and 'Estimated Direct Costs' of £114,550. As was the custom, the TUCCS were supplied confidentially with an 'Amplification of Financial Information', but while the 'Direct Costs' figure was the same as in the Heads of Information, inexplicably 'Receipts' of just £25,000 were shown (comprising 'Net Earnings' of £24,100, plus £900 'Contributory Value' generated by travel elsewhere on the network). The movement cost was high, at 9s 11d per train-mile, reflecting in part the use of steam traction, rather than DMUs, for additional peak-hour trains.

But Kilmacolm (and Bridge of Weir, four miles down the line) did not lack for motivated local residents – including 'movers and shakers' commuting to Glasgow offices – and 181 objections were lodged with the TUCCS, from individuals and organisations such as the local authorities and the Quarrier's Home near Bridge of Weir. A public hearing was held in February 1965 in Glasgow and the TUCCS report was submitted to the minister a month later. The committee's verdict was clear: there would be 'considerable hardship' at Kilmacolm, Bridge of Weir, Houston & Crosslee and Elderslie, and 'substantial hardship' at Corkerhill, Mosspark, Crookston and Paisley Canal on the secondary route from Elderslie to Glasgow. Unsurprisingly, there would be no hardship at Greenock Princes Pier: a total of 75 boat trains to and from Glasgow in 1963 had declined to 64 in 1964 – and the last liners would call at Greenock in the late 1960s, as air transport almost entirely eclipsed the traditional transatlantic passage.

The minister's verdict came in December 1965: all the stations where hardship would be incurred were to be reprieved, with the exception of Elderslie – and Kilmacolm to Princes Pier would close. After the reprieve, BR in due course undertook sensible economies, shutting Bridge of Weir signal box in 1966, and then in 1973 singling west of Elderslie[10] so that the 7¾-mile line to Kilmacolm became a wholly DMU-operated 'basic railway' with 'One Train Working'. While evening train services were withdrawn in 1966, local residents and campaigners must have felt that the line's future was assured – but they had reckoned without railway politics . . .

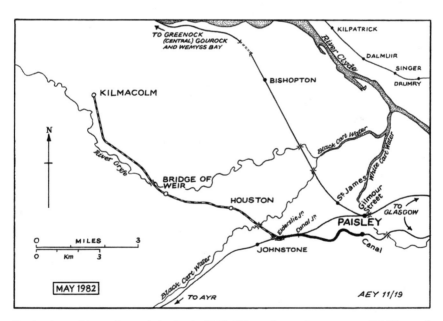

By the time of its undeserved demise in 1983, Kilmacolm station was on a DMU-served 'basic railway' over a single 'long siding' from Elderslie Junction. The railway crossed the River Gryfe near the line's mid-point; ironically, Lord Taylor of Gryfe was a Member of the British Railways Board from 1968 to 1980, and Chairman of the Scottish Railways Board from 1971 to 1980 – and was therefore spared the embarrassment of any association with the Kilmacolm line closure three years after his retiral. (Alan Young)

101

Long after rail closures had generally become regarded as an outdated solution to BR's financial problems, the truncated Kilmacolm line was the victim of a spat involving the Labour-controlled Strathclyde Passenger Transport Executive (SPTE) and the railway trade unions. The latter were opposed to the plans of the former (who funded the rail service) to introduce 'driver-only' trains across the Greater Glasgow suburban network, and SPTE opted to show their determination to pursue the policy by withdrawing financial support for the train service serving a traditionally Conservative-voting district.

The TUCCS received no fewer than 737 objections, and two petitions containing 794 and 295 signatures were received at the public hearing held on 9 January 1981 in Glasgow. The evidence submitted focused in particular on the inadequacy of the alternative bus services, the major problem of road congestion and car parking difficulties in Glasgow – and it was noted that usage of the train service had increased slightly over the previous two years. In the TUCCS annual report for 1981,[11] to the Conservative Secretary of State for Transport, David Howell MP, the committee summarises its deliberations, including two robustly worded conclusions: 'After carefully considering all the oral and written evidence the Committee unanimously concluded that undoubted and in some cases extreme hardship would be experienced by users of the rail service if it was withdrawn . . . The Committee's unanimous recommendations to you were that the whole railway line to Kilmacolm via Paisley Canal should remain open.'

This was 16 years after Beeching had departed BR, and it might reasonably have been assumed that such unequivocal verdicts on hardship and closure would have strongly influenced the minister. But it was not to be, and the final paragraph of the TUCCS report commentary on the Kilmacolm case suggested considerable frustration with his October 1981 consent to closure: 'The Committee subsequently learned that you had decided to allow British Rail to withdraw the service but not before 1st January 1983 in order to allow British Rail and Strathclyde Passenger Transport Executive to examine whether the financial performance of the service could be increased. We welcome this postponement, but somewhat regret that you did not accept our recommendations that the line should remain open in view of the hardship that we feel closure will inflict on users. We would earnestly ask you in future cases to make the fullest possible disclosure to the public of the reasons for non-acceptance of our conclusions and recommendations.'

As the *Herald* put it many years later: 'The line was closed as Strathclyde Region refused to pay the six-figure subsidy demanded by British Rail as the line was a loss-maker.'[12] A key principle in any PTE jurisdiction was that if a local line was not subsidised by the PTE then BR had to put it up for closure, as otherwise the costs fell on BR's nationwide 'Passenger Service Obligation' agreed with the government. The last train left Kilmacolm on Saturday 8 January 1983. Ex-Beeching implementation officer John Edser, writing in *Beeching: the inside track*,[13] places the Kilmacolm story in a much wider context: 'Apparently the Scottish Region took some visitors from SNCF to see the line before it closed. They asked why it was being closed, were quoted the passenger usage and said if the same line existed in France, it would be electrified both for the social good and the potential for growth.'

Ironically, the eastern third of the route formerly used by Kilmacolm trains – from Paisley Canal to Glasgow (over most of which operational track remained to service an oil terminal at Hawkhead and the Corkerhill DMU depot) – was re-opened in 1990 and electrified in 2012, demonstrating the folly of the 1983 closure.

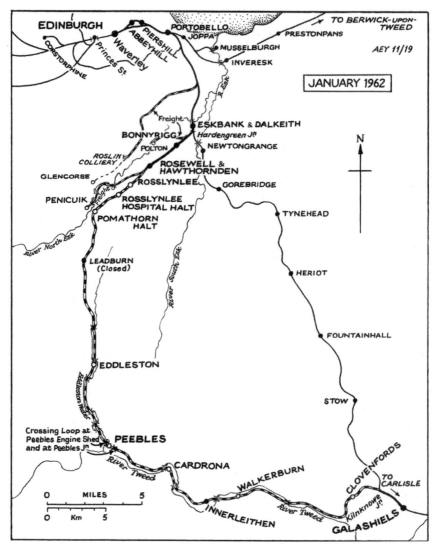

The Peebles line climbed continuously from near its junction with the Waverley Route at Hardengreen Junction through Hawthornden Junction (just south of Rosewell & Hawthornden station) to its 935-foot summit a mile south of Leadburn. Both railway and road skirted the western end of the Moorfoot Hills then east of Peebles shared the Tweed valley over generally gentle gradients, other than around Clovenfords where the line climbed out of the valley then descended at 1 in 60 into the valley of the Gala Water and re-joined the Waverley Route at Kilnknowe Junction. (NB: the loop beside the Peebles Junction block post was not a conventional loop for crossing trains on the running lines, but did allow locomotives to run round goods trains in the yard there.) (Alan Young)

7

A bus man knifes the railway: Peebles

The Peebles Railway Company opened its 18-mile line from Eskbank, on the Edinburgh–Hawick route, to the county town of Peeblesshire in 1855. By 1866 this had been extended a further 18½ miles along the Tweed Valley via Innerleithen and Walkerburn to Galashiels, by then a key staging point on the North British Railway's Waverley Route via Hawick to Carlisle, which had been completed in 1862.

The Caledonian Railway-sponsored Symington, Biggar & Broughton Railway opened to Peebles in 1864, but its station was on the other side of the Tweed from the NBR station, and the connecting line built across the river was used only for freight traffic. For a while, through trains ran from Peebles to Glasgow, but the Caledonian branch from the WCML served few places of any size and lost its passenger services in 1950, with freight trains to Peebles ceasing four years later.[1]

A false dawn, then closure threatened – and all before the Beeching Report

As we saw in Chapter 2, in 1956 the Edinburgh–Peebles–Galashiels line was one of the first routes in Scotland to benefit from the introduction of lower-cost and (in theory) faster DMUs. The route also saw an increase in weekday frequency – from four trains each way in 1957 to seven / eight when DMUs were introduced to regular service in 1958. Over the first year of DMU operation this generated a mighty 111.5% improvement in revenue performance compared to the last year of steam. According to Peter Marshall, in his history of *Peebles Railways*: 'The new trains were warmly (literally) welcomed by the Borders folk who found their clean interiors an improvement on the previous steam-hauled coaching stock. Many remember the clear view forward through the glass screen behind the driver's cab, giving a hitherto unseen panorama.'[2]

But, inexplicably, the introduction of DMUs – with their superior acceleration – did not produce a faster timetable. On the crucial Peebles–Edinburgh transit, the average journey time by DMU remained the same as in steam days: one hour.[3]

With no speed-up, an irregular frequency, and gaps of over three hours between some trains, it is perhaps little wonder that after the undoubted initial novelty, Year 2 of DMU operation saw only a 4.3% improvement compared to Year 1. At a time when the hourly bus service and the flexible car faced little road congestion, the Peebles line needed a comprehensive – rather than half-hearted – response to this competition. And in 1960 BR had considered abandoning the line between Peebles and Galashiels, combining the existing Peebles service with the Edinburgh 'Outer Suburban' service to Rosewell & Hawthornden in Midlothian.[4] This sensible-sounding proposal (in the context of the then prevailing culture) was not taken forward, but might it have improved the finances of the core Peebles–Edinburgh section sufficiently to avert its closure? We consider that scenario later.

BR's annual loss on operating account nationally had risen to £68 million in 1960 (and would be £87 million in 1961), and Dr Beeching was by now chairman of the BTC when, on 25 August 1961, the BR General Manager's office in Glasgow wrote to the TUCCS advising that complete closure (passenger and freight) was planned for the Peebles line. Losses in the mid 1950s – 'estimated under steam operation to approach £50,000 per annum' – had led to the introduction of 'an accelerated and augmented' DMU service.[5] The latter adjective was appropriate, but to claim that the service had been accelerated was simply untrue. The letter continued with reference to a 50% increase in passenger carryings and receipts (over three years), implying – on the basis of the figures above for Years 1 and 2 – that there must have been a substantial *decrease* in Year 3. A recent costing survey had indicated that 'working and terminal costs still amount to twice the earnings'. An impenetrable three-page appendix sets out details of cost savings and lost receipts, with costs disaggregated in a confusing format – unlike the simple division into movement, terminal and direct track & signalling expenses used in the Beeching Report and supplied to the TUCCS for proposed closures post-1962 Transport Act. The latter approach at least had the virtue of ease of understanding, even if the assumptions and methodology behind the figures were opaque.

KELSO, KILMACOLM and PEEBLES

On 13 June 1964 the smartly turned-out Guard of the final St Boswells–Berwick passenger train checks the doors prior to departure from Coldstream, with its solid signal box and distinctive footbridge. The station served the most significant settlement on the 'English' section east of Kelso. *Frank Spaven*

As the last train to St Boswells prepares to leave Kelso on 13 June 1964, there are four times as many observers as the pitiful total of six official objectors to closure. *Norman Turnbull*

This undated (possibly 1950s) shot of Kilmacolm station looking north illustrates the once-generous provision of track and station infrastructure while still on a through route to Greenock Princes Pier. *Alan Young Collection*

Just one man and his dog – plus the train crew – in evidence at the 'basic railway' terminus at Kilmacolm on a late afternoon in early September 1982, four months before closure. *David McCrossan*

On 11 November 1961, seven years after complete closure, the relative grandeur of the former Caledonian Railway station at Peebles is still very much evident. *WAC Smith / Transport Treasury*

Rail traffic with no future in any scenario: Class J38 No. 65915 shunts a sparsely-loaded wagonload freight at Innerleithen in an undated shot looking west. *Norris Forrest / Transport Treasury*

Rosslynlee Hospital Halt recorded an average daily (Monday to Friday) number of 21 passengers alighting from trains and just five joining – a rather mysterious contrast! *RW Lynn Collection*

BRITISH RAILWAYS

CLOSING OF STATIONS

AT

CARDRONA	POMATHORN
CLOVENFORDS	ROSSLYNLEE
EDDLESTON	
INNERLEITHEN	ROSSLYNLEE
LEADBURN	HOSPITAL HALT
PEEBLES	WALKERBURN

On and from

MONDAY, 5th February, 1962

with the approval of the Transport Users' Consultative Committee for Scotland the above-mentioned stations will be CLOSED and the following arrangements will apply :—

PASSENGERS

Alternative bus services, operated by Scottish Omnibuses Limited, are available in the areas served by the stations to be closed.

PARCELS AND OTHER MERCHANDISE TRAFFIC BY PASSENGER TRAIN AND FREIGHT TRAIN TRAFFIC

Alternative facilities are available at PENICUIK STATION for the above-mentioned traffic now dealt with at Pomathorn and Leadburn stations and at GALASHIELS STATION for traffic now dealt with at the other stations concerned.

A collection and delivery service covering the areas will be provided as required from PENICUIK and GALASHIELS respectively.

PEEBLES RAIL TICKET AGENCY AND RECEIVING OFFICE

Railway tickets for journeys commencing at EDINBURGH or GALASHIELS may be purchased in advance from Scottish Omnibuses Limited, High Street, Peebles where railway timetables may be consulted. At this address orders may also be placed for the collection of parcels or goods by British Railways motor for despatch by rail.

BRITISH RAILWAYS

The final closure notice at Peebles station, in January 1962, does not go out of its way to help displaced rail passengers with future travel, bluntly advising that 'Alternative bus services, operated by Scottish Omnibuses Limited, are available in the areas served by the stations to be closed'. *Norman Turnbull*

Seen here on 20 January 1962 with the 12.21 p.m. Edinburgh–Peebles–Galashiels train, Pomathorn (only half a mile from Penicuik) was the second-busiest parcels station on the line. *WAC Smith / Transport Treasury*

Winkston Level Crossing, north of Peebles – photographed on 20 January 1962 – was one of 16 which contributed to the line's high operating and maintenance costs. *WAC Smith / Transport Treasury*

The 826 yards of single-track between Peebles Engine Shed and Peebles Junction signal boxes served the most important station on the line. Here the Driver of the 7.44 a.m. Edinburgh–Galashiels train exchanges single-line tokens with the Engine Shed Signalman on the final day of operation, Saturday 3 February 1962. *Frank Spaven*

The photographer's sons, with the author on the left, head away from the 7.44 a.m. Edinburgh–Galashiels service at Peebles' single-platform station – cramped by the topography – on 3 February 1962. *Frank Spaven*

On 3 February 1962 the Stephenson Locomotive Society ran a farewell excursion train, seen here at Rosewell & Hawthornden waiting to cross a Galashiels–Peebles–Edinburgh service. *WAC Smith / Transport Treasury*

In effect, there was plenty of data about the Peebles line's finances, but not much *useful* information from which to make robust judgements. A cynic (like me) might conclude that BR was happy to bamboozle a committee which was, in any case, seemingly reluctant to challenge the BR line of argument, but other factors were at play, too, as suggested by David Prescott: 'Traffic costing started in the 1950s but the evidence from 1960–61 is that it had not yet evolved into a useful management tool at a route level – it was at best only indicative.' Both perspectives lead us to the generic conclusion reached by Faulkner and Austin on closure data: 'In short, do not trust the statistics. At best, they tell only half the story; at worst, they can be manipulated to support any argument.'[6]

James Ness, General Manager of BR Scottish Region, wrote to the General Secretary of the NUR on 25 August 1961 to intimate the proposed closure. This letter advised bluntly: 'The circumstances of [the Peebles branch] have been investigated and from an examination of the passenger traffic it is clear that the use of the trains is so small that their continuance can no longer be justified . . . In these circumstances it is proposed to close the branch completely. Substantial economies will accrue; from staff alone these will amount to £42,000 a year, and there will be further savings from train working costs, and from Maintenance and renewal of rolling stock, permanent way and structures.'[7]

BR was taking a liberty by referencing savings from renewal of rolling stock, permanent way and structures: the DMUs had been in operation for only three years, extensive concrete re-sleepering had been undertaken in recent times, and the structures – which had been built to last – were likely to have many decades of life left in them.

The extent to which the line was burdened with infrastructure and facilities requiring staffing well beyond what was required for a sustainable passenger-only operation, was laid bare in a November 1961 memo to staff from the chief civil engineer's department in Glasgow.[8] Over the 34½ miles of single-track between Hawthornden Junction (just south of Rosewell & Hawthornden station) and Kilnknowe Junction (in north Galashiels) there were no fewer than:

- 13 level crossings
- 2 signal boxes at level crossings
- 2 further signal boxes
- 1 unstaffed halt with a level crossing

- 1 unstaffed halt with a private (freight) siding
- 2 further unstaffed halts
- 5 goods and passenger stations
- 1 goods and parcels station
- 4 private (freight) sidings
- 1 public (freight) siding

However, BR looked to be on stronger ground on passenger numbers, the memo noting that 'the average throughout loading of trains equipped to carry 118 passengers was under 15'. The average daily number of passengers using the trains was barely in double figures for six of the nine stations, with Clovenfords said to have nobody joining or alighting on an average weekday or Saturday, and Pomathorn seeing just three joining and six alighting on an average weekday. Only Peebles and Innerleithen (the largest settlements) had reasonably respectable numbers, with joining / alighting totals of 113 and 44 respectively on an average weekday, and Saturday figures of 340 and 128.

Particularly striking – and perhaps reflecting the generally lower volume of commuting (and, in particular, longer-distance commuting) in the early 1960s, as much as the deficiencies of the train service – is the memo's reference to 28 season tickets being sold in the 12 months ended January 1961, 14 of them at Peebles. One might hazard a guess that if the railway had still been open today the equivalent figure would have been well over 10 times that number. But the reality was that towns such as Peebles were much more self-contained and self-sufficient than today – and its population had declined from 6,000 in 1951 to 5,600 in 1961. As veteran Borders rail campaigner Bill Jamieson comments: 'Peebles had its own Town Council as well as being the administrative and economic centre of Peeblesshire, and no doubt it had its own cottage hospital too. In short there would be very little reason for most residents to travel out of town during the week, with the exception of the smallish number of professionals (presumably) who commuted to Edinburgh.'[9]

But the questions which should have been asked were: How much cost can we lose by sensible rationalisation of the infrastructure for a passenger-only operation? By how much can we increase revenue by speeding up trains and introducing a more frequent, regular-interval service? And we do not know what BR's 1960 analysis of a service cut back to Peebles–Edinburgh concluded about the impacts on costs and revenue.

The NUR predicts 'chaos'

Twenty-two members of the Galashiels branch of the NUR gathered at the town's station on 21 September 1961 to discuss the proposed closure. In the opening paragraph of a letter sent four days later to Sidney Greene, general secretary of the union in London, the branch secretary suggested that the closure would cause 'chaos'. But the two pages of text were not concerned with existing passengers or any impact on local roads – although brief mention was made that closure 'will seriously affect our [goods and parcels] customers interests, and will affect the taking of overspills from other city populations and the bringing of other industries to the Borders'.[10]

What was exercising the local NUR members was the difficulty of coping with the loading of a six-ton lorry to convey goods and parcels traffic to customers along the Peebles branch after closure. Having concluded that 'it is obvious to the most illiterate [ironically, the latter word had been mis-typed and then corrected] that it is impossible for this extra Peebles branch traffic to be dealt with under present staffing', the next 50 lines of text address – in astonishing detail – 'the problem of Passenger rated Perishables', a sample of which reads:

> At 6 am a Pcls clerk books on but the Ldg Porter who calls off the Traffic has now become the Ticket Collector in readiness for the 6.15 am to Edinburgh. After tis [sic] the Ldg Porter proceeds to call of [sic] Parcels until 6.50 whence he again becomes Ticket Collector for the Midland [the overnight train from London St Pancras via the Waverley Route to Edinburgh] at 7.5 am and the local at 7.24 am so therefore time is lost until 7.26 am in the sheeting of traffic. Thence again at 7.40 am he agin [sic] becomes Ticket Collector for the 7.55 am. Sheeting of traffic again takes place until 8.15 am whence Leading Porter again become [sic] Ticket Collector until dep of 8.42 am after which he may take up sheeting duties to complete the parcels traffic. It must be noted that during this time the clerk has constantly to answer the phone in regard to passenger train queries, and to book traffic for out going trains.

From my own experiences as a Railman and Senior Railman at Invergordon and Inverness in 1973, 1974 and 1975, I have plenty of sympathy for the staff workload caused by peaking of traffic. But what is striking in the NUR letter is the total focus on current operational detail – including the unrealistic suggestion that 'the Goods train be kept on from Galashiels with a General Porter at least at Peebles to deal with this traffic and a motor maintained at Peebles' for an average of only four wagons per day. Perhaps it is not reasonable to expect grassroots railwaymen to have properly appreciated in 1961 the wider market and political forces at play, but the reality was that just 10 years later *all* the passenger, parcels and freight traffic at Galashiels to which the NUR branch referred in great detail had completely disappeared from BR – lost to road competition and the vagaries of national politics.

On 12 October 1961, BR management and staff representatives met in Glasgow to discuss the proposed closure. The chairman of the management side provided a modicum of additional financial data, but no details of the 1960 investigation, in his gloomy verdict on the line's future: 'Mr. Fleming said the plain fact was that the Line is earning approximately £30,000 per annum whereas the costs are in the region of £60,000. Very full thought was given to the matter before deciding to go forward with the proposal to close the branch. Consideration was given as to whether we could not partially close the line but after weighing up all the factors, the conclusion was reached that the only satisfactory solution was to close the whole branch. Mr. Fleming added that the bus route ran parallel to the railway and the buses were also running half empty. The traffic was just not there.'[11]

Remarkably, the staff side pursued neither a breakdown of the quoted costs, nor the details of the 1960 study. Indeed, the minutes record only statements and assertions rather any penetrating questions for management, with the staff chairman limply concluding his contribution: 'Mr. McLaren reiterated that, despite the figures, the Staff Side were quite emphatic this branch line should be kept open in fulfilment of the Government directive that we should look after the needs of the community and they wished to lodge the strongest protest in regard to the withdrawal.'

With this standard of trade union opposition, BR management must have felt confident that closure could be secured without undue difficulty.

The TUCCS process: busy but superficial

The minutes and appendices of the TUCCS meeting held in Edinburgh on 20 October 1961[12] demonstrate that – at least in terms of quantity – much effort was devoted to discussing the Peebles closure proposal. No fewer than 58 pages were concerned wholly with the closure, including: a memorandum setting out the objections; copies of letters from organisations objecting; notes of a discussion earlier in the day with a deputation representing the objecting organisations; details of the train service, patronage and financial information; and notes of the TUCCS discussion leading up to its final decision.

The deputation comprised representatives from Peebles County Council, Peebles Town Council, Innerleithen Town Council, the Burgh of Bonnyrigg and Lasswade, Peebles and District Trades Council and local industry. The local authorities had earlier (on 29 September) written to advise that they and nine other interested bodies had met a week earlier in Peebles and wished to send a deputation to the TUCCS meeting considering the future of the railway. The letter also enclosed a written protest signed by members of the public, 'comprising 148 sheets and containing almost 3,500 signatures'.

The notes of that earlier meeting covered a wide range of arguments which were aired in some detail during the Edinburgh TUCCS meeting on 20 October. One contribution from the 22 September meeting in Peebles was a particularly succinct articulation of the case against closure, by the Honorary Secretary of Peebles & District Trades Council, which, unfortunately, he expressed much less clearly at the subsequent, crucial Edinburgh meeting:

Mr. David W. Taylor pointed out that if Peebles was to expand as a dormitory town of Edinburgh, it was a matter of extreme importance to retain the branch railway. He stated that in his view British Railways were now in the position of operating the line with modern equipment but encumbered by outmoded regulations, and appeared to be prepared to waste the considerable expenditure recently incurred re-laying the line.[13] He pointed out that the experimental timetables introduced with the diesel service had never been altered, although the times of the trains were by no means satisfactory from the point of view of the travelling public. He posed the query whether or not additional halts to serve housing schemes in the area would not increase passenger traffic and went on to describe the present fare structure as illogical and unattractive. He mentioned the high cost of maintaining manned crossings, of which there is a considerable number, and felt that there was a case for the introduction of the continental type of crossing barrier. He suggested that it should be possible to reduce staff considerably, as for example by the employment of guards to take fares on trains and ended by stressing the need for a railway if the area was to develop its industrial potential.

Taylor would be proved wrong about the need (as opposed to the desirability) for a railway if Peebles was to expand as a dormitory town, but his sound challenges to BR on economies and service improvements would never be satisfactorily answered.

Provost Lawrie of Peebles spoke at the Edinburgh meeting on behalf the three Borders councils. The transcript of his address takes up nearly four pages of the TUCCS record of the event, with the sheer length of his case forewarned in an early comment: 'I wish to submit to you eleven considerations. They are already, I believe, in your hands. No single one is sufficient and conclusive in itself, but in their cumulative merit, I think absolutely overwhelming.'

Briefly, these were the impacts on the existing county economy, on efforts to attract new industry, on the 'over-burdened' road system, on civil defence needs in the event of a national emergency, and on the cost of road transport of domestic coal (10,000 tons annually to Peebles alone). Plus: the scope for economies (including closing 'some of the smaller intermediate halts' to speed up the service); an improved service and fare structure (including the return half of tickets being valid on either bus or train, as had been introduced on the Workington–Keswick–Penrith service); a proposal to increase patronage as rapid housing development for commuters progressed in Peebles, and Edinburgh's parking places became more choked; the impact on the tourist trade; the opportunities for automatic level crossings – '[in Germany] the only roads without level crossings are the autobahns, all other roads have automatic crossings, and there are hundreds of them. They are efficient, they are money-saving, they are safe.'; the inadequacy of the replacement bus service; and, finally, the role of the railway as a public service, like schools, post offices and electricity supply to the most inaccessible places.

Baillie John Moffat of the Burgh of Bonnyrigg and Lasswade finished by asking for a stay of execution of at least 12 months.

And then BR Scottish Region began its response, led by Mr H.M. Lattimer (Operating Officer), supported by Mr J.M. Fleming (Traffic Manager) and Mr J.L. Stevenson (Traffic Costing Officer). Lattimer introduced BR's case bluntly: 'because of this volume of traffic, its lowness, the taxpayer – let us call him by the proper name – is paying half the train working costs, the whole of the station costs, and the whole of the engineering costs of the line'. He went on to reject the claim that BR had not done enough to cut costs, because '[we] have devoted to this line management time and energy out of all proportion to what it is earning', quoting first the example of level crossings: 'We already have one lifting barrier in Scotland, and you will have another by the end of the year, and more may follow, but . . . it all costs money. If I may say briefly the cost of these barriers works out to something like £4,000 a piece, and the maintenance and interest charges would bear more heavily on the annual accounts than the cost of manning the existing level crossing . . . there are many of them, and the capital sum of £50,000 might be involved.'

This sounded damning for the Peebles railway, but BR's evidence should have been presented in the form of a cost comparison (capital and annual operating / maintenance) with manned level crossings over perhaps 20 or more years – yet evidently the members of the committee did not feel motivated to offer such basic challenges to the BR claims. Was the presence on the committee of the Chairman of the Scottish Area Board of the BTC (Cameron of Lochiel) and the General Manager of BR Scottish Region (James Ness) an inhibiting factor?

The burden of level crossings proved to be a key factor in the closure of a number of other lines in the 1960s – such as Beverley to York and the East Lincolnshire line from Peterborough to Grimsby (which at the time was the main London–Grimsby route) – although other lines in Lincolnshire survived and their crossings were automated in the 1980s. As David Prescott points out in relation to the Peebles line: 'It appears that most crossing keepers were resident on site in railway cottages. Resident female crossing keepers were paid very little at that time, but got the crossing cottage virtu-ally rent-free, and their husbands were usually either signalman or worked on the Permanent Way, so had a cash wage. This would have changed if the line had been stripped back to a "basic railway" operation, with fewer signal boxes and less infrastructure to maintain, and labour costs for level crossings would have begun to rise in real terms – eventually changing the balance of financial advantage to automation in the 1980s, as elsewhere. But BR had more pressing, short-term concerns in 1961.'[14]

Back in the Peebles line debate in October 1961, the next suggestion to be rejected by BR was issuing tickets on trains (and, by implication, de-staffing stations) and adopting 'the many other methods which might be construed as cheapening the cost of passenger trains': 'They would bear little fruit, and have little effect on the economics of the railway line.' As for further improving the service, for example by trebling the frequency in 1958 (rather than doubling it, as happened), then an additional DMU set would have been required 'at the expense of someone else', and earnings would have had to be quadrupled to cover the increased working costs – more than quadrupled if fares were cut. Ignoring the role of the car as a key competitor, Lattimer then concluded: 'If there is the potential, then it must be travelling by other methods of transport, and I can say that if we can double or treble the number of passengers here, then the Scottish Omnibus Service must have some very contented and regular customers.'

Pursuing another option for economising, the Town Clerk of Peebles referenced Lattimer's earlier concession that it would be possible if the railway branch line stopped at Walkerburn to give a more advantageous timing of trains. Lattimer's response was vague – and devoid of any details which would allow the TUCCS to make their own judgement: 'We have tried every sort of permutation on this line – cutting it short at every Station, keeping the Galashiels end open, keeping the other end open, we have tried all permutations and the answer still comes out the same. They are different figures, but the same answer.'

The answer was not supplied, and nor were the figures – but none of the evidently docile, or compliant, 19 members of the committee present was moved to challenge this sweeping dismissal of different approaches to running the railway.

An ill-informed decision

The notes of the TUCCS discussion after the meeting reflect overwhelmingly unquestioning attitudes to the proposal, and not a single reference to the scope for economies and an enhanced service. The discussion was opened by a Mr J. Bennett with a confused, and confusing, statement: 'I am putting forward a purely personal point of view. I was very much impressed with the Deputation as to what they said and how they said it. I was not the least bit impressed by the British Transport Commission representatives on this occasion or the answers given to the questions raised. I, for one, was not struck in any way. I was much happier reading the submission than hearing it from the British Transport Commission representatives. Having said that, however, and consequent upon our visit to the area concerned this morning, I am of the opinion that the British Transport Commission have made their case.'

Other members were generally satisfied with the BTC submission, albeit with a number of references to suggested delay to (a) resolve the question of delivery of household coal to the county by road, and / or (b) try to develop tourist traffic. There was but one mention of the impact of closure on rail passengers, and it was not sympathetic. Mr J. Urquhart commented: 'I have heard nothing to-day to suggest any conceivable hardship or inconvenience.' Either the discussion had been hopelessly narrow, or Mr Urquhart was not readily capable of relating to individual train travellers' needs.

The TUCCS Chairman (Sir John G Banks, CBE, JP) gave a preliminary – and disjointed, not to say pompous – summing-up, prior to giving the floor to the two members representing the BTC: 'I have the feeling that there has been little enthusiasm down there for the railway. There is an unfortunate "could not care less" atmosphere throughout the country at the present time. It is no good these people thinking they will work up enthusiasm for Diesel trains, and I would be disposed to agree to the complete closure.'

Cameron of Lochiel argued that the diesel service had had a reasonable chance to prove itself (over nearly four years) and rejected the scope for developing tourist traffic: 'Personally, I feel that tourists do not go a short distance by train. Tourists use a train when they have a beautiful scenic route, but I think to go to Peebles they almost certainly use private cars, and I do not believe whatever advertising we did or alterations we made to the time table, would attract much more tourist traffic.' In other words, he did not know, and no research had been done by BR. This went unchallenged by any members of the committee (who might have been expected to cite the town's slogan, 'Peebles for Pleasure', and the popularity of Peebles Hydro hotel and spa resort).

James Ness then focused on the annual patronage changes following the introduction of DMUs in early 1958: Year 1 had seen 75,000 additional passenger journeys compared to the last year of steam, Year 2 a further 30,000, while Year 3 saw numbers drop back by 19,000, and a further 20,000 had been lost in the first nine months of Year 4. In other words, although he did not spell it out, in Year 4 the railway was still generating 66,000 more passenger journeys than in the last year of steam. But his verdict was simple – the bus, 'which carried most of the traffic' had 18 services per day compared to eight by train: 'There is, therefore, no case for keeping this line open a day longer than is necessary for me to meet the needs of Mr. Adamson [who had raised the issue of coal transport]'.

Nobody thought to ask for any further explanation of *why* the big increases in rail journeys (equating to a 111% increase in receipts in Year 1, as we saw in Chapter 2) had partly been reversed – nor for a BR explanation of how much cost could be lost through economies in infrastructure, etc. The stage was now set for the Chairman of Scottish Omnibuses to put his knife into the unwanted competition for his Edinburgh–Peebles bus service. The contribution of Mr James Amos was short, and sour:

If ever there was a case for keeping a railway open, this would not have been it. I know the railway line very well and have studied it closely. I should have liked to have questioned the Provost on the adequacy or inadequacy of the bus services.

I will quote the Peebles local newspaper in the case of the recent Edinburgh Holiday, when they said they had an excellent bus service. Trains run on the same fuel as buses.

I agree with what Mr. Ness has said on this occasion. I disagreed with him when he put Diesels on the Peebles route because I knew there was no hope for them, and the quicker the line is closed the better it will be. There are other railway services in Scotland which show more signs of progression, and I would have no hesitation in re-iterating my view that the quicker the line is closed the better.

The TUCCS Chairman then noted that eight members had voted for closure, while four had voted for a delay of either six or twelve months. After further discussion, it was finally agreed to approve the BTC proposals and allow it to close the line when arrangements had been made for the transportation of coal.

In his history of *Peebles Railways*, Peter Marshall records that Peebles Town Council subsequently complained to Ernest Marples, the Minister of Transport, that there had been insufficient time to organise a case against closure and there should be a period of further experiment to promote the service. The minister's reply indicated that he could not agree, and that, 'as the TUCC did not make any recommendations on the proposals, he had in any event no power to direct the British Transport Commission in this matter'. What Marples was presumably trying to say was that the committee had not made a *recommendation*, but rather had made a *decision*, to authorise closure. As Robert Drysdale writes in a forthcoming book on the demise of Edinburgh's suburban railways: 'It was a statutory fact that if the TUCC, whether deliberately or unwittingly, recorded its conclusions as a "decision" rather than a "recommendation to the Minister", then the BTC was free to proceed in line with the TUCC's verdict, and the Minister had no say in the matter. This was particularly perplexing for the Scottish Secretary, who was thereby denied any scope for lobbying Marples.'[15]

In any event, the town council then concluded that there could be no purpose in pursuing the matter further. In the words of the town clerk: 'When we lost at the hearing, it was the end of it.'[16]

It was then only six weeks until the sad end of the rail service, as recorded by Peter Marshall: 'With a great deal of gloom and some little ceremony, the final train on the Peebles Railway ran on Saturday 3rd February 1962 – the 11.00 pm, Saturdays only, from Edinburgh (Waverley). On Peebles station platform, a reception party of a piper and around 200 people met the train. The diesel multiple unit announced its final arrival to the sound of detonators, which had been placed on the rail. Once the train had completed its journey at Galashiels, the Peebles line between Hawthornden Junction signal box and Kilnknowe Junction . . . was closed to all traffic.'[17]

Peeblesshire thus became the first county on the Scottish mainland to lose all its passenger train services.[18] It would not be the last.

A very strange closure

A.J. Mullay uses the experience of the Peebles line closure process to illustrate his wider point that the TUCCs were not always seen as impartial: 'In 1962, the TUCC's decision not to oppose the much-lamented decision to close the Peebles line, led to accusations of lack of impartiality – the head of Scottish Omnibuses was a member of the committee (at the chairman's invitation), and the company was on record as complaining about the introduction of DMUs on the route four years earlier. No wonder there appears to have been a lack of public confidence in the TUCC system.'[19]

Mullay describes the loss of trains to Peebles as 'one of Scotland's most puzzling closures', and implicitly links this to the presence of Amos on the TUCC, which 'was curious, if not downright wrong . . . It seems impossible to explain how the company's representation on the Committee could be justified.'

While it is not possible, without much more data from the period, to assess full cost and revenue projections for a railway rationalised to secure significant cost-savings while also enhancing the service provided, we can reasonably identify the broad scope of potential economies.

The operational curse of the Peebles line was the 16 staffed level crossings, of which 14 were not controlled by signal boxes otherwise required to control train movements. Level crossing automation, while still in its infancy in 1961, would ultimately have resulted in significant staff cost savings. Two years after a fact-finding trip to mainland Europe by the BTC, Her Majesty's Railway Inspectorate and the MoT, in 1957 a report advocating the use of automatic and automated level crossings in Britain was completed. Although it then took four years of sorting out new regulations to control their operation and use, the first automatically operated level crossing opened in Staffordshire in May 1961,[20] more than six months before the decision was taken to close the Peebles line.

Doubtless the pressure to secure early cuts in BR's financial losses squeezed out any consideration of local automation economies – which of course would have involved up-front capital expenditure and an inevitable time-lag before the revenue expenditure benefits were realised. BR's 25 August 1961 letter setting out the case for closure makes reference to the exceptional number of manned level crossings, 'which adds considerably to working and signalling costs', but then states: 'No simplification is capable of introduction which would conform to Ministry standards and which would at the same time allow a passenger service to traverse them at normal speeds.' Given the precedent in Staffordshire earlier that year – and BR's failure to speed up the service when DMUs were introduced – this was a breathtaking and disingenuous claim.

Of the nine stations south of Rosewell & Hawthornden – the latter enjoying a greater frequency of trains partly linked to Edinburgh's South Suburban Outer Circle service – Peebles, Innerleithen and Walkerburn were fully staffed, while dual-function crossing keeper or halt / station attendants were deployed at Pomathorn Halt, Eddleston and Cardrona; just Rosslynlee and Rosslynlee Hospital Halt were completely unstaffed – so only limited economies had been implemented on this front.

The August 1961 BR management memo to the staff side listed a total of 37 operating staff posts to be withdrawn on the branch, plus 10 train crew and platform staff at Galashiels, while the November 1961 memo detailed a total of 23 Permanent Way and signal technician staff posts to be withdrawn at Walkerburn, Peebles and Leadburn. With 70 staff, this was a labour-intensive railway – but not untypical for the time.

Turning to track and signalling infrastructure, south of Hawthornden Junction (where the Penicuik freight branch diverged) there were four unevenly spaced crossing loops / block posts[21] to control the 34½ miles of single-track railway to Kilknowe Junction on the Waverley Route. Most of the eight Up and seven Down trains crossed other trains on the branch, but in each of these instances there was only a single crossing made. With conversion to a 'basic railway', including automated level crossings, two of the conventional crossing loops could have been eliminated, particularly if transits had been speeded up by closing the smallest intermediate stations. And BR could have, at long last, accelerated a timetable which still reflected pre-1958 steam haulage timings.

Galashiels to Edinburgh via Peebles, with typically 12 or 13 intermediate stops, took around 1 hour 35 minutes. A brief perusal of the timetable suggests that a minimum of two or three DMU sets were required to maintain the (irregular) service pattern.[22] Eliminating six of the seven least-used stations – Clovenfords, Walkerburn, Cardrona, Eddleston, Rosslynlee Hospital Halt and Rosslynlee – would have allowed a cut in journey time to perhaps 1 hour 20 minutes for the 45½ miles from Galashiels to Edinburgh. Would it have been realistic to operate an hourly frequency to match the bus service? Bill Jamieson has his doubts, given Peebles' relatively small population, and the largely self-contained character of the Borders town in those days: 'I have some difficulty in imagining how, in the socio-economic circumstances of the early 1960s, the potential patronage could ever have justified an hourly regular-interval service; two hourly perhaps – in fact the DMU service in 1960 wasn't far off being that, albeit irregular – but I still suspect that the potential for generating Monday to Friday traffic was very limited at that time.'[23]

Not only the demand side would have been problematic – an hourly frequency from Galashiels through Peebles to Edinburgh would have required the retention of crossing loops at Innerleithen and Leadburn (half an hour running-time apart) and hence reduced the scope for economies.

In any event, assuming a reprieve for the whole route, all goods facilities and associate track and signalling – at six stations, five private sidings and one public siding – would have been removed. However, even a 'basic railway' would sensibly have retained a service, at partly marginal cost, for parcels (carried on DMUs) handled at probably the only two staffed stations – Peebles and Pomathorn (the latter also a park-and-ride facility) – as BR retained a nationwide parcels service until the late 1990s.

A compromise solution: retain only Peebles to Edinburgh?

If the viability of the whole branch looked dubious, what about the option of closing Galashiels to Peebles, and only retaining the service from the latter to Edinburgh, as BR explored in 1960? Peebles to Edinburgh took an hour, typically with eight intermediate calls. Closing the three smallest intermediate stations – Eddleston, Rosslynlee Hospital Halt and Rosslynlee, but retaining Pomathorn as a passenger and parcels railhead for Penicuik – together with acceleration to take full advantage of the DMUs' speed capability, would have allowed a cut in journey time to perhaps 45–50 minutes for the 27 miles from Peebles to Edinburgh. Bill Jamieson suggests that this might have required more powerful DMUs than the 300hp 'Gloucester' model used – perhaps the 360hp Metro-Cammell – particularly for the long climb from Eskbank to the line's summit just south of Leadburn.

A minimum of two DMU sets would have been needed to operate a self-contained hourly-interval service, or only one DMU for a two-hourly service (compared to the two or three needed for the final Edinburgh–Peebles–Galashiels timetable). And, as David Prescott points out, an hourly Peebles–Edinburgh frequency 'would have enabled the separate Rosewell suburban service to be withdrawn and the revenue transferred to the Peebles service'.[24] For the two-hourly service, the line could have been worked as a 'long siding' south of Hawthornden Junction – once all the level crossings had been automated or simplified – removing the loops at Leadburn and Peebles Engine Shed. Even an hourly service could (just) have been accommodated on a long siding, assuming closure of three of the intermediate stations – but to cope with out-of-course running and charter trains it would have been sensible to retain the loop at Peebles as a train crew-operated 'ground frame' facility and the loop at Leadburn, at least as long as the signal box was needed to control the level crossing there.

It would have meant 17½ miles of track between Peebles and Kilnknowe Junction becoming redundant, and it would reduce operating costs (but also the passenger revenue) to zero between Peebles and Gala. However, at 60 years' remove we can only guess how far the revenue / cost equation for Peebles–Edinburgh would have been brought into better balance by the creation of a 'basic railway' with an improved service. Bill Jamieson takes the view that Peebles–Gala should have been sacrificed in 1962:

> Even on Saturdays, perhaps barring when rugby fixtures were on, it's difficult to imagine there was much patronage east of Walkerburn. Why would anyone go in that direction? Peebles probably offered a better selection of independent shops than Galashiels back then (as it still does today) and, crucially, there were no supermarkets. Also there was no Borders General Hospital, nor Scottish Borders Council HQ at Newtown, although there was a central hospital facility at Peel, but that was two miles from Clovenfords station and more conveniently served by bus.
>
> I would certainly agree with the thesis that if the Peebles–Edinburgh line had remained open, it would now be thriving. The population of the town today is probably over 9,000, and adding in Walkerburn, Innerleithen and Cardrona, the catchment

population for a 21st century railhead would be something like 14,000, the same order of magnitude as Galashiels, which has proved to be a highly successful rail re-opening.[25]

It would be fascinating to unearth what infrastructure and service changes BR envisaged in its 1960 analysis of this option. Given that it was not implemented, we can speculate that at that time there was no great appetite for exploring what became known only a few years later as the 'basic railway' concept. By the end of the decade such enlightened thinking became mainstream in the rail industry, but in the early 1960s there was a powerful attraction to the simplicity of complete closure, against a background of widespread assumptions that railways were in terminal decline.

The aftermath

The Peebles line features prominently in a little-reported aspect of closures: the financial benefit which accrued to BR (and presumably the taxpayer) through the recovery of redundant assets. In his research for *BR Scottish Region*, A.J. Mullay unearthed much line-by-line detail from BR records: of 30 lines listed in the 'reporting years' 1955 to 1971, only the Waverley Route (in 1971) yielded a higher recovery figure than the £3,465 per mile for Hawthornden Junction–Peebles–Galashiels.[26] Reviewing data for all the lines listed, Mullay notes a 'similarity in recovery figures per mile, whether the closed railway was single-track or double-track. This suggests that the actual materials making up the permanent way – rails, sleepers (especially if concrete), ballast – were budgeted as reusable, with the principal income coming from the sale or rental of lineside accommodation, inflated no doubt on grounds of increased amenity. This would explain why the recovery figure for the Peebles line, with its numerous crossing-keepers' cottages, was so high.'[27]

How did former rail passengers fare after they were obliged to use bus or car, or curtail the journeys previously made? We can reasonably assume that the nationwide pattern of dislocation and disadvantage discovered by Hillman and Whalley was replicated on the Edinburgh–Peebles–Galashiels corridor, but the TUCCS 1962 annual report could only comment – in relation to the Peebles line and two other concurrent closures – that 'despite the strong representations which were made by the Local Authorities and others for the retention of the facilities, no complaints have been received by the Committee regarding the alternative services available'.[28] But given the British reluctance to complain, former rail users may simply have been suffering in silence.

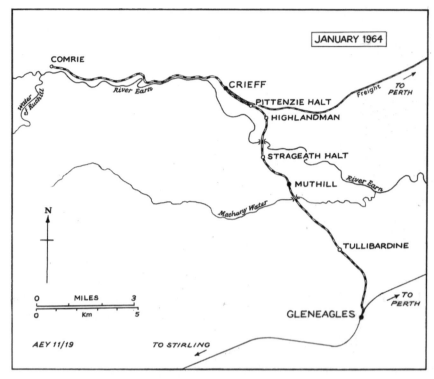

The nine-mile railway from Gleneagles to Crieff climbed north towards Strathearn, crossing the Machary Water and the River Earn on substantial bridges. Always single-track, the line latterly had one crossing loop at Muthill and no fewer than three tracks through the grand station at Crieff. Comrie signal box was closed in 1961, and thereafter the 5¾ single-track miles to Crieff were operated by the One Engine in Steam method of working. However, an unsignalled loop – operated by train crew – was retained at Comrie to allow rounding of locomotive-hauled trains when these had to be substituted for railbus failures. (Alan Young)

8

The wrong kind of train: Crieff / Comrie

Crieff's original station – the terminus of the nine-mile Crieff Junction Railway from Crieff Junction (later 'Gleneagles') opened in 1856 – had to be rebuilt when the line was extended a further 5¾ miles through to Comrie in 1893, and it appears that the Caledonian Railway spared no expense. The town may have been the second largest in Perthshire, but its population was still less than 6,000 in 1861, yet the Caledonian – renowned for its 'belle époque' style – constructed a grand station building with, unusually for a secondary line, three tracks between its two through platforms. Further enhancement followed – with the platforms lengthened to 700 feet – during the extension of the line to St Fillans, Lochearnhead and the junction with the Callander & Oban at Balquhidder (opened in 1905).

St John Thomas cites Crieff station as an example of over-ambition resulting from 'genuine mistakes in forecasting traffic volume'.[1] The latter task was to prove a perennial problem for the rail industry well over a century later, with several Scottish line re-openings in the 21st century – notably the Borders Railway – suffering from *under-provision* of infrastructure due to seriously pessimistic traffic forecasts.

A little-known pre-Beeching closure proposal

As we have seen, the early 1950s saw an acceleration of closures in Scotland, with a subsequent lull followed by the axing of half-a-dozen lines in 1955. A lesser-known aspect of that decade is that the BTC was unsuccessful in some bids to withdraw passenger services, largely due to the opposition of the TUCCs established by the 1947 Transport Act. Gleneagles–Crieff / Comrie is a notable example, with the minutes of the 24th meeting of the Transport Users' Consultative Committee for Scotland – held on 10 June

1955 at the North British Hotel in Edinburgh – only hinting at the depth and breadth of discussion devoted to the line's future earlier that day: 'A Deputation consisting of Mr. Alex. Thomson, Advocate, and representatives of the Joint County Council of the Combined County of Perth and Kinross, the Town Council of Crieff, the Central District Council of the County of Perth, and the Scottish Tourist Board, as well as The Convention of Royal Burghs, who had not intimated their intention to be present, was received, and Mr. C.J.H. Selfe, Assistant Commercial Manager, Scottish Region, British Railways, presented the case for the Commission.'

Attached to the meeting minutes are: a 17-page memorandum (including written objections from a variety of bodies objecting to closure, perhaps the most unlikely coming from The Scottish Licensed Trade Association); 18 pages of notes of the discussion with the deputation; and four pages of notes of the subsequent committee discussion of the proposed closure.[2] If weight of paper was the determinant of TUCC decisions, the Crieff / Comrie opposition had certainly played its cards right.

The BTC case – at first sight – was not without its merits. Figures for the average number of passengers per train showed that the busiest carried only 28 people, and the least-used only four. That said, Crieff was served by only seven trains a day, while Comrie had just one. It was stated by the BTC that after making allowance for loss of receipts 'and without calculating Technical Department economies, it is estimated the proposal will improve the Commission's annual net revenue by £13,735'. The National Farmers' Union of Scotland – which supported closure of the small intermediate stations – had voiced its doubts about the losses, a refrain that would become very familiar throughout the Beeching era, the notes recording that 'it is significant that British Railways have not given the break-up figures for which they asked'.

A submission from the local authorities sought to challenge both the demand and supply situation, in the former case suggesting the need for a better train service: 'It is believed that increased passenger traffic could be attracted to the existing branch line by the improvement of rolling stock, the provision of extended and more reasonable cheap day return tickets from Crieff to Edinburgh and Glasgow and later train services back to Crieff from Edinburgh and Glasgow.'

Interestingly, at least the first and third of these suggestions would be taken on board by BR three years after the reprieve, when the line was dieselised. The local authorities also highlighted the need for economies, such as

(i) closure of intermediate stations, (ii) closure of the Crieff locomotive shed, with work to be taken over by Stirling, which already sent a steam engine and crew to Crieff early each morning, and (iii) 'as an alternative to the steam engine some other form of locomotion could be used with great saving in running cost – e.g. diesel car or electric battery coach'.

Far from closing intermediate stations, three years later BR actually opened two new low-cost halts – Pittenzie and Strageath – to coincide with dieselisation. While it was diesel rather than a battery car which came to the Comrie / Crieff line, the TUCC papers reveal that BR had to be dragged kicking and screaming to introduce a battery car *anywhere* in Scotland, although one would ultimately appear on Deeside in 1958. Sir George McGlashan, representing Perth and Kinross Joint County Council, was politely scathing:

> May I . . . refer to electric battery coaches. It has already been pointed out to the Commission, they are well aware of the fact, that in Germany 76 of these vehicles are in operation and have been found to solve problems of branch line operation which previously were insoluble. So far as we know the Commission have made no attempt whatever to experiment with that system before continuing their policy of closing down branch lines. They contend that they do not have technical officers available, and they have also said that in any event a minimum expenditure of £50,000 to make the experiment would be required. I happen to be a member of the North of Scotland Hydro Electric Board, and we have obtained reliable estimates from actual makers, and the cost of a complete battery coach unit is £18,000, including batteries . . . May I say, having those comparative figures in mind, that is the Commission's estimate of £50,000 and the actual figure of £18,000, it is hardly surprising that the authorities who are making these representations to you, sir, hesitate a little to accept the estimate of loss on the Crieff branch line.

BR's Mr Selfe (with no colleagues to support him) struggled to respond: 'It has been said that the cost of a unit is £18,000. That is the estimate from the makers, but there is surely a very great deal more to be taken into consideration than the mere cost of one unit. You have to set up a servicing depot, and there are a number of other things which I, as a non technical man, would not know about, but which the technical men would probably advise you on.'

Provost Maclean of Crieff had done his homework and took up the cudgel on the question of attracting additional passengers to the railway: 'I happened to pick up the Railway Staff Magazine last month and I saw a very enthusiastic leader there about the success of the introduction of diesel trains in some of the busier areas of England, but also in a place like Westmorland, which is much more comparable with Perthshire, where an increase of between 70 and 140 per cent in receipts had been recorded.'

Mr Selfe was not persuaded: 'The fact that diesels had made savings of 70 per cent to 140 per cent is perfectly true in certain areas, but before we can decide to put in diesels we must know all the circumstances in the particular area to which they are to go in. Certainly an increase in traffic of 140 per cent would still not make the Gleneagles–Crieff section profitable. We are a long long way from that, and if we cannot get sufficient passengers to justify it, to bring us into parity, there would be no real point in doing it.'

Perhaps Selfe was mis-quoted in confusing 'savings' and 'receipts', but presumably not even in his wildest dreams (or would they be nightmares?) could he have anticipated that in only four years' time the first year of dieselisation of the Crieff line would yield an increase in receipts even greater than 140%. In any event, to view dieselisation as pointless unless the line were made 'profitable' seems an extreme view of the purpose of railways, even in 1955.

After some further exchanges, the deputation withdrew and the TUCCS members considered what decision to reach. Despite protestations from Sir Ian Bolton (Bt, OBE, and the Scottish representative on the BTC), the committee agreed to recommend that the passenger train service should be retained.

So, the passenger service continued, but BR also sought to make sensible economies. Comrie station, specifically, was an example of proposals for rationalisation – short of closure – which would routinely be considered by the TUCCS in the 1950s. At its 42nd meeting on 14 July 1959, the committee was presented with the BTC's case for de-staffing Comrie station, citing a total of only 4,655 passengers (booked, inwards and seasons) in the 12 months ended December 1958.[3] This certainly did not justify employing a 'Station Master and one Porter Signalman' – but with three trains a day, what did BR expect?

As we have seen, BR began trialling DMUs on passenger service on the Peebles line on 11 July 1956, often described as the first such operation in

Scotland, but photographic evidence[4] indicates that DMUs were already in operation between Gleneagles and Crieff at least two days earlier. Passenger numbers evidently did not justify a two-car unit, however, and in September 1958 the line became the first in Scotland to have a regular railbus service.

The type of lightweight railbus normally used on the branch could seat only 48 passengers and had a top speed of just 60mph, but they boasted 'large windows which gave good all-round views and a light and modern feel to the passenger area'.[5] On each side they had an air-operated door and a set of extending / portable steps for use where there was no station platform, as at the new halts at Strageath and Pittenzie. Two of the three other intermediate stations – Tullibardine and Highlandman – became unstaffed halts. To coincide with dieselisation, BR upped the train service frequency from seven to 10 from Gleneagles to Crieff, and from one to three between Crieff and Comrie – and devoted substantial publicity to the new service. Overall, one could argue that this was a text-book example of BR trying to breathe new life into a branch line while making (some) sensible economies – but there was one fundamental flaw.

The railbuses proved to be unreliable in regular operation, and often had to be replaced by traditional steam traction – and this was presumably a contributory factor to the phenomenon of 158% patronage growth from the last year of regular steam service to the first year of diesel operation, followed by 29% decline in the second year. However, the 1960 BR report on dieselisation (see page 36) does note that a factor in Comrie / Crieff was the presence in 1958 of 'a squad of workmen on a construction contract' which finished part-way through 1959. But *structural* traffic decline was, of course, a key factor behind the sweeping closure proposals in 1963's Beeching Report.

Fifteen minutes of fame in the Beeching Report

Gleneagles–Crieff / Comrie – unlike the overwhelming majority of lines mentioned in the Beeching Report – featured not only in the lengthy list of routes proposed for closure, but also in his table of 10 case studies illustrating the assessments made of the annual revenue and expenses for a variety of threatened passenger services, variously categorised as commuter / holiday / inter-urban / rural, or a combination of these. (This table, and indeed the whole Beeching Report, can readily be viewed online.)[6]

Only three of the 10 services are addressed specifically in the report text, one of these being Gleneagles–Crieff / Comrie, which is categorised as 'holiday / rural' – and concerns about the impact on tourism were indeed regularly voiced by objectors. Just how important this economic sector was to Crieff specifically is illustrated by a list – derived from the 'National Register of Accommodation' for 1964, published by the Scottish Tourist Board – of towns with hotel and boarding house accommodation which would be deprived of their rail service by closures proposed in the Beeching Report. Crieff came top of the list of 132 towns, with 747 single-room-equivalent places.[7]

Crieff would therefore suffer particularly from an inherent flaw in the closure proposal process nationally, which was set out in the official BR notices for all individual proposals: 'In accordance with the requirements of the Act, it is necessary to publicise in two local newspapers details of the proposed withdrawal and to post notices at the stations affected during two successive weeks. These intimations provide for a period of six weeks, during which objections from any user of the service or any body which represents such users may be sent to the Secretary of the Transport Users' Consultative Committee.'[8]

On the face of it, this all looked very proper – for *local* rail users. 'The stations affected' were deemed to be those directly served by those trains proposed for withdrawal. So, for the Crieff / Comrie branch, whose trains originated no further away than Gleneagles (apart from one through train daily from Stirling), a substantial proportion of users may well have been unaware of the statutory process by which they could formally lodge an objection with the body which (in theory) had a significant bearing on the fate of the railway. Arguably, the majority of branch lines considered in detail in this book therefore faced an uphill battle to garner sufficient official objections to convey the scale of hardship involved – albeit that 'hardship' would be harder to attribute to day-trippers and tourists than regular local users, given the narrowly drawn unofficial definition used at the MoT.

The excerpt below from the Beeching Report text on Crieff / Comrie illustrates the failure to justify closure of the Gleneagles–Crieff section, as opposed to its conversion to a 'basic railway':

> Some 340,000 passenger miles accrue to this service which accounts for 65,000 train miles a year. On average, there are 5 passengers on a train at any one time. Earnings are £1,900 and these represent little more than a quarter of the train movement expenses of £7,500. Station terminal expenses bring the total of

direct expenses to nearly £11,000, less than a fifth of which is covered by the earnings of the service. When track and signalling expenses are added – £8,200 – the total expenses [£19,260] are ten times as great as the earnings of the service.

Passengers using this service in combination with other services contribute more than £12,000 to the earnings of other rail services, and it is estimated that withdrawal of the service would result in the loss of £9,000 of this contributory revenue. Because there would be no alternative rail service on this line after withdrawal, none of the earnings on the service would be retained.

Despite the estimate of contributory loss, which is probably high, bearing in mind that holidaymakers may travel elsewhere, the overall net financial improvement expected from withdrawal is nearly £8,400, or more than two-fifths of the present level of total direct expenses attributable to the service.

The first paragraph above quickly conjures up a picture of a hopeless financial case. However, we then learn that no less than £9,000 of contributory revenue to the rest of the BR network was expected to be lost. But Beeching's text swiftly skips forward to his bottom-line conclusion that the overall net financial improvement expected from withdrawal is 'more than two-fifths of the present level of total direct expenses attributable to the service'.

Even a quick perusal of the accompanying table reveals some illuminating points about the viability of the service, which Beeching's text (perhaps carefully) ignores. Unlike eight of his 10 case studies, in which the expected loss in total gross revenue as a result of closure is less than even the 'movement expenses' (i.e., the direct cost only of operating the trains), in the case of Crieff / Comrie (and Aberdeen–Ballater) the revenue loss from closure is less than the combined movement and 'terminal' (i.e., stations) expenses. It is only once 'direct track and signalling expenses' are included that 'withdrawal of the service becomes financially justified'. This is a clear pointer that Crieff (but not Comrie) and Ballater were not 'basket cases', but with sensible rationalisation could have had an ongoing future based on relatively modest subsidy.

Some care needs to be taken in not over-stating the case. The movement expenses attributed to the service are only 2s 4d per train-mile, presumably based on optimal railbus operation – but the railbuses often did *not* operate optimally (and an earlier page of the report suggested a generic figure of

3s per mile). A longer-term solution would have required two-car DMU operation, at somewhat greater movement cost, perhaps of the order of 4s per train-mile – or alternatively BR also had four-axle single-unit DMU 'railcars' with significantly more capacity (65 seats) than any type of railbus (46–56 seats). The former certainly proved their reliability, with the Class 121 being Britain's longest-serving DMU type, operating in passenger service for 57 years until 2017.[9]

The direct track and signalling expenses allocated to threatened passenger services assumed, as throughout the Beeching Report, that freight was the basic *raison d'être* of the railway and would continue to operate, leaving the passenger service to pick up only the marginal costs for the additional capacity needed for, and higher train speeds of, a passenger service. This was not a credible long-term solution, as Beeching's analysis of wagonload freight's loss-making characteristics – particularly in the context of rural branches – inevitably led to widespread freight withdrawals over the following two decades. Advocates of the closure solution can therefore argue that BR's figures understated the extent of losses – albeit that the scope for infrastructure economies had been ignored.

BR consults with staff – and marshals its arguments for the TUCCS

Consultation papers issued by BR management to staff in May 1963[10] included details of traffic conveyed in 1962: Crieff station had booked 13,109 passengers (but this excluded the significant volume of inbound holiday passengers who would have added further contributory revenue), 27,090 parcels had been handled and a total of 20,211 tons of freight had been forwarded / received (55% being inward coal traffic). The staff complement was 25 (excluding train drivers) and the 'Cartage Strength' showed two 'Motors' – but no longer any 'Horses'.

Interestingly, prior to standing down as BR Scottish Region's General Manager in 1963, James Ness – who was sympathetic to preservation – had made a tentative approach to the embryonic Scottish Railway Preservation Society (founded in 1961) about the possibility of their preserving the by-then freight-only Perth–Methven Junction–Crieff branch. Crieff would have made an excellent base, with its grand station facilities, turntable, engine shed and goods shed, but the offer – presumably in anticipation of freight being withdrawn (as it would be in 1967) – had to be declined as the SRPS suffered a severe shortage of funds in its early years.[11]

Four days before the 26 November 1963 TUCC public hearing in Crieff, BR produced its 'Brief for Liaison Officer',[12] a substantial internal document prepared in advance of all such post-1962 hearings organised by the TUCCS (allowing objectors to provide oral evidence and BR to be cross-examined). The briefs typically comprised:

- a summary of objections
- copies of letters received from objectors, and BR's private comments on these
- BR's publicly available Heads of Information on the closure proposal and any supplementary details
- financial information, including a limited breakdown of receipts and costs supplied confidentially to the TUCCS

The Crieff brief opened with a damning statistic: there had been only 25 objections to closure, 20 from individuals and five from organisations. The National Farmers' Union of Scotland was objecting (as it had done in 1955), as was the Scottish Railway Development Association, but there was silence from the three local authorities (including Crieff Town Council) and the Scottish Tourist Board. Eight years of growing car ownership – and the unhappy experiment with railbuses – had evidently been enough to transform the reaction to proposed closure, from one of engaging an advocate to argue the case against, to one where four key organisations did not even bother to write a letter of objection to the TUCCS.

The BR Heads of Information included a comparison of bus and rail fares and journey times; the grounds of the objections to closure related mainly to the inadequacy of the alternative bus service and the condition of roads in the area. As was often the case for threatened rail services, the Special Cheap Day Return fare and season tickets by train were the same price or within a few pennies of the return bus fare for key journeys. But rail's Ordinary Returns compared poorly: for example, 13s 6d from Crieff to Stirling, as opposed to 5s 8d on the bus.

Nine to 10 trains a day between Crieff and Gleneagles would be replaced by seven to eight bus journeys taking 28 minutes, against 20–23 minutes (although there was little difference in journey time to Stirling, given rail's necessity for a change at Gleneagles.) There was an honest admission in the brief: 'The objector who mentions that there is no guarantee that any new bus service will be continued is correct' – and that indeed is the case today between Crieff and Gleneagles. The availability of an hourly bus service from Crieff to Stirling (as an alternative railhead) was cited, with the blasé verdict that 'the distance between the railway and bus stations should cause little inconvenience as these places are less than ½ mile apart. If burdened with luggage, etc. passengers can obtain taxis to and from the bus station.' This was not a vision of high-quality, integrated public transport.

The brief commented on a number of other aspects of bus travel stated by objectors as offering less comfort than the train, including the incidence of travel sickness: 'Remedies to combat travel sickness e.g. KWELLS and MARZINE, are readily available. Buses are fitted with heaters. The journey time of 35 minutes [sic] by bus between Crieff and Gleneagles should impose no strain on anyone. It should be noted that the diesel railbuses operating between Crieff and Gleneagles at present have no facilities for non-smokers or for dining.' The thought of railbus passengers tucking into dinner with silver service is truly delicious.

Several objectors had made suggestions for service improvements and one suggested reducing the number of staff, especially at Crieff, but the brief's commentary rejected all these out of hand: 'None of the suggestions made would result in any appreciable increase in net revenue – in fact, the reverse might well be the case.' Various criticisms based on the limited financial information provided by BR's Heads of Information were repudiated, with an interesting statement that 'the financial details are supplied simply as background information and are not the subject of discussion by T.U.C.C.s'.

The comment that 'the effect [of loss of contributory gross revenue] on main line revenue is quoted in the Re-shaping report as £9,000 per annum and is relatively small' was breathtaking in its audacity. The £9,000 was (a) more than four times the line's self-contained earnings (to be lost in their entirety), and (b) represented 73% of the total contributory gross revenue to the rest of the network (£12,280) – the highest proportion of any of the 10 case studies in the Beeching Report.

With contributory value brought into the equation, there was a much healthier ratio of receipts to costs. Yet the travelling public were denied this information (unless they had examined Table 1 of the Beeching Report). The staff side made important points of principle about the line's finances at a consultation meeting on 14 June 1963 in Glasgow,[13] but the prosaic was never far away: 'Mr. Watt raised the question of extra work for the staff at Gleneagles and particularly the pushing of laden barrows of Crieff Branch traffic up the ramp to the station entrance.' However, a further consultation meeting on 21 June in Perth[14] heard union representatives once again question the financial detail, and on this occasion request a breakdown of the figures 'to give a clear indication of the method of costing which had been employed'. The staff side made a variety of constructive suggestions, including retiming some branch trains to make better connections at Gleneagles, provision of better car parking facilities at Comrie and Crieff stations, and the replacement of the railbus by a DMU in light of 'the regular failure of the present railbus operating on the Branch, leading to considerable inconvenience to the passengers'. The response of the management side to this latter, crucial point was bewildering: 'Mr. Crighton stated that these were regrettable and everything possible was done locally to provide a dependable service . . . [he] explained that he did not think there was justification for [DMU operation] as the railbus adequately met requirements.'

BR takes credit for its improvements – and the TUCCS reaches a verdict

The BR Brief for Liaison Officer made comparison with the circumstances in 1955 when the TUCC had rejected closure: 'Gross revenue in 1955 was estimated at £12,100, whereas the corresponding figure in the Re-shaping report is £14,180. Bearing in mind the increases in fares which have taken place since 1955, the indications are that passenger traffic has fallen away slightly but, even if one takes the most optimistic view, there are no grounds for thinking that this traffic has done more than remain static.'

The number of passengers carried per train was not impressive, although arguably it did not need to be, given the lower threshold for viability of a limited-capacity railbus. The busiest train (on 'representative' summer Saturdays) in the Down direction averaged 38 passengers, while in the Up direction the 3.51 p.m. service from Crieff to Gleneagles on Mondays to Fridays averaged 29. Several trains daily ran with one or no passengers.

Perhaps predictably, the BR brief was silent about the mammoth increase in patronage in the year following dieselisation (and the downturn the following year), but – 'in view of the criticisms that we have not done enough to reduce costs or to improve the service' – it did highlight the four constructive measures undertaken since 1955: the introduction of railbuses; increased train services; opening of new halts; and de-staffing three stations. The final paragraph looked damning: 'It is still being said that we could reduce costs. Assuming this to be true, any such economies could not be substantial. With our experience since 1955, it has already been established that the additional passenger potential is negligible. The conclusion is obvious: there is no course of action open to us which would ensure that this line could attain viability.'

The closing assertion was probably correct, but was viability the sole or right criterion for an important piece of rural infrastructure (certainly between Crieff and Gleneagles, which had initially seen substantial passenger growth following dieselisation)? We shall return to the scope for additional economies later.

The TUCCS annual report for 1963[15] records that 'a considerable number of written objections' was received – an odd way of describing only 25 objections. In any event, just nine of the objectors attended the 26 November hearing at Crieff's Masonic Hall to further their representations orally.

The following day's (Dundee) *Courier and Advertiser* led its story with the headline 'Sir Malcolm Knox attacks rail closure'. Knox, who was a director of Crieff Hydro (and Principal of St Andrews University) told the public hearing that the financial information provided by BR was 'grossly misleading' if compared with that in the Beeching Report. It does seem strange that BR, having incorporated details of the line's contributory revenue (and how much of this was expected to be lost) in the Beeching Report, then excluded it from the public Heads of Information supporting the closure proposal. Of course, the TUCCS had been specifically supplied with this information – although it was marked 'confidential', despite being in the Beeching Report! That the TUCCS accepted the narrowest interpretation of its role was confirmed by the *Courier*-reported comment by the committee's Chairman, Sir John Greig Dunbar: 'We are not concerned with suggestions as to how the railways should be run or the representations from the railway company as to how much money they will save if these stations are closed.'

Unfortunately, following the 1962 Transport Act, transcripts of the proceedings of the TUCC public hearings were no longer made available, so we are reliant on the annual reports and surviving press cuttings for details of the deliberations. The TUCCS annual report records that in response to concerns about the proposed replacement service, a Scottish Omnibuses representative had stated that they would arrange 'for certain buses on the Comrie–Crieff–Gleneagles route running to Gleneagles Station forecourt at times to connect with the North and Southbound trains'. That was good enough for the committee, which 'unanimously agreed that there would be no case of hardship in the event of the passenger train service being withdrawn between Crieff and Comrie'.

Opinion was more divided on the core section of the service: 'With regard to the service between Gleneagles and Crieff; a motion to the effect that this service should be retained as the withdrawal would cause hardship to the inhabitants of Strageath, Highlandman and Pittenzie [a strange argument, focusing on three of the smallest settlements on the line] as well as being harmful to the Tourist industry, was tabled and seconded. Another member stated that, in his view, it was invariably found that a bus service was more suitable to inhabitants of rural areas than a rail service, and moved an amendment, which was seconded, to the effect that no real hardship would be incurred by the complete withdrawal of the passenger service. The amendment was carried by ten votes to five.'

The Prime Minister gets involved

The committee's verdict was submitted to the minister in late December, and it took him only five months to reach a decision. Behind the scenes, however, an interesting debate developed. In the aftermath of the Profumo Affair, Harold Macmillan, having fallen ill in October 1963, had resigned as prime minister and been replaced by Sir Alec Douglas-Home – and in a November 1963 by-election he was elected as MP for Kinross and West Perthshire, the safest Conservative seat in Scotland.

Comrie and Crieff both lay within the constituency, and a note from the PM's office on 28 February 1964, following a meeting that day between Douglas-Home and Marples on Scottish rail closures, stated: 'The Prime Minister suggested that there would be no objection to closing the railway from Crieff to Comrie but he hoped that the Crieff to Gleneagles line could be kept open.' This suggestion for reprieve (and Douglas-Home's alternative suggestion to postpone closure until October) did not win the support of Marples or Lord Blakenham, Chancellor of the Duchy of Lancaster, who cited the fact that 'damaging comparisons' might be drawn between the Crieff / Comrie railway and two other doomed lines over which summer traffic was higher, namely Porthcawl and Silloth: 'It would be very difficult to explain why the Gleneagles–Comrie service was being continued through the summer when these two much busier ones are not. I am sure you will agree that that if the apparent disparity in treatment were attributed to the fact that the line is in your constituency you could be placed in considerable embarrassment. You may feel that in all the circumstances it would be better for the Minister of Transport to approve the discontinuance of the service from Gleneagles without making any condition as to the date when it is to take effect.'[16] Douglas-Home clearly understood the political realities, and he quickly assented to Blakenham's recommendation.

Marples gave his (public) consent to closure on 25 May 1964 – and only six weeks later, on Saturday 4 July, Crieff saw the departure of its last passenger train, holidays or not. And the inferior replacement bus service from Comrie and Crieff to Gleneagles 'was not well patronised, and a little over three years later Alexander's [the bus company] applied for and were granted a variation [to the condition of consent to rail closure] which effectively meant the end of the route'.[17] As in too many cases in the 1960s, the end of the railway was just a precursor to the end of public transport.

Was there scope for rationalisation – and further service improvement?

As in other closures, there is no evidence that the TUCCS used the availability of additional financial information from BR to probe the finances and explore the scope for running the railway better. Indeed, as we have seen, the TUCCS Chairman explicitly rejected such suggestions. But it seems beyond doubt that further substantial economies could have been made, while still retaining and increasing revenue through a faster train service – using a DMU rather than the railbus – focused solely on Crieff (which had four times the population of Comrie). The running time for the six miles from Gleneagles to Crieff, with up to five intermediate stops, was 22 minutes – so a non-stop service would have taken around 15 minutes, easily allowing one DMU to provide a service as frequent as hourly in each direction. However, the main line service at Gleneagles – around 15 trains daily in each direction – was largely *not* on a regular-interval basis, so key connections from Crieff would have required an irregular pattern of departures.

At the time of closure, although all intermediate stations were unstaffed, there were signal boxes at Crieff and Muthill,[18] level crossing keepers at Highlandman, Pittentain, Pittenzie and Strageath,[19] a crossing loop at Muthill, and no fewer than three tracks through Crieff's grand station. The labour-intensive nature of the rail operation at the time of closure is illustrated by Bernard Byrom in *The Railways of Upper Strathearn*,[20] in which he quotes a list of no fewer than 12 BR employees at Crieff station alone, comprising a station master, two porters, two ticket office staff, three signalmen, two railbus drivers and two railbus guards. While the geographical catchment for this list, and the types of staff included, are evidently not the same as for the 1962 list of 25 employees, the staff complement had definitely shrunk over those two years, with clerical staff halved and signalmen cut by a quarter.

BR therefore cannot be accused of failing to make economies, but they could have done much more. If a 'basic railway' operation had been implemented, abandoning the six miles of track from Crieff to Comrie – with freight from Perth to Crieff withdrawn, as it would be three years later, and all intermediate stations closed – then a 'long siding' from Gleneagles to Crieff, with 'open' (un-barriered) or remotely-controlled automated level crossings, would have required perhaps only eight operating staff *on the entire railway*: two ticket office staff at Crieff to handle the key longer-distance business connecting at Gleneagles (and perhaps parcels), two train drivers and two train guards, plus relief staff (excluding track maintenance requirements).

A radical alternative suggested by John Yellowlees[21] would have involved closing Comrie–Crieff–Gleneagles and replacing it with a DMU-operated service from Crieff over the existing freight railway (closed to passengers in 1951) to the county town of Perth, which had been operated by the simple 'Telephone & Notice Board' signalling system since 1962. While less convenient for onward travel to Glasgow, it would have better served the local market, while also providing a line-of-route connection towards Edinburgh. Steam-hauled services from Perth to Crieff in 1946 took 40 minutes for the 17¾-mile journey, with eight intermediate stops, so it is reasonable to assume (subject to track upgrades to improve line speeds, and automation of level crossings) that a non-stop DMU service would have taken around 20–25 minutes, enabling a frequency of up to hourly to be maintained by one unit.

But such imaginative approaches to rural rail operation were not welcomed by the 'bandwagon of nihilists' in BR management described by Gerry Fiennes – in the rush to strip out branch lines and (supposedly) move the national railway system to financial break-even. As a contemporary footnote, the pre-Covid Crieff–Perth bus service – serving more intermediate locations than the former railway – provided a remarkable (commercially operated) half-hourly frequency for much of the day, while Crieff–Stirling still enjoys an hourly service, with the bus and rail stations at the latter now much closer together than in the Beeching era.

Despite being located in a rural district, where development pressures are typically fewer than in urban areas, the Gleneagles–Crieff solum has suffered many breaches over the 58 years since closure, and this inevitably has had an impact on the prospects for re-opening, as we shall see in Chapter 15. Reprieving and rationalising a rural railway in the 1960s was an altogether different financial proposition to rebuilding it from scratch in the 21st century.

137

9

Two contrasting cases:
Fraserburgh and Peterhead

The Formartine & Buchan Railway opened to the fishing port of Peterhead in 1862, striking off from the Aberdeen–Inverness railway at Dyce, then heading north to Ellon and Maud, where it turned abruptly eastwards to reach Peterhead – a circuitous 38-mile route compared to the more obvious alignment north–east from Ellon by Cruden Bay and Boddam. The 16-mile 'branch' from Maud to Fraserburgh – a somewhat smaller, but nonetheless important, fishing town at the extreme tip of north-east Scotland – began operations in 1865. One hundred years later the railway to Fraserburgh had become the 'main line' – but both lost their passenger services that year.

Boddam got its branch line in 1897 – also serving a new hotel built by the Great North of Scotland Railway (GNOSR) at Cruden Bay – and the Buchan network was completed with the late arrival, in 1903, of the low-cost Light Railway from Fraserburgh to the nearby fishing village of St Combs. As recorded by Thomas and Turnock, the growth of fishing and food processing renewed agitation in Peterhead, in 1919, for a more direct rail link to Aberdeen via Boddam, cutting the journey by 11 miles, but: 'The GNOSR was naturally guarded in its response. It had endeavoured to meet local requirements by building the Boddam branch and saw little to be gained by extending this branch over a few [topographically] difficult miles into Peterhead when the town already enjoyed a railway service.'[1]

Although motor cars had been seen on Scottish roads since the last years of the 19th century – and regular bus services would soon emerge nation-wide – the railway company could not have foreseen just how drastically road competition would affect the rail system. But, as David Fasken has pointed out, the GNOSR was the first railway company in Scotland to get

CRIEFF, FRASERBURGH AND PETERHEAD

Highlandman, seen here looking south on 25 August 1955, was one of five locations on the Gleneagles–Crieff section with manual level crossing gates which could have been automated. *WAC Smith / Transport Treasury*

Some of the first rail passengers in Scotland to sample DMUs: at Crieff on 16 July 1956 a two-car Metro-Cammell unit awaits its 5.25 p.m. departure to Gleneagles. *WAC Smith / Transport Treasury*

A fine array of semaphore signals at the north end of Gleneagles' island platform on 26 August 1961. All these disappeared in 1966 when Gleneagles signal box was closed and control of this section of the main line was transferred to Auchterarder box, two miles to the north, and Blackford box, two miles to the south. *David Murray-Smith*

At Strageath Halt there was a simple, slabbed concrete area beside the track. This view is from the 11 a.m. Gleneagles–Crieff service on a summer Saturday in 1961. *Frank Spaven*

A throng of passengers at Crieff following the arrival of a limited-capacity railbus from Gleneagles on the last day of service, Saturday 4 July 1964. *Stuart Sellar*

On 4 July 1964, the 4.48 p.m. train from Gleneagles to Crieff passes the junction with the overgrown freight siding to the BR-owned Gleneagles Hotel. *WAC Smith / Transport Treasury*

The Crieff Signalman receives the single-line token for the block section from Muthill from the Driver of the 7.30 p.m. train from Gleneagles on 4 July 1964. The freight-only line to Perth is to the left of the railbus. *WAC Smith / Transport Treasury*

NBL Type 2 D6138 heads a lightweight Buchan parcels train north through the Bucksburn suburb of Aberdeen c.1961, with an ex-LMS 'Full Brake' and ex-LNER Gresley Full Brake in tow. *David Murray Smith*

The sometimes untaxing train weights behind NBL Type 2s is also illustrated by this 1 July 1963 shot of a Peterhead-bound service headed by D6148 at Maud Junction. *Sandy Murdoch / Transport Treasury*

NBL Type 2s allocated to north-east Scotland had cab-side recesses for tablet catchers, seen here below the side window in this undated shot of a southbound freight leaving Strichen. *Sandy Murdoch / Transport Treasury*

Traditional hand-exchange of single-line tokens for a northbound train headed by D6150 at Maud Junction's bi-directional Fraserburgh track and platform on 1 March 1965. *Sandy Murdoch / Transport Treasury*

Youthful fascination with steam – in this case Ivatt 2MT No. 46461 – is seen here at St Combs on 9 August 1956. Steam (and the rounding loop) would last only three more years. *Stuart Sellar*

St Combs on Saturday 1 May 1965, the last day of service. The sign in the cab window reads: 'Farewell oor trainie, we shed a tear. The Beeching axe, has fallen here.' The author and his grandfather stand far right. *Frank Spaven*

Taken soon after Fraserburgh signal box closed in mid-1966 this panoramic view of the freight yard, and the former passenger station (beyond the loco), shows an NBL Type 2 shunting a mixed rake of wagons. *Carl Marsden, courtesy of Alan Young*

This undated shot of Maud Junction was probably taken between 1966 and the 1969 closure of the signal box. EE Type 1 D8098 – now preserved on the heritage Great Central Railway – sits on the Up Peterhead line. *Sandy Murdoch / Transport Treasury*

involved in the bus industry – perhaps reflecting a protectionist response to the perceived threat from bus companies.[2] In any event, by the early 1960s the circuitous rail route was certainly a contributory factor to the dire economics of the Peterhead line, which helped to ensure the withdrawal of its passenger train services. And the Boddam branch had lost its passenger services in 1932 and closed completely in 1945.[3]

False hopes – then Beeching's brutal prescription

North-east Scotland was relatively far from major coalfields, and the opportunity to eliminate expensive haulage of locomotive coal to the area – plus the undoubted speed and operating / maintenance cost benefits of a switch from steam – led to some of the earliest diesels to emerge from the Modernisation Plan beginning trials north of Aberdeen in 1958. The BR 'Report on the progress of diesel schemes in the Scottish Region'[4] issued in 1960 indicates that full dieselisation of passenger services on the Buchan lines – using DMUs, initially – coincided with the start of the summer 1959 public timetable. Conversion to locomotive haulage followed the arrival of the large majority of an allocation of 20 Glasgow-built North British Locomotive Company (NBL) Type 2s in Aberdeen in 1960.

The report categorised the Buchan lines among those where dieselisation was 'designed to reduce costs in areas known to have little to offer in the way of potential traffic', but Aberdeen – Fraserburgh / Peterhead did see receipts increase by 7.2% from seven steam-operated months in 1958 to the equivalent months in 1959.

Of the three last-surviving Buchan lines, only the Fraserburgh–St Combs passenger service was entirely DMU-operated from dieselisation until closure. Latterly, a single DMU service operated daily in each direction between Aberdeen and Fraserburgh on an otherwise loco-hauled operation – to enable the isolated St Combs unit to be fuelled and serviced at Kittybrewster engine shed in Aberdeen. It has been suggested[5] that the limited van space of a DMU could not accommodate all the parcels, mail, newspaper and 'passenger-rated' agricultural traffic on the Fraserburgh line, although they were able to haul a separate parcels van as a 'tail load',[6] and bespoke parcels railcars could operate in multiple with most passenger DMUs.[7] There may have been operational synergies in inter-working locomotives on both passenger and freight trains, but the latter could have dealt with at least some of the non-passenger traffic beyond the capacity of DMUs. A further argument

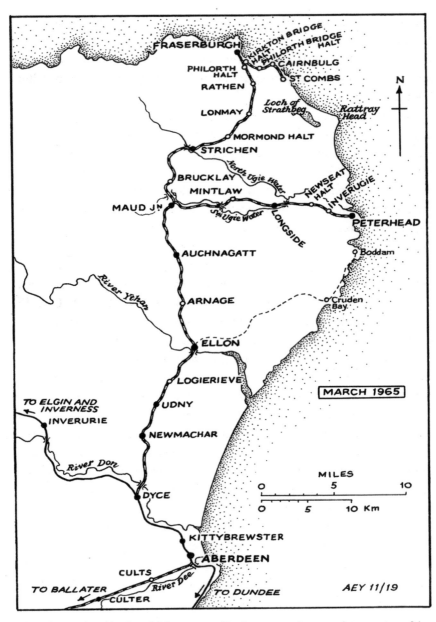

The rich agricultural lands and fishing ports of Buchan were early targets for expansion of the railway network north of Aberdeen. Traversing generally low-lying terrain and rolling hill country, the main Buchan lines required few substantial structures, but they were not free of steep gradients, the most severe being a one and a half mile climb south from Strichen at 1 in 60. The circuitous nature of the line to Peterhead contrasts with the more logical route of the branch to nearby Boddam from Ellon (shown in a pecked line). (Alan Young)

against loco-hauled operation is that DMUs potentially could have taken advantage of differential speed limits, as was the case at the time on the Peebles line, where DMUs were authorised to exceed the maximum 50mph speed limit for locomotives (the same as the Fraserburgh line) by 5mph.[8] But it was not to be.

Less than four years after the false hopes raised by dieselisation, the front page of the *P&J* of 28 March 1963 was full of reactions to the Beeching Report, one of the more melodramatic of the many headlines being: 'NEW HIGHLAND CLEARANCES ARE FEARED' – with Provost Forman of Peterhead (not conceivably within any definition of the Highlands) warning: 'This is just another nail in our coffin.'[9] Some wild claims were made in response to Beeching, and, as predictions go, this was one of the least accurate – for what is now Britain's top fishing port.[10]

Fraserburgh – with its trains to Aberdeen being significantly faster than the bus – had much more to lose than Peterhead with its circuitous rail route. Under an editorial page headline of 'BROCH PROVOST – "DOOM, IF . . ."' Fraserburgh provost Alex Noble commented: 'We did not expect cuts on this scale. We are one of the highest areas of unemployment in the country and this will mean more men out of work unless the railways in their wisdom have alternative work for the men who will be out of a job.' He added that it would be doom for Fraserburgh if the goods service was lost.

The *P&J* also reported a perceptive comment by Provost Forman which implicitly touched on Beeching's blind spot: 'It is the easiest thing under the sun to close down the railways, but it takes a really big man to find a way of maintaining them.' However, the provost lost his sense of proportion by adding: 'And if Dr Beeching closes down the rail goods transport, he might just as well close down Scotland.'

Unsurprisingly, the newspaper was able to report the opposite of doom and gloom from the bus sector: 'Mr James Kindness, Traffic Manager of Simpson's Motors, Rosehearty and Fraserburgh, who serve a considerable area of the North East between Aberdeen and these centres, said he was confident his firm could cope with any increase in traffic caused by the passenger service closures.'

Three months later, Simpson's was one of 'several omnibus operators' – identified as linking rail-served Buchan settlements – in the small print of the statutory BR public notice announcing the specific closure proposals for the lines to Fraserburgh, Peterhead and St Combs (and no fewer than 23 stations served). If the MoT had wished to bury some bad news, then

18 June 1963 was an ideal day to do so: the media was awash with the fall-out from the Profumo Affair, and so the proposed fate of Kirkton Bridge Halt, Mormond Halt and Newseat Halt was not likely to distract many *P&J* readers from all the intrigue and salacious detail of the scandal.

The railway trade unions had been advised by BR in May 1963 that closure notices would be posted at the stations affected on 17 June.[11] It was a firm intention (which was carried out) to retain freight services to Fraserburgh and Peterhead after passenger closure, and therefore the scale of 'Occupied Posts to be Closed' was less severe than it might have been – but nevertheless 31 traffic staff on the Buchan lines were to go, plus 25 motive power staff at Fraserburgh, Kittybrewster and Peterhead, eight chief civil engineer's staff at Aberdeen, Dyce and Fraserburgh, and '4 other occupied posts . . . the Grades and locations affected to be determined following re-organisation' – a total of 68 jobs.

Amazingly, the staff remaining on the Buchan lines would total no fewer than 108 (excluding civil engineering posts) – to handle only two freight trains daily from Fraserburgh to Aberdeen, and two daily from Peterhead to Maud (one continuing independently to Aberdeen), plus local road deliveries. Compared to the lean staffing of road haulage companies, this was a heavy cost burden for BR's freight business to bear. Although all passenger services were to disappear, one of the quirks of the post-closure situation was that BR would retain clerks at the goods office in Fraserburgh to handle passenger ticket sales for local people still travelling south by train from Aberdeen.

BR marshals its arguments for Fraserburgh closure

The BR Heads of Information issued in May 1963 as part of the statutory closure process for the Fraserburgh line[12] provided a 'Statement of numbers of passengers using existing rail services on representative days', but no information was provided on which days these were. And were they really representative? This was a question raised by campaigners the length and breadth of Britain.

Northbound in winter, the five trains daily were patronised by a total of 278 passengers on Mondays to Fridays, and 228 on Saturdays. Summer patronage was more than 50% higher on Saturdays. Peak travel on the line in winter was determined by 'about 50 schoolchildren' who travelled to Ellon from the three stations south thereof, while 'apart from this . . . the heaviest trains tend to be the first morning train from Fraserburgh and the last two trains from Aberdeen [i.e., 40% of the northbound service]. These trains are used by workers and students travelling from Fraserburgh and intermediate points to Aberdeen and back. There are also similar flows between intermediate points, e.g. hospital workers travelling from Strichen to Maud.'[13]

The numbers were not massive, and only six out of 10 daily trains on winter Mondays to Fridays carried more than a typical single-decker busload of 40 passengers. However, passengers (excluding schoolchildren) were largely concentrated on four of the 14 stations north of Dyce – Ellon, Maud, Strichen and Fraserburgh – and this lent weight to a suggestion at a consultation meeting of Scottish Region 'Sectional Council' No. 2 held on 14 June 1963, where the staff side commented that 'the time was opportune for a speeding up of the Buchan Passenger Services and suggested that serious consideration should be given to reducing stopping places and proposed that stops be only made at Kittybrewster, Dyce, Ellon, Maud Junction, Strichen and Fraserburgh – on the Maud / Peterhead Branch no intermediate stops. At present the hand exchange of tokens reacted against speeding up and if the system which is operating on the Aberdeen–Inverness services was introduced, it would allow for the journeys involved in the Buchan lines to be covered in approximately 75 minutes.'[14]

The system mentioned was the 'Manson automatic token exchange' system – invented by the fourth Locomotive Superintendent of the GNOSR, James Manson[15] – use of which had evidently died out in the late 1950s in favour of traditional hand exchange, probably precipitated by the 1959 arrival of DMUs, which were not fitted with the automatic apparatus. Hand exchange had, in any case, routinely applied in the case of stopping trains and for at least one of the trains when two trains crossed. The auto exchanger (including ground-based equipment) did not work well with diesel locos as their springing made alignment of apparatus more difficult, and standards of maintenance of equipment, track and locos were not so good by the 1950s – so their use became unpopular with railwaymen.[16]

But in any event, in late 1963 the loops on the Fraserburgh line numbered no fewer than nine,[17] equating to an average block section length of 4½ miles – much more capacity than was needed for five passenger trains, and three freights (south of Maud), in each direction daily.[18]

Figures in BR's 'Heads of Information: Supplementary Details'[19] indicate that of the 13 intermediate stops between Fraserburgh and Dyce no fewer than 10 had populations of less than 1,000 – the majority no more than several hundred. Stripping out the nine least-used stations would have left a passenger service – and crossing loops – at Fraserburgh (population 10,462), Strichen (1,040), Maud (1,374), Ellon (1,456) and one other location to split 13 miles of single-track from the latter to Dyce – and would indeed have cut journey times from Fraserburgh to Aberdeen from around 90 minutes to under 75, potentially facilitating an enhanced service of six or seven trains daily with the same number of train sets. As well as being attractive in its own right, this would have allowed a further improvement in service suggested by the staff at the 14 June consultation meeting: 'A retiming should take place with a view to introducing departure times from Aberdeen giving a good connection with the trains arriving from the South and the trains leaving Peterhead and Fraserburgh be retimed to give connections to South bound trains.'

With a service of only five trains daily, there was inevitably tension between timings designed to suit the local market to Aberdeen (including commuting, shopping trips, etc.) and those to optimise long-distance connections. The latter market was particularly poorly served, with no southbound connections within 30 minutes of the five Aberdeen arrivals from Fraserburgh, and limited to three in the northbound direction.[20] Increased train frequency would have made it easier to serve both markets, although this would not necessarily have allowed the '[regular] interval services' between the main centres of population, as advocated by the staff.

However, there was much to be said for their view that such a service, 'having regard to the increased difficulties of car parking in Aberdeen, [would] encourage the public to travel by rail if parking facilities were available at the stations on this route'. On the face of it, the staff side was far more perceptive of the opportunities for rail than the management side, narrowly focused as it was on Beeching's holy grail – closures.

The Heads of Information also provided the bare details of the passenger service finances – and the equation did not look good. Yes, the service could have been much better, and costs could have been substantially cut – but 'Estimated Receipts' of £15,460 (excluding contributory revenue) were dwarfed by 'Estimated Direct Costs' of £63,940. That was one of the poorer revenue-to-cost ratios among the branch lines examined in greatest detail in this book; however, as David Prescott has pointed out: 'This was in part due to retention of loco haulage for parcels etc, but the revenue for this traffic was almost certainly not credited to the service.'[21] The confidential 'Amplification of Financial Information'[22] supplied to the TUCCS provided more detail, but – unlike the Ballater and Comrie / Crieff case studies in the

Beeching Report – did not indicate what proportion of the contributory value of £7,100 was expected to be lost to the network.

With the large majority of trains loco-hauled, the movement cost of 4s 7d per train-mile was significantly higher than it would have been with DMU operation. What really would have assisted the TUCCS – assuming they were willing to stray that far from their narrow official remit – and transformed the wider debate, would have been an additional column of figures setting out estimates for a 'basic railway' operation, founded on:

- stripping out at least four of the nine crossing loops
- closing all stations except Fraserburgh, Strichen, Maud, Ellon and one other
- retaining clerical / platform staff only at Fraserburgh and Ellon
- converting the service to DMU operation
- increasing frequency from five to six or seven trains a day
- improving onwards connections at Aberdeen
- revising fares to better reflect market conditions

At 60-odd years' remove it is no easy task to calculate the possible financial impact of such an approach. But in 1966 Gerry Fiennes reckoned that the cost of running the 45-mile East Suffolk line could be cut from around £250,000 to £84,000 per annum.[23] Admittedly, this was a rough calculation and included conversion from double-track to single-track – as well as what became standard 'basic railway' measures: de-staffing stations (with conductor-guards issuing tickets on 'Paytrains') and automating (or introducing simpler, low-cost) signalling and level crossing barrier systems.

One might reasonably hazard a guestimate – based on outcomes elsewhere – that a faster, more frequent and DMU-operated service on a rationalised railway from Fraserburgh to Aberdeen could have boosted receipts by a third, to around £20,000, while also cutting costs by a third, to some £40,000: thereby yielding a relatively healthy revenue-to-costs ratio of close to 50% for a service contributing more to social and economic wellbeing in Buchan than in its 1963 guise.

The wrong kind of locomotive

As John Yellowlees has pointed out, DMUs would have been much more reliable than the notorious NBL Type 2s – later Class 21 or Class 29 – whose poor performance may well have been a factor in undermining Buchan rail demand.[24] Built in Glasgow, these were one of the worst products of the 1955 Modernisation Plan, and the entire fleet of 58 locomotives was withdrawn from service by 1971. A veteran railway colleague of mine, Neil Macdonald, recalled once asking a St Rollox (Glasgow) driver: 'What's the best thing about these NBL Type 2s?' to which he replied, quick as a flash: 'The fire extinguisher, son. I use it more than the throttle.'

This was a classic example of the BTC being panicked, in the late 1950s, into swift and wholesale replacement of steam without properly trialling diesel prototypes or initially small fleets of the many different diesel models. Bill Jamieson[25] wonders if the haste to get rid of steam was 'ideologically driven': 'It's not as if the Buchan lines were being operated by ancient relics – on 1st January 1958 Kittybrewster shed had an allocation of five Standard Class 4 2-6-0s and five Standard Class 4 2-6-4 tank engines, all of them less than a year old! It would have been far more sensible to hang on to steam for two or three years and then replace it with the by-then demonstrably more reliable models of Type 2 diesel, with a leavening of DMUs on purely passenger diagrams.'[26]

In his exhaustive study of the NBL Type 2s, Anthony Sayer argues that if the first 10 'Pilot Scheme' locos of 1,000hp (delivered in 1958–59) 'had been fully tested before further orders were placed [for the subsequent 48 'Production' locos of 1,100hp], no further North British diesel-electric Type 2s would ever have seen the light of day.'[27] It was Fraserburgh's misfortune not only to have missed out on DMUs for its Aberdeen service, but also to be saddled with one of BR Scottish Region's less reliable locomotive classes.[28]

By contrast, other 'peripheral' routes, such as those north of Inverness and the West Highland Lines, benefited from the superior performance of the Type 2 diesels built by the Birmingham Railway Carriage & Wagon Co. (later Classes 26 and 27) and by various BR Works (later Class 24). It was understandable that BR would want to allocate the more powerful (1,160–1,250hp) and more reliable locos to the Highland routes. In practice, the 20 NBLs which had been allocated to north-east Scotland (none of which would be re-engined as Class 29s of 1,350hp) would disappear from the region not long after the Buchan passenger closures – the bulk being stored or withdrawn in 1966–67. The Fraserburgh line's final 14 freight-only years (see page 155) would largely be operated by the more reliable Type 2 classes, not least the Class 26, the last of which would survive on BR operations until as late as 1993.

A sub-standard bus alternative

Back in 1963, the Heads of Information for the Fraserburgh closure included a summary timetable of alternative bus services – spread across three operators and no fewer than 17 separate bus services – demonstrating graphically that no single bus service replicated all the station calls of the train. Indeed, the highest number of station calls made by any one bus service was only six. The contrast with the simplicity of the rail timetable – and its scope for enhancement – could hardly have been greater.

The bus would also be slower for key journeys: Fraserburgh to Aberdeen would increase from around 90 minutes to 104; Maud to Aberdeen from an hour to 87 minutes; but Ellon to Aberdeen by bus (38 minutes) would show little change from the train. Of course, road congestion – particularly in and around Aberdeen – was clearly going to get worse at a time when rail congestion was very much *not* a problem. The return bus fares of 9s 6d from Fraserburgh to Aberdeen, and 3s 6d from Ellon to Aberdeen, were matched by 'Special Cheap Day Returns' on the train, but – as was usual – the rail Ordinary Returns (at 23s 6d and 10s respectively) were stratospherically more expensive than the bus.

Alternative bus services – or more specifically the potential hardship which would result from rail passengers having to use them – were at the heart of the statutory closure process. But an even more fundamental issue would be raised again, as in many individual closure cases, by railway staff and campaigners: the vexed question of finances, and BR's unwillingness to provide more than the most basic statistics. The Sectional Council meeting on 14 June 1963 was no exception, where the staff side commented that 'it is difficult to understand how the financial figures are calculated. They should be broken down and explained in more detailed form.' That was a request, together with questions about the scope for economies, which would repeatedly be rebuffed up and down the country.

As objections to closure had been submitted to the TUCCS, a mandatory public hearing was arranged – for 13 November 1963, in Aberdeen – and, as was customary, BR prepared its internal Brief for Liaison Officer.[29] This clarified that while the number of objections was relatively modest – at 33 – four of the objections were representing in total (in one case in the form of a petition) a further 184 people. The SRDA was quick off the mark with Objection No. 1 (representing a further 68 individual objectors) sent by the association's Honorary Secretary, Tom Hart: 'The principal grounds of objection relate to the alleged inadequacy of the alternative bus service and to the effect that the withdrawal of the passenger train services will have on the facilities for the conveyance of merchandise – fish, meat, seed potatoes etc.'

A summary of the 'alleged' problems with the bus raised by objectors – together with BR's comments on these – occupied no fewer than 12 pages of the brief, under five headings: frequency and timing; comfort; capacity; operation in winter; and holiday traffic. As in the case of the Crieff closure, BR advocated taking medicine prior to bus journeys, and their further commentary on bus comfort did not conjure up a vision of civilised modern transport: 'Remedies to combat travel sickness e.g. MARZINE AND KWELLS, are readily available and smoking is normally prohibited in certain sections of buses. On longer bus journeys on buses with no toilet facilities, any juvenile incontinence may be relieved by asking bus conductors to make a short stop.'

Nine objectors raised the issue of unreliability of buses during the winter, and a particular seasonal objection came from Peter Jones, a Consultant Surgeon at Aberdeen Royal Infirmary, who held an out-patient clinic at Fraserburgh every fortnight. The impact of his objection was rather blunted by the admission that 'I usually go by car as the train leaves both Aberdeen and Fraserburgh at awkward times', although 'I rely very much on rail transport during the winter': which turned out to be 'once or twice' a year. Here was a classic example of the availability of a railway being valued in exceptional / emergency circumstances, but not for regular use. Granted, the Fraserburgh timetable was sub-optimal, but even the objections in relation to the seasonal unreliability of buses turned out to be on somewhat shaky grounds, the brief noting that 'Messrs Alexander's records show that during the severe 1962 / 63 winter the Aberdeen–Fraserburgh bus service was disrupted on one occasion only (6th February 1963)'.

The Scottish Housewives Association had travelled on the Buchan lines in July, asking passengers for their opinion on the closure proposals, and its findings were salutary:

> It is apparent that most of those using the line regularly are 1) Young People, 2) Mothers with Young Children, and 3) Elderly folk. Such people, by reason of their diffidence, are less likely to actively protest although asked to do so and this protest is submitted with their interests in mind.

The hardships of these people if the rail closes are 1) Financial & Longer [sic] time spent travelling to Work (young people), 2) Lack of accommodation for prams and carricots, and for children (young mothers), and 3) Lack of comfort (the Elderly): there are also health hardships, bus sickness being not uncommon, especially among children, and the impossibility of those with chronic chest complaints to avoid smoke polluted atmosphere.

Objections in relation to merchandise traffic on passenger trains, such as fish, meat and seed potatoes, were countered − not unreasonably − by the continuing availability of freight trains, and this was suggested even for 'hundreds of puppies [which] are despatched each year from Ellon to towns in Scotland and England'.

Other grounds for objection, including the effect on holiday traffic, industrial development and the condition of the roads, were answered adequately within the brief, including the most bizarre objection − from the Scottish National Party − which considered that 'the closure is a contravention of Articles IV and VI of the Treaty of Union, 1707'. Fortunately, BR could breathe a sigh of relief: the articles were attached to the brief and 'the Legal Adviser is satisfied that there is no substance in this complaint'.

Where the brief, perhaps inevitably, fails to convince is on certain objectors' suggestions for improving the service, including: closing Philorth, Rathen, Lonmay, Mormond and Brucklay stations, and closure or reduction to unstaffed halts of Auchnagatt, Arnage, Logierieve, Udny and Newmachar stations; acceleration and retiming of trains; and revision of both fares and timetable. BR's cursory comment was: 'None of the measures would be sufficient to enable the passenger service to attain viability . . . Most of the places specifically mentioned are either unstaffed already or function with the bare minimum of staff.'

The latter point was fair only in the case of clerical / platform staff (as opposed to signalmen), and the maintenance / operating cost − and journey time − benefits of closing these stations were ignored, as was the scope to further improve the timetable (and reduce costs) by eliminating crossing loops and associated speed restrictions. Nor was the scope for a more imaginative fares policy explored.

While issues wider than the nitty-gritty of personal hardship would play a part in the fate of some threatened lines, the regional economic development argument would not come to the aid of any of the Buchan passenger services. The provisional views of the Scottish Development Group were summarised at a meeting in St Andrew's House on 9 July 1964: 'In view of industrial developments in Fraserburgh assurance of continued provision for freight service at least should be required.' The verdict on Peterhead was blunt: 'No objections.'[30]

Poor Peterhead: a closure hard to criticise

The BR Heads of Information[31] provided a detailed statement of the numbers of passengers using the Peterhead trains 'on representative days'. With only three trains on weekdays from Maud to Peterhead (connecting out of services from Aberdeen to Fraserburgh) and four in the opposite direction – supplemented by a summer Saturday train in each direction – it was little surprise that numbers were low. Adding in the circuitous rail route compared to bus or car journeys, and the need to change trains at Maud, it is no wonder that the utility of the rail service was highly questionable.

During the winter a total of 30 passengers travelled daily in each direction on Mondays to Fridays, and 40 on Saturdays. In summer these figures increased to 50 on Mondays to Fridays and to 60–80 on Saturdays. The busiest train – the 3.20 p.m. from Peterhead to Maud on summer Mondays to Fridays – averaged 25 passengers, which was not much more than half a single-decker bus load. The three quietest trains had three or four passengers: a taxi load.

While the comfort of the train was appreciated by passengers, the existing bus services had much to offer in strictly quantitative terms: 20 or 21 services a day from Peterhead to Aberdeen, and even five a day from Peterhead to Maud (albeit that the journey time was twice as long as the train, at 50 minutes). At 80–85 minutes on average from Peterhead to Aberdeen, the bus was marginally quicker than the train, and the bus return fare of 7s 8d was (just) cheaper than BR's Special Cheap Day Return fare of 7s 9d, and, in particular, the rail Ordinary Return of 22s 6d. Not unreasonably, no additional bus services were proposed to replace the train.

Given the foregoing, it is perhaps no surprise that there were only 11 objections to closure, with the internal BR brief[32] summing these up almost identically to the Fraserburgh case: 'The principle grounds of objection relate to the inadequacy [not "alleged" in this case] of the alternative bus services and to the withdrawal of trains conveying fish and meat traffic.' Despite Peterhead's 12,497 population (all four intermediate stations to Maud served populations well under 1,000), 'the patronage of the service is so poor that no clearly defined flows of travel are readily discernable [sic]'. For trains hauled by a 1,100hp locomotive this was a gross mis-match between supply and demand, and it showed in the stark details of the financial information supplied to the TUCCS: an operating cost of 8s 2d per train-mile (worse than any of the 10 case studies in the Beeching Report), 'Net Earnings' of £760, 'Contributory Value' of £800 and 'Estimated Direct Costs' of £19,980.

Yes, a 'basic railway' operation with a single-car DMU (and no change of train at Maud) would have improved the service and its financial performance, but these could not have overcome the fundamental geographical disadvantage of the Peterhead line's circuitous route to Aberdeen. This must have been one of the more clear-cut Beeching closure cases.

St Combs: plucky but isolated

The proposed closure of all three Buchan lines had been announced together, on 18 June 1963, and the response 10 days later from the NUR General Secretary, Sidney Greene, to the four local branches of the union[33] made no distinction between the lines as he referred to the steps which should be taken 'to ensure the strongest possible protest' to the TUCCS. In management / staff consultation meetings, the arguments made for retention were predominantly collective for the three lines – although the circumstances were very different. Peterhead was effectively a lost cause, while the Fraserburgh–Aberdeen service was reasonably competitive and offered significant scope for both service enhancement and cost reduction. Fraserburgh to St Combs – a DMU shuttle – had the best revenue-to-cost ratio of the three (£5,470 estimated receipts and £15,030 estimated direct costs) but could only survive if Fraserburgh–Aberdeen was retained. Receipts were almost certainly less than they should have been, given the problems faced by conductor-guards collecting fares in the space of no more than 15 minutes from passengers travelling between the four unstaffed halts.

The St Combs line – the last operational Light Railway in Scotland – had a good service: 11 trains a day in each direction (12 on Saturdays); a journey time which was five minutes faster than the bus; and a Special Cheap Day Return of 1s 6d comparing well to 1s 9d on the bus. Here was a classic low-cost operation – a 'long siding' with no signalling, all branch stations unstaffed, and operated by DMUs – performing a useful local function, years before Gerry Fiennes labelled the concept as 'basic railway'. Patronage was healthy – with the busiest train averaging 128 passengers, and only a handful of services having single-figure loads. In an interesting twist – anticipating future criticisms of Beeching's failure to address the *actual* engineering costs which would be saved by a specific line closure and how long it would take to achieve such savings – the Heads of Information noted zero 'estimated expenditure over the next 5 years'.

An alternative view is that BR had sensibly exhausted all possible movement, terminal and track economies after St Combs and Cairnbulg stations were de-staffed and freight services withdrawn in 1960 (the line had always been 'One Train Working' with no signalling) – and yet the service *still* (allegedly) cost nearly three times as much to operate as the revenue earned. This was essentially Beeching's central argument about rural lines, which sought 'to dispose of any idea that stopping-train services could be preserved, as an economic alternative to buses or private transport, if only some ingenuity were shown by railway operators. This really is not so, and it is obvious that a high proportion of stopping passenger train services ought to be discontinued as soon as possible.'[34]

Nevertheless, an intriguing thought is that, had the Fraserburgh service been reprieved, would there then have been a case for St Combs also being retained, with some synergies between the two operations if Fraserburgh–Aberdeen had been converted to DMU working?

The TUCCS verdicts – and ministerial consent to closure

Following public hearings on 13 and 14 November 1963 in Aberdeen, the TUCCS reached verdicts on all three services and submitted these to the minister by the end of the year. The committee devoted two pages of its 1963 annual report[35] to the Fraserburgh case, a further two pages to Peterhead and half a page to St Combs.

The key grounds for objection and BR's response were summarised in the Fraserburgh section, and it was noted that a bus company representative had indicated that arrangements could be made for a new service linking Strichen and Maud, and 'they would be prepared to speed up the running time of certain bus services between Fraserburgh and Aberdeen'. The verdict was not, however, clear-cut: 'After considering the written and oral objections six members of the Committee considered that, if the passenger train service was withdrawn, there would be hardship to the present users of the service, and five members were of the view that, if the alternative services suggested by the Road Transport Representatives were provided, no real hardship would be incurred.'

The Peterhead section of the annual report recorded that the only hardship would be in the Newseat area – where around 100 people lived – and this would be alleviated if one bus a week in each direction (on Fridays) was diverted via the village. However, given the high rate of unemployment in Peterhead, 'certain members of the Committee were rather concerned as to the effect which the withdrawal of the passenger train service would have on the area'. It would not be enough to save the railway.

Interestingly, the committee took a tougher line on the diminutive St Combs railway, noting objectors' concerns about the narrow alternative road. Having heard from the BRB representative that there were formerly 200 regular travellers on the line, but '50 per cent of these were school children, who now travelled by contract bus', the annual report concludes: 'After considering all the representations, the Committee unanimously agreed that there would definitely be hardship if the passenger train service was withdrawn before the necessary road improvements had been carried out, and some suitable arrangements come to regarding the visits by mothers with very young children to the Welfare Clinic in Fraserburgh.'

In all three cases, the TUCCS had been supplied with limited additional figures in the confidential financial information. Unfortunately, the proceedings of the public hearing and the private committee session thereafter were not made available to the public, so we do not know what discussions, if any, took place on the route finances and the scope for reducing losses. The TUCCS annual report is silent on this, and one is tempted to conclude, given the committee's narrowly drawn remit, that the supply of additional information was simply window-dressing, designed to make BR's case look slightly more transparent (or rather, slightly less opaque).

The minister's consent for closure of all three Buchan lines came on 28 July 1964, and in the case of the Fraserburgh line was subject to the condition that certain additional bus services must be provided, including from Maud and Strichen to Aberdeen. At least five subsequent letters were sent from the MoT to the BRB – one as late as 25 July 1968 – allowing for variations to the new services in light of changing travel patterns (including people deserting the bus). It is not clear whether the Fraserburgh rail closure conditions were ultimately formally abandoned or just quietly forgotten. But, as we have seen more widely, few replacement buses lasted more than three or four years. The Peterhead consent was also subject to additional bus services being provided, while the St Combs closure was not to be implemented before 1 May 1965,[36] presumably to allow road improvements to be undertaken.

The last St Combs train ran on Saturday 1 May 1965. The following Monday's *P&J* provided an eloquent – and near-poetic – report by Ken Jones on the 'Sad last journey from St Combs', illustrating the feelings experienced by diverse individuals connected with this unique little railway:

> Sad for Mrs Barbara Buchan, 29 North Street, Fraserburgh, who rode on the first train out of St Combs 62 years ago. She was 10 years old then, and it cost her fourpence.
>
> Sad too, for Mr Jim Murray, 82 Forsyth Street, Fraserburgh, who in four months would have retired with 46 years' service on the railways. But, with the 8.25 [train to St Combs], he became redundant.
>
> Sad for driver George Gray, a third generation of railmen. George, 20 Grattan Place, Fraserburgh, makes a habit of firsts and lasts. He brought the last steam engine into Fraserburgh from Aberdeen and drove the first diesel out. He was at the controls of the 9.45 [the last train from St Combs].
>
> Sad for the fisher wife, head shrouded in a shawl, who left the comfort of her home to voice a final protest to the driver as the train rolled through Cairnbulg.[37]

As David Fasken comments, however, Mr Murray might not have been entirely sad: 'Being made redundant four months before normal retirement after 46 years, presumably with a hefty redundancy package and healthy pension, I suggest he was doing cartwheels round the town with a bottle of champagne!'[38]

In any event, by contrast to the '150 St Combs villagers as they watched the last train draw into the dank Saturday night', that same evening – 15 miles along the coast – the town of Peterhead seemed to have much less sentiment about the loss of its passenger railway, 'which has operated for 103 years, [and] came to an end when the last diesel drew out of the station in a no-ceremony farewell. About 50 passengers, mostly youngsters, made a sentimental last trip.'

The situation might have been altogether different if the GNOSR had extended the Boddam branch three miles to the established Peterhead station. As Alan Young's map on page 140 illustrates, such an extension (albeit over not the easiest of terrain) would have cut the rail distance to Aberdeen by 11 miles.

The last day of passenger operation at Fraserburgh was Saturday 6 October 1965. In a short news report the following Monday,[39] the *P&J* recorded that the final Buchan passenger service ended 'amid a flood of memories and sadness', with the six-coach 6.42 p.m. train from Fraserburgh to Aberdeen (hauled by one of the ill-fated NBL Type 2 diesels) watched by 'many people with sentimental attachments to the service'. There were 120 people on board – 'the most to travel on the train for a long time' – but only 70 on the last inbound train an hour later. And 'the main part of the crowd awaiting its arrival consisted of newspaper delivery boys waiting for the Saturday evening sporting papers'. The report noted that 'the crew of the 7.44 are now all redundant, as are 17 of the 50 people employed at Fraserburgh', and concluded sombrely: 'So the Buchan line closed for passengers with a bang from detonators, the shouts of schoolboys, and a lump in the throats of the many who have been associated with it during a lifetime of almost 100 years.'

Only two weeks later, a banner advert in the *P&J* lauded an altogether different aspect of Beeching's strategic vision: 'British Rail Inter-City ... The fast way to travel in crowded Britain.' The remaining clerks at the Fraserburgh goods office must have had mixed feelings as they issued the occasional long-distance rail ticket to passengers now 42 miles by road from the nearest station.

Freight long outlasts passengers

As we have already seen, the direct track and signalling expenses allocated to threatened passenger services assumed that freight would continue to operate. In many cases this was a flawed assumption, as Loft illustrates: 'Life might have been easier had freight and passenger closures been taken together, as the inclusion of the balance of track and signalling costs could have a dramatic effect on the financial case (for example in the Aberdeen to Fraserburgh and Peterhead case, an annual saving of nearly £60,000 from passenger closures would be increased by £150,000 if freight was withdrawn).'[40]

However, unlike the large majority of the branches examined in this book, freight services to Fraserburgh (in particular) and Peterhead significantly outlasted passenger closure – suggesting there was a network benefit in not following the path outlined by Loft. And cost reduction was a key part of the equation for freight-only operation, with rationalisation of the infrastructure beginning the same year as the passenger trains ceased.[41]

Freight to Peterhead survived until 1970, ironically just as the North Sea oil era was emerging. The key traffics had been empty cans from Metal Box at Arbroath to Crosse & Blackwell's Peterhead factory and substantial flows of the finished product by rail: tinned sausages and beans as well as Branston Pickle in glass jars. Unfortunately, their Kirktown plant was never directly connected to the railway, necessitating a local lorry movement to Peterhead goods yard. The unavoidable cost associated with transfer from road to rail meant that when Aberdeen Freightliner Terminal opened in 1966, it made commercial sense for BR to switch this wagonload traffic to lorries feeding into fixed-formation 75mph container trains from Aberdeen to major markets in London and Glasgow. The local loss of the Crosse & Blackwell flows undermined the economics of the daily train, and other traffics such as domestic coal (in long-term decline) were not enough to support the cost of running the train and maintaining the 12 miles of track to Maud, which intermediately generated no other revenue-earning business.

Fraserburgh freight (and parcels traffic) continued until 1979, latterly with a simple One Train Working arrangement for the entire 41-mile railway from Dyce. The formerly staple traffic of fish to London had been lost from the branch before the end. In the mid 1970s traditional railway vans were replaced by intermodal containers – which were lifted from the branch freight train on to the Freightliner service for London at the Aberdeen Guild Street hub – but latterly (post-1977) the containers were shuttled by lorry between Fraserburgh and Aberdeen,[42] in something of a re-run of the loss of Crosse & Blackwell traffic from the Peterhead branch.

In its final freight-only years, the line handled domestic coal, fertilisers, caravans and – at Maud – seed potatoes, and pipes for the North Sea oil industry, the latter transported in dedicated trainloads from Invergordon on the Far North Line.[43] During the freight-only period there were occasional calls for a low-cost passenger service to be reinstated – including from me – suggesting the use of DMUs on what was not an excessively steep route (and certainly comparable gradient-wise with the formerly three routes from Cairnie Junction / Keith Junction to Elgin, which had seen DMU operations from 1960 onwards).[44] But the appetite for rail re-openings was still in its early days – it would be the mid 1980s before this really took off.[45] Throughout the 1970s the line continued to operate with minimum maintenance, with speed latterly restricted to 20mph, 'but even so by 1979 either money had to be spent or the line closed'.[46] And so it closed.

Back in 1963, Provost Alex Noble had warned of 'doom' for Fraserburgh if the railway freight service was withdrawn, but – although the town has had its problems – the population has now grown to its highest-ever level (13,000) since 1961, doubtless reflecting the general buoyancy of the fishing industry. The Dyce–Fraserburgh track was lifted in the early 1980s, but fortunately the vision of Grampian Regional Council led to the entire route (including the Peterhead arm) becoming the Formartine and Buchan Way, a long-distance footpath and cycle way, preserving its integrity as a transport corridor (other than some bridges removed to improve sightlines for motorists), and holding out opportunities for a passenger train revival in the future, as explored in Chapter 15.

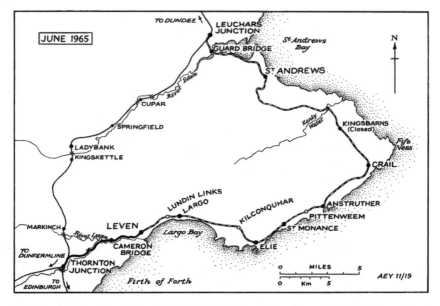

The East of Fife railway followed the Firth of Forth coastline for much of the Leven to Crail section. North of Crail, the railway turned inland, serving four intermediate stations (all closed in 1930) before reaching St Andrews. Prior to the line's demise in 1965, most of the five weekday trains operated throughout from Thornton to St Andrews or Dundee, but on summer Saturdays all but one of the augmented service of seven trains (four of these originating in Edinburgh or Glasgow) went no further than Crail. The closed station at Kingsbarns is shown here as it retained a crossing loop until the end. (Alan Young)

10

Cut the trunk and the branches wither: Crail, Leven and St Andrews

The cross-country – largely coastal – railway linking Thornton Junction (on the Edinburgh–Aberdeen main line) with Leven, the main East Neuk towns and villages (such as Anstruther, Crail, Elie and Largo), St Andrews and Leuchars Junction (on the main line, 20 miles north of Thornton), came into being as the work of four separate railway companies: the Leven Railway, the East of Fife Railway, the Anstruther and St Andrews Railway, and the St Andrews Railway. The 39½-mile through line was a long time coming, being completed in various stages between 1852 and 1887.

The western end of the line (ultimately double-track, unlike the rest of the railway) became very busy with export coal traffic through the expanded harbours at Leven and Methil. Eastwards, the line served the fishing industry and agriculture, while holiday traffic to the East Neuk coastal towns and villages dominated the passenger business every summer. From 1910 the North British Railway (which had taken over all the constituent railway companies) began operating, over summer weekends, the *Fifeshire Coast Express* from Glasgow to Crail on Friday evenings, returning on Monday mornings. This enabled businesspeople to locate their families on the coast in the summer, and to travel there themselves at the weekend. The train was a success and ran from Mondays to Fridays in subsequent summers.[1]

What later became the *Fife Coast Express* – operating from both Glasgow and Edinburgh – was suspended during both World Wars, but was reinstated between Crail and Glasgow in 1949, using the former *Silver Jubilee* streamlined stock displaced from the ECML, and ran until September 1959. That year also saw the first DMUs on the East of Fife line, including through trains to Edinburgh and Glasgow. As noted by Hajducki, Jodeluk and Simpson in one of their three comprehensive histories of the constituent railways of the through line: 'The diesel units on local services were popular with the travelling public because of their speed, perceived modernity and comparative cleanliness and, not least, because of the fine views that could be had through the cab windows.'[2]

By 1960 the majority of passenger services were DMU-operated, cutting costs and boosting demand, but 'many felt that an opportunity had not been taken to make further savings by eliminating steam-haulage altogether and by introducing conductor-guard working with the sale of tickets by the train crew and the consequent de-staffing of the passenger stations . . . Although dieselization was a welcome advance on the life-expired passenger stock which had operated the line in the 1950s, traffic over the line in the winter months was dwindling almost to nothing and the bus and private car had, effectively, already won the battle.'[3]

Official figures a few years later, as we shall see, would arguably challenge that damning description of the line's patronage, but there was no doubt that frequent and regular bus services – penetrating to the heart of virtually every town and village served by the railway, whose stations were not all conveniently located and whose trains were relatively infrequent and irregular – had become a big challenge for the East of Fife line.

By 1962 it was clear that a major threat to the future of branch lines generally was in the offing, and in December of that year the SRDA sent letters to the various local authorities along the line, warning that 'the rumours circulating in relation to the proposed closure of the Fife coast line were almost certainly based on fact and that the Association was prepared to offer what help they could if, and when, these proposals became a reality.'[4]

The warning was duly noted and, at a public meeting held on 19 February 1963 in Pittenweem, a committee was formed of the provosts of the five East Neuk burghs, with a remit to arrange meetings with Sir John Gilmour, the local Conservative MP, the Scottish Tourist Board, the Scottish Council, Development and Industry, and the BRB, to make the case for retaining the railway.

Beeching threatens Leven–Crail–St Andrews closure

On its publication on 27 March 1963, the Beeching Report's Map 3 – 'Distribution of passenger traffic station receipts' – showed that every intermediate station between Leven and St Andrews fell into the lowest revenue category. And it was therefore no surprise that the infamous Map 9 – 'Proposed withdrawal of passenger train services' – marked the Leven–St Andrews section in black, denoting 'All passenger services to be withdrawn'. Formal closure proposal notices for the withdrawal of trains between Thornton Junction and Dundee via Crail (but leaving Leven and St Andrews stations unscathed) were posted in local newspapers and at the stations affected on 2 September 1963 – part of a 'second wave' of Beeching closure proposals to be published in Scotland (the first having come in June). There was, mostly, a quick reaction locally: 'With the exception of the St Andrews Town Council, who seemed to have adopted a somewhat laconic and disinterested position, the response of the local authorities was swift and vociferous and the Five Burghs Committee resolved that they would fight the proposals all of the way and that "every possible protest should be lodged by the people living between St Andrews and Leven".'[5]

In accordance with the normal practice, the railway trade unions had been given advance notice, in August, of the proposed closure, as part of the formal consultation process. The memo supplied by management showed that more than 75 staff were employed to operate and maintain a 28-mile railway carrying only five passenger trains in each direction daily, and – bearing in mind that the Beeching Report's Map 4 of 'Distribution of freight traffic station tonnage' showed all stations in the lowest tonnage category – a modest freight service.

The publicly available BR Heads of Information, which accompanied the memo to the staff side, gave details of the numbers of passengers using each train on representative days. Between Leven and Dundee (not including the more frequent St Andrews–Leuchars / Dundee trains), a total of 320–400 passengers used the service daily in each direction throughout the year, rising to over 750 on summer Saturdays when additional trains ran – plus 200–300 beyond Leven on summer Sunday excursion trains.

The East Neuk had long been attractive for holidaymakers and the line itself hosted three 'camping coaches': at Elie, Lundin Links and St Monance (or St Monans). Camping coaches were old passenger vehicles no longer suitable for use in trains, converted to provide basic sleeping and living space at static locations in rural or coastal areas – and there were over 30 such coaches sited in Scotland in 1957.[6] BR's 1963–64 timetable for Scotland[7] advertised this opportunity 'For Carefree Holidays' in a coach which was 'fully equipped with crockery, cutlery, table linen, blankets and bed linen, etc., and accommodates six persons', but it was also made clear that guests had to purchase return rail tickets 'from their home station to the station serving the Camping Coach'. As well as getting you to your holiday resort, the train was a practical way of exploring the area after arrival, with 25s weekly Holiday Runabout tickets offering unlimited travel in a wide area bounded by Dunfermline, Mawcarse, Crail and Leuchars Junction.[8] Whether Holiday Runabout ticketholders – and those with the sister 'Freedom of Scotland' tickets – ever had their journeys on the East of Fife line credited to its finances is doubtful.

The official statistics are (half-heartedly) challenged

For a railway heavily dominated in summer by holiday traffic, the absence in the Heads of Information of revenue for those who booked elsewhere to travel to stations on the line was a major omission. In one of at least four consultation meetings held by BR to discuss the proposed closure (in this case on 6 September 1963, in Edinburgh) the first question posed by the staff side focused on passengers originating outwith the threatened stations and the associated financial implications: 'a completely unrealistic picture is being presented to the public by the B.R.B. From these figures it is clear that approximately 50% of the passengers using this service join the trains outwith the stations listed for closure and we contend the logical approach to the financial set up on this Branch is to take into account all receipts for bookings to and from the stations concerned.'[9]

The management response was brief and opaque: 'as had been mentioned before, the revenue was related to the portion of the line concerned'. Once again, BR had failed to provide any meaningful clarity on a threatened line's finances, not least in terms of inbound holiday traffic. Nevertheless, despite the limitations of the statistics, it is remarkable that the 'Estimated Receipts' (£31,420) in the Heads of Information represented no less than 52% of the 'Estimated Direct Costs' (£59,850) – the best receipts-to-costs ratio of those identified in this book's detailed case studies, on perhaps one of the most unlikely lines. The two largest intermediate towns served (Anstruther and Largo) had populations of around 3,000, while the other four significant settlements served were all 1,500 or less.[10]

The validity of BR's revenue figure of £31,240 is in any event brought into question by different data contained in the confidential 'Amplification of Financial information' for the TUCCS (contained in the BR Brief for Liaison Officer). While the 'Direct Costs' are the same as in the Heads of

Information (£59,850) – but additionally broken down into movement, terminals and track and signalling costs – the entry for 'Receipts' totals £43,700 (not £31,420), comprising £17,500 net earnings and £26,200 'Contributory Value'. This discrepancy – evidently unchallenged by the TUCCS – lends weight to the conclusion that the approach to such figures in the Beeching period was often cavalier. Even two decades later, dubious accounting practices were still around, as David Prescott recalls: 'I was told by a senior manager when I was being required to sign my name to the income for the Settle–Carlisle route during the potential sale phase (where we had to warrant the operation for a prospectus for potential purchasers) that the grossly inaccurate revenue allocation arrangements did not matter as it was going to close anyway. I refused and said if you want to warrant it – you sign! He didn't, and I got my APTIS [Advanced Passenger Ticket Issuing System] machines installed at Settle and Appleby stations, which as I predicted, once true tickets sales data was being captured, led to an apparent surge in passengers and revenue, and the rest, as they say, is history.'[11]

At the 6 September 1963 consultation meeting the staff side raised – among a variety of challenges about the management of the line – the question of holiday traffic: 'At a time when Management should be endeavouring to publicise the speed and comfort of rail travel we find that the pattern of service on this Branch has not changed to any great extent since the trains were steam hauled. Some of the Staff representatives present at the meeting went so far as to state that in their view, there had been a deliberate attempt to rundown the services in this area. It was maintained that no effort had been made to exploit the scenic beauty of this coastline; that whilst land cruises had proved profitable in other areas, no attempt had been made to run such trains from the industrial centres to St Andrews.'[12]

'Land Cruises' had been introduced by BR following the arrival of DMUs in Scotland; they offered inclusive day excursions linking Central Scotland towns and cities with scenic / holiday areas which did not normally enjoy through timetabled services. Perhaps the classic example was the circular *Six Lochs*, which on eight dates in summer 1964 operated variously from Coalburn, Fauldhouse, Glasgow Queen Street, Gourock, Grangemouth, Rutherglen and Wishaw Central (and intermediate stations) via the West Highland Line and the Callander & Oban, encompassing Lochs Gare, Long, Lomond, Tay, Earn and Lubnaig.[13]

The management's limp response to the suggestion that the East of Fife railway had been insufficiently developed and promoted – 'over the years much effort had been put into trying to persuade the public to make use of rail facilities' – should have prompted some searching supplementary questions from the staff as to what had and hadn't been done, but the discussion moved swiftly on. The NUR archives do point to a tendency for staff representatives to fail to grill management adequately on the whys and wherefores of proposed closures, but in their defence, Philip Bagwell, in his history of the NUR, argues that the union headquarters provided little help to hard-pressed local branches:

> The union's Closure of Branch Lines sub-committee was not a very effective body. Roy Trench, a member of the EC [Executive Committee] in 1962–64, who served on the sub-committee, recalled that its members were sometimes confronted with a pile of papers up to a foot high and that a good deal of the work comprised 'rubber stamping' the closure proposals. Apart from what the local branches were able to supply, the sub-committee had little evidence to go on, there being no headquarters research team to provide factual information and suggest alternative solutions to outright closure. In these circumstances, it depended a great deal on the zeal and initiative of branch and district council secretaries as to how far it proved possible to delay or stop the closure of lines and reduction of services.[14]

Rae Montgomery echoes that view of the workload – from a management perspective – having attended a number of consultation meetings on closures in the Inverness-managed Northern Division: 'Everyone involved was weighed down by the volume of paperwork. My colleague Hugh Gowans and I used to be called into the office of the Divisional manager, Miles Herbert, which we compared to being run under a grain hopper, as yet another stack of correspondence, consultation papers, etc, was unloaded upon us.'[15]

In the case of the NUR, one has to ask *why* there was no headquarters research team? Lack of funds was not the explanation for the NUR's half-hearted resistance to closures: the union's total assets at the end of 1962 were over £6.5 million. Negotiating better redundancy terms – rather than stopping closures – was the key objective of the NUR's General Secretary, Sidney Greene. Bagwell also records an insider view that 'the General Secretary was not fighting all-out against the Beeching Plan, because he was led to believe that once the closure programme was completed the staff who remained to run a more efficient service would be a well-paid elite'.[16]

It would not be until the 2000s – well into the era of privatisation – that this prediction would come true, at least in terms of train drivers. In 2016, ScotRail drivers were on a basic annual salary of nearly £45,000 – compared to £25,000–£30,000 for bus and lorry drivers, who bear the additional safety responsibility of steering their vehicles (and have a direct interface with customers).[17] In fairness, train drivers generally travel at much higher speeds and can be responsible for a much greater number of passengers than bus drivers, but the contrast is still stark.

At a further consultation meeting held in Glasgow on 26 September 1963 to discuss the proposed closure of a number of lines (including the East of Fife railway), a fundamental question was raised about the figures supplied by BR:

> The Secretary of the Staff Side asked for a breakdown of the financial statements in respect of the lines under consideration. The Chairman of the Management Side stated that as this information was not available, he was, therefore, unable to give the details asked for by the Staff Side. The Secretary of the Staff Side said this counted as a refusal to provide the information and Staff Side of the [Sectional] Council deplored the fact that past practice of providing this information no longer obtained,[18] and stated that they would require to follow up this aspect of the matter with their Headquarters, as they considered Consultation could not be properly completed without this information.
>
> The Chairman of Management Side said this complaint would be noted.[19]

Noted, but doubtless not followed up.

The process leads to closure

The BR Brief for Liaison Officer[20] records that there had been 119 individual objections – a much larger number than in any of the other detailed case studies in this book (albeit that several of these also had either petitions or were objections on behalf of multiple others). However, the consequences of the restricted geographical distribution of public notices about the proposed closure were evident: despite this being very much a holiday route, only 12 objections came from outwith Fife.

Just 16 objections were identified as coming from regular travellers, but overall there was a considerable diversity of objectors, notably including hoteliers, landladies, local authorities (no fewer than eight), the SRDA, teachers and local traders. BR summarised the main grounds for objections as 'the adverse effect on tourist industry, inadequacy of alternative bus services, road congestion and lengthening of travel time'. No fewer than 56 objectors had raised the adverse effect on the tourist industry, including the managing director of Anstruther Holiday Camp, who had read 'with dismay' the notice of the proposed closure, and had written on 17 September 1963:

> We are in an excellent position to know the value of the passenger line as far as holiday traffic is concerned, and our records show that during the latter part of June, the whole of July and the early part of August this year, approximately 3,500 holidaymakers arrived here by train.
>
> An important fact to note on this subject is that very few of the railway passengers arriving at the Holiday Camp supported Anstruther Station financially, because they were travelling with return tickets bought at the station at which they started their journey . . . Furthermore it is not true to say alternative bus or motor coach transport would be equally good. A family with children and luggage would suffer considerable inconvenience . . . It is highly probable that when holidaymakers, who otherwise intend to spend their holidays at Anstruther, discover that they cannot reach their destination direct by train, they will decide to spend their holidays somewhere else more accessible.

He was probably correct, but perhaps not necessarily appreciating that the 'somewhere else' would increasingly become Spain, by plane. BR's internal brief made a surprisingly honest comment on the tourist trade issue, conceding that east of Largo (where the bus service was less frequent) 'the other points along the coast may well suffer to a greater degree in view of the necessity to change from train to bus at Leven. It is thought, however, that the biggest loss would be on day-trippers, particularly on Sundays.'

Inevitably, a significant number of objectors (26) raised the inadequacy of bus services, while 28 (partly overlapping) objectors also drew attention to the lack of bus facilities for heavy luggage, prams and cots. BR's brief not unreasonably pointed out the availability of an hourly interval bus service along the length of the route, supplemented by additional peak-hour services, but conceded that 'some duplication would be necessary during the busy summer months'.

It is surprising that only 13 objectors cited one of the greatest deficiencies of the proposed replacement bus service: the walking distance from the nearest bus stops to Leven station – variously six, seven or nine minutes – and the absence of convenient timetabled bus–train connections. The BR brief was blunt and honest: 'The allegation by some objectors that trains and buses do not run at co-ordinated times is true to a large extent.'

The TUCCS annual report for 1964 recorded that objectors at the public hearing on 17 February in Leven had brought out that 'the economy of the East Neuk of Fife depended to a large extent on Summer visitors, mostly composed of families whose practice is to rent accommodation for a fortnightly period'. This was a pattern which was changing markedly with growing affluence, but the committee nevertheless reached three pretty firm conclusions, the last of which looked to be stretching the narrow definition of 'hardship' beyond the existing conventional wisdom:

> If the train service were withdrawn, passengers requiring to change to the bus at Leven rail-head would have a walk of approximately half a mile and this would create hardship to elderly people and passengers with heavy luggage.

> The Committee concluded that the *only* [emphasis added] hardship would be to the existing users of the passenger trains at the stations from Leven to Crail inclusive, as the withdrawal of the train service would involve them in increased travel expenses, plus the fact that they would have a considerable walk between the Bus and Railway Stations at Leven.

> It was also agreed that the Hoteliers, Landladies and Merchants in the coastal area would suffer financial hardship if the proposals were given effect to in their entirety.[21]

'Only' seems a strange way to describe hardship at eight out of the 10 stations proposed for closure. The other two were Guardbridge and St Fort, both between St Andrews and Dundee on lines which would stay open.

Wider regional development considerations would not help this threatened railway. In a 1 May 1964 letter to the SDD, the SCDI advised, somewhat confusingly, that it 'does not oppose these proposed closures of passenger services on the grounds that the probable consequent loss of the existing rail goods service would have a serious economic effect on the area. Nevertheless the Scottish Council is of the opinion that the withdrawal of the passenger services on the line serving the East Neuk Burghs would have a serious effect on their prosperity as summer resorts unless or until in its place there was provided a bus service from the appropriate rail-head which would be capable of handling the holiday season Saturday peak traffic as it arrives by rail and without delay.'[22]

The TUCCS submitted its report on the line to the MoT on 3 April 1964, but it would not be until 11 February 1965 that the minister (Labour MP Tom Fraser) publicly announced his decision to axe passenger services if there were improvements to the bus–rail interchange at Leven.

Hajducki, Jodeluk and Simpson record that the local MP, Sir John Gilmour, and Provost Braid of St Monance remained 'indomitable in their fight to prevent the East Neuk from losing its passenger services but the seemingly inevitable was now impossible to resist'. As a small consolation to the tourist trade, closure was postponed until 6 September, with replacement buses to be operated by Alexanders over a variety of routes, 'most of which gave a connection to the remaining railheads at Cupar, Leven or St Andrews'.[23] The poor quality of the interchange at Leven would continue to be a source of protest until that town in turn lost its passenger station five years later.

The final throw of the die was a 30 July meeting in Glasgow between the BRB, representatives of the East Neuk burghs and Sir John Gilmour MP, with the latter 'expressing the view that Leven itself would only be a temporary railhead and that, within a couple of years, the station there would also be facing closure'.[24] He was right. And the meeting was not a success. Even at that late stage, Provost Braid was making the case for de-staffing stations, automating level crossings and boosting patronage by running more through trains from Edinburgh to Dundee via Crail, 'but these further proposals fell on stony ground'.[25]

The final day of service was Sunday 5 September, bringing the last day-trippers from Edinburgh and Glasgow to enjoy a visit by train to the

East Neuk: 'Excitement mounted all day among locals who were determined to give the local line a good send-off and Alexanders put on a special bus from Leven to take those who wished to travel on the last train, the 18.20 Crail to Glasgow, the last eastbound train having gone several hours before. Before 6 o'clock the ticket office at Crail had run out of tickets and paper certificates had to be issued in their place.'[26]

Doubtless most of the excited crowds witnessing the last train were no longer regular rail travellers. There was a nostalgic attachment to the railway, but as in many closure cases the length and breadth of Britain, not enough people had heeded the warning to 'use it or lose it'. However, for former rail users without access to a car, there was only one alternative mode of transport, whose inadequacy – as cited by objectors – would quickly be demonstrated on the ground: 'On Monday 6th September the buses took over with a nominally hourly bus from Newport and St Andrews to Leven station. Within days public protests were being made about the poor service provided and of the failure of the buses to maintain any proper connections – hardly a surprise, given the attitude towards rail passengers exhibited by the management of Alexanders.'[27]

What could have been done to cut the losses?

The quoted BR figures showed, surprisingly, that the rail service revenue covered more than half its attributed movement, terminal and track and signalling costs. And yet there was still substantial scope for cutting costs in all three cost categories. Six signal boxes at block posts / crossing loops[28] – meaning the single-track block sections averaged only four miles in length – were not needed for a passenger service of five trains in each direction (taking around 70 minutes to traverse the 28 miles of railway between Leven and St Andrews). Freight traffic was not a long-term proposition, and at most two signal boxes would have sufficed, splitting the line into three block sections: more than adequate for even an enhanced passenger service. The six level crossings could have been automated. Staff were not required at more than a couple (if that) of the 10 intermediate stations. And movement costs – at 5s 1d per train-mile (as revealed to the TUCCS) – were higher than they would have been for an entirely DMU-operated service.

Most of the line's traffic was over the section from Leven to Crail, and so an alternative to complete closure, or an entire reprieve, would have been to close the 11 lightly-trafficked miles between St Andrews and Crail, leaving

169

the balance of 17 miles from Crail to Leven to be operated as an even more simplified 'basic railway'. A single loop, part-way along the branch, would have allowed an up-to-hourly frequency to operate – but the loss of the through route (and its tourist charter potential) would have been unfortunate, bearing in mind that a single-track block section between Crail and St Andrews would have incurred a relatively low maintenance and operating cost for lightweight DMUs running over track with half a dozen permanent speed restrictions of 50mph or less (the maximum line speed being 60mph).[29]

And then came St Andrews and Leven

In the third of their three histories of the constituent parts of the railway from Thornton Junction to Leuchars Junction, Hajducki, Jodeluk and Simpson suggest that the six-mile Leven stub 'seemed to have been granted a new lease of life' following the closure of the line from St Andrews and Crail: 'Leven remained, at least nominally, as the railhead for the East of Fife line bus replacement services, notwithstanding the fact that the services latterly did not actually run up to the station and a transfer between the two modes involved a walk. The timetable was revised, and the passenger service of through DMU trains between Leven and Edinburgh, obviating the need to change at the increasingly decrepit Thornton Junction station, consisted of eight trains per day from Leven between 6.44 am and 8.25 pm, with 10 regular journeys in the opposite direction, and was relatively well patronized.'[30]

On the face of it, therefore, it was perhaps surprising that a subsequent positive shift of direction in national policy actually involved the proposed demise of train services to Leven (and St Andrews). By the time that the 'British Railways Network for Development' map was published in March 1967, government thinking had moved on from one key aim of the Marples / Beeching era – with an effective acknowledgement that the rail system's financial losses could not be eliminated, and that it was unrealistic for BR to have such terms of reference. The 1967 White Paper on Transport Policy acknowledged that the government should – instead of underwriting BR's annual global losses – financially support specified socially necessary passenger services which would otherwise be withdrawn. The 1967 map set out the 'basic rail network' of some 11,000 route miles which the government and BRB had concluded was needed to meet these objectives – and neither Leven nor St Andrews (nor several other routes in Fife and along the Forth Estuary)

CRAIL, ST ANDREWS, LEVEN AND CALLANDER

Plenty of passengers (including the photographer's family in the foreground) wait to board a St Andrews–Edinburgh train at Crail in summer 1964, a year before closure. *Frank Spaven*

An excursion train hauled by J37 No. 64602 crosses a DMU at Elie on 1 May 1965. The excursion, which had started from Dundee Tay Bridge station, terminated at Dundee West station, which closed that day.
Robin Barbour (courtesy of Bruce McCartney)

B1 No. 61116 crosses Largo Viaduct with the 12.17 p.m. service from Thornton Junction to Crail on 25 July 1964. *WAC Smith / Transport Treasury*

The layout at St Andrews station as seen from an incoming DMU from Leuchars in the early summer of 1967, a few months before track rationalisation. *Frank Spaven*

Watching the ball or the train? A DMU from Leuchars trundles past two golfers on the final approach to St Andrews, on the penultimate day of service – Friday 3 January 1969. *Norman Turnbull*

The benefits of cross-platform connection: on 3 January 1969 a branch train for St Andrews sits in the bay platform at Leuchars while a Dundee service pulls away on the left. *Norman Turnbull*

'Aye, the pram'll nae be so easy on the bus…' On 1 August 1969, two months before closure, passengers at Leven are perhaps contemplating a future without trains. *Norman Turnbull*

On 27 August 1969, passengers leave the 12.30 p.m. Edinburgh–Leven train at Cameron Bridge. The service would be withdrawn just five weeks later, but freight trains would continue to serve the adjacent grain distillery until the mid-1990s. *WAC Smith / Transport Treasury*

On Sunday 21 August 1960, two separate 'Six Lochs' Land Cruise sets stand at Callander, where passengers were allowed time for lunch. *WAC Smith / Transport Treasury*

NBL Type 2s began operating to Oban in 1961. Here D6130 and D6133 prepare to depart from Callander on the 12 noon from Glasgow Buchanan Street on Monday 3 April. *WAC Smith / Transport Treasury*

The Secondman of the 5.15 p.m. Oban–Glasgow Buchanan Street service, hauled by NBL Type 2s D6114 and D6135, awaits the Guard's green flag at Doune on 5 August 1961. *WAC Smith / Transport Treasury*

A local train for the south prepares to depart from Callander on 23 May 1964 hauled by V2 No. 60818 – an expensive operation compared to DMUs. *Stuart Sellar*

On 17 June 1967, Doune station (rebuilt in typically grand Caledonian Railway style in the early 1900s) is showing no signs of vandalism, despite more than 18 months having elapsed since closure. *Norman Turnbull*

A delightful station falling into rack and ruin. With its attractive setting and architecture, Callander station – seen here in February 1968 – had been one of the gems of the journey to Oban. *Norman Turnbull*

were part of the Network for Development. And while – a year after the map was published – the 1968 Transport Act enshrined the principle of grant aid for specific socially necessary passenger services, this did not save the two remaining stubs of the East of Fife railway.

The St Andrews debate

DMUs had first reached St Andrews in 1959, and were popular with passengers, including visitors who – through the glass partition behind the train driver – could enjoy 'such delights as the crossing of the Tay Bridge and the run along the banks of the Eden with the ever increasing prospect of the beach, Old Course and city'.[31] In the first seven months of DMU service, patronage grew by 13.7% compared to the equivalent final period of steam operation.[32]

However, in March 1967, following substantial traffic losses in the wake of the opening of the Tay Road Bridge the previous year, BR announced its intention to withdraw passenger services from St Andrews (freight had finished in 1966). The trade unions were sent a memorandum on the proposal in June, noting that economies short of closure had already cleared staff consultation: notably 'the substitution of "One Engine in Steam"[33] method of working between Leuchars and St. Andrews to replace the present Electric Token system'.[34] Surprisingly, once this was implemented, only six of the 17 posts involved in the 5¼-mile branch operation would be closed. The remaining posts at St Andrews would comprise two clerks, two foremen, one porter, one office cleaner and one guard, while Guardbridge would have two posts of 'Male Crossing Keeper', and the two signalmen at Leuchars Junction South signal box would remain.

The Heads of information[35] set out particulars of the number of passengers using the service. Between September 1966 (the month *after* the Tay Road Bridge opened) and March 1967, the average number of passengers joining trains on Mondays to Fridays at St Andrews had declined from 608 to 361 daily, a drop of no less than 41%. On Saturdays the decline was 25%, suggesting that commuter traffic had suffered more than other travel purposes. The nature of (part of) the competition was also noted: while there were 20 or 22 trains in each direction daily (a very intensive service, by any standard), buses between St Andrews and Dundee ran 'basically hourly with additional buses on Saturday afternoons', and during July and August a half-hourly service operated for most of the afternoon. A significant constraint on rail patronage was the absence of any Sunday services, so weekenders always had to use a bus in one direction.

On the 20 trains daily from St Andrews to Leuchars / Dundee / Arbroath, in the week ended 3 June 1967, average passenger loadings on Monday to Friday ranged from two to 59 per train, with five of the six poorest-patronised trains being evening services after 7.15 p.m. The Saturday service (across 19 trains) generated 25% more patronage, including healthier evening numbers.

A comparison of bus and train services had to consider more than frequency – cost and journey time were also important. The rail Cheap Day Return from St Andrews to Dundee was 6s 9d, while the bus cost 6s 11d; the rail Weekly Season cost 29s, while a 10-journey weekly ticket on the bus was 27s 10d. The difference between journey times was much more dramatic: 25–36 minutes by train from St Andrews to Dundee, but 48 minutes by bus. One might therefore speculate that the major transfer of passengers away from the train was to car rather than bus.

The NUR archive at Warwick University includes a reasonably detailed (but undated) BR financial statement which shows that estimated direct earnings from the service were £23,370, while estimated direct expenses were £51,050: a relatively respectable revenue-to-costs ratio of 46%. Later advice from BR about the impact of One Engine in Steam / One Train Working from 4 September 1967 would reduce estimated costs to £47,110, yielding a revenue-to-costs ratio of 50%. But what was particularly striking about the earlier statement was its reference to £66,350 'contributory gross revenue' – of which BR expected to lose only £9,010, presumably on the assumption that travellers heading for destinations beyond Leuchars (in particular) and Dundee would overwhelmingly transfer between bus / car and train, despite less than satisfactory interchange arrangements at these locations at that time (and, indeed, still the case in Dundee today).

At a management and staff consultation meeting on 8 September in Glasgow, the staff side suggested that further cost reduction was an alternative to complete closure, railway employees at St Andrews having pointed out the scope to withdraw three poorly patronised evening trains. The management response – which begged a number of questions – unfortunately went unchallenged: 'Management Side Chairman indicated that unless a set or sets of men could be saved, little actual savings would accrue and, having regard to the wide disparity between revenue and direct costs, the withdrawal of these trains would only have a marginal effect.'

But given the large number of train crew based at Dundee at the time

– and the consequent scope to amend 'diagrams'[36] to match resources more closely to demand – there would surely have been opportunities to devise a plan for withdrawal of all evening services, giving significant direct savings in fuel and manpower. And did St Andrews really need six staff working at the station? The disparity between revenue and costs was nothing like as wide as in the case of some earlier closures, and there was reason to believe that patronage could yet be boosted, as well as further costs cut: the staff side had highlighted the proposed city centre parking bans / charges in Dundee, which 'might have the effect of attracting local car users back to rail'.

A unique issue aired at consultation meetings, and indeed throughout the closure saga, was noted in the BR Heads of Information: the large quantities of 'Luggage in Advance' associated with students at St Andrews University and pupils at two large boarding schools for girls, with these being 'drawn from all parts of the British Isles'. These heavily peaked traffics would fail to be a clincher for the TUCCS, given alternative railhead availability at Leuchars and Cupar, but arguably there would have been many more formal objections to closure from such users if BR had been obliged to advertise its proposal much more widely than only at those stations with a direct train service to St Andrews – which meant that not even Edinburgh Waverley was on the list. And the four newspapers which carried the closure proposal notice – *Glasgow Herald, Scotsman, Courier and Advertiser* (Dundee) and *St Andrews Citizen* – would doubtless have had few student readers 'from all parts of the British Isles' on the chosen dates of 30 June and 7 July.[37] A conspiracy theorist could have had a field day.

In October 1967, BR prepared its customary Brief for Liaison Officer, in advance of the TUCCS public hearing on 2 November in St Andrews. This was a hefty document, incorporating information supplied to the TUCCS, a summary of objections, BR comments on the objections and copies of the letters of objection.[38] The 'General Comment' unsurprisingly homed in on the unique competitive circumstances: 'Since the opening of the Bridge, stations South of the Tay, have lost passenger traffic to a marked degree to road transport, both public and private. This particular theme runs like a thread throughout the Sections of this Brief and the importance of the impact of the Road Bridge on our stations bookings, passenger carryings, etc., cannot be overstressed.'

The number of passengers booked at St Andrews had dropped from 80,244 in 1965 (the last full year before the opening of the road bridge) to 66,203 in 1966 (which saw four months of road bridge operation). A hand-written addendum (presumably made in early 1968) recorded a 1967 figure of 43,017, which represented a decline of 46% between 1965 and 1967. Even major golf tournaments were deemed to be of marginal importance to the railway, BR's Area Manager in Dundee having advised that his investigation into travel to the 'Alcan Golfer of the Year' event had established that 'very few people travelled by rail' – yet if the railway had survived until the 21st century that would most certainly not have been the case, with ScotRail's 'Golflink' timetable being a core part of the logistics for major tournaments at the likes of Carnoustie, Gleneagles – and St Andrews (from the Leuchars railhead).

Surprisingly few objections

Remarkably, the TUCCS received only 23 objections to closure, including submissions from the university and local authorities and 15 individuals. Given that there were 71 season ticket holders at St Andrews in May 1967 (during the school and university terms) and 47 in August 1967, it seems astonishing that so many of them were evidently not motivated to lodge objections to the loss of their daily transport mode.

Fife County Council's objection that the bus could not be a substitute for the train was based on two grounds: 'The bus service between St Andrews and Leuchars does not contact [sic] the railway station at Leuchars which is at least ½ a mile distant from the nearest bus stop', and 'on account of the unsatisfactory bus connection, people travelling with luggage would require to hire a taxi from the bus stop to Leuchars station'.[39]

The BR brief noted that it proposed peak-period connecting buses at Leuchars station and dismissed 'remaining travel [as] so small that it does not justify additional facilities'. There were 'three points where suitable bus stops are located' which 'in order of merit, by our reckoning' involved walking times of seven, 10 and 12 minutes. Integrated transport this would not be, but the situation on the ground was even worse, as only the 12-minute walk had any street lighting. Pathetically, BR sought to invoke an argument that the length of walk faced by travellers would be no worse than the seriously sub-optimal situation in Scotland's capital (which still pertains today): 'The walking time of 7 minutes between Leuchars Junction station and the nearest main road bus stop is no worse than exists in, for example, Edinburgh. From Waverley station to St. Andrews [sic] bus station the walking time is around 10 minutes.'

A large majority of journeys from St Andrews to Dundee would take substantially longer by bus (typically 48 minutes compared to 25–36 minutes by train) but the brief could not resist highlighting one case where the bus would be six minutes quicker than train (due to a change of trains at Leuchars), reaching the dismissive conclusion: 'The unfortunates who end up with an increase rather than a decrease are nevertheless merely inconvenienced and nothing more.' It was just as well that this was an internal BR document.

A public hearing was held on 2 November 1967 in St Andrews. Two days later, *The Citizen* newspaper reported that a representative of the town council had handed over a petition against closure, signed by no fewer than 2,174 people. This, however, got a fairly dusty response from the TUCCS: 'The chairman [Mr E.W. Craig] said he thought it was a great pity the petition had been handed in only now. Ample time had been given to people to make individual representations on hardship, and from the figures of passengers submitted it was obvious that it had been signed by people who did not use the line much and therefore were not likely to suffer hardship.'[40]

Less than three weeks after the hearing the TUCCS submitted its seven-page report to Barbara Castle, the Minister of Transport. It noted that one additional peak-hour bus journey in each direction between St Andrews and Dundee on Mondays to Saturdays was proposed, as was re-routing of certain buses 'at peak periods' to connect with 11 trains at Leuchars – and that the additional travelling time from St Andrews to Dundee would range from three to 24 minutes, depending on the service selected. Despite the latter, the conclusion was typical for closure proposals in the 1960s: 'After carefully considering all the written and oral objections and the statements made by the representatives of British Railways and The Scottish Bus Group, the Committee unanimously concluded that, in the event of the passenger train services being withdrawn, any hardship which may be caused to users will be alleviated by the adequate alternative transport arrangements.'[41]

As well as the grounds of hardship contained in the written objections, the committee had taken the following factors into account in reaching its decision:

> The assurance given by the British Railways' representative that arrangements would be made to allow elderly or disabled persons and mothers with prams to use the sleeper crossing at Leuchars Junction Station under the supervision of railway staff [to avoid the footbridge to the station's 'island' platforms].

The necessity for full co-operation between the University of St. Andrews, St. Leonards and St. Catherine's Schools, St. Andrews, and British Railways to obviate hardship to students / pupils at term times.

The intention at present of British Railways not to close Leuchars Junction Station.

Given the TUCCS conclusion, it would have come as no surprise when – eight months later – the MoT advised that the minister (now Richard Marsh MP, who had passed sentence on the Waverley Route 11 days earlier) had decided to give his consent to closure, subject to the additional bus services to which the TUCCS report had referred.

One of the bitter ironies of the St Andrews case is that only a month before Marsh's announcement, British Transport Hotels (a BR subsidiary) opened the new Old Course Hotel on the site of the former goods station at St Andrews (Links). For a brief period, 'the forlorn DMUS trundled past the new building', which was said to resemble 'a chest of drawers with all the drawers sticking out'.[42] Hajducki, Jodeluk and Simpson comment:

> Whether the hotel was ever destined to cater for rail passengers was a matter of some controversy but it seems likely that those likely to patronise the 'Old Course' would have been expected to travel by road from Leuchars rather than have to endure the rattling DMU on the branch which would pass by and terminate half a mile distant . . . The initial overnight rates for a room with facilities was £6 5s. 0d. for a single and £7 0s. 0d. for a double . . . breakfast in all cases was an extra at 14s. 6d. per person. A contemporary guest house establishment in St Andrews was charging between 15s. 0d. and 21s. 0d. for a double room with breakfast.[43]

Could more have been done to improve the economics?

Harsh to regular travellers as the loss of the St Andrews branch seems from a modern-day perspective, in some ways it is hard not to defend the TUCCS verdict (which only suggested that hardship would be *alleviated*, rather than *eliminated*). Train patronage had been drastically affected by the new Tay Road Bridge – albeit that the decline was artificially exaggerated by the earlier temporary boost to rail use caused by curtailment of passenger ferry services between Newport-on-Tay and Dundee during the three years of construction of the bridge.[44] BR had provided a frequent service and had rationalised the infrastructure down to single-track throughout, so what more could they have done to get the ratio of receipts-to-costs to a healthier level than the 50% achieved? David Prescott comments:

> BR could have done more to cut costs – the model was already there with Gerry Fiennes' East Suffolk Line, and North Berwick would get similar treatment when it was reprieved in 1969. At most, three staff were needed at St. Andrews – together with motorisation of points[45] at Leuchars South junction, automation of the level crossing at Guardbridge and withdrawal of evening trains it should have been possible to get costs down to £40,000 or so. Combined with better marketing, including getting the fares right – and bearing in mind that the initial post-Road Bridge changes in travel patterns would not necessarily be sustained, as road congestion became a growing problem – a performance getting close to break-even would not have been out of the question.[46]

Nevertheless, the combination of the road bridge, a frequent bus service providing much better penetration of Dundee city centre than the train (as Tay Bridge station was now hemmed in by roads linking to the road bridge), and growing car ownership, would not have eased the competitive pressure on the timetabled rail service. And infrastructure rationalisation had effectively ended the possibility of developing the charter train market. With hindsight, it is not difficult to see both sides of the St Andrews argument.

Once the minister had given his verdict, a last-ditch attempt was made by St Andrews Town Council to explore ways in which the line might be kept open. Citing a recent decision by Dundee Corporation to subsidise the Dundee–London air link, the idea of the town council and Fife County Council contributing to the annual subsidy was floated. BR, which offered to meet the council, insisted that the full cost of running the service would have to be met, but the SRDA suggested that possible methods of operating the line more cheaply could be discussed. It all came to nought: 'As if to scupper any possibility of Council support, British Rail told them on 4th November that the estimated cost of maintain the service had now increased to some £20,000 per year . . . [however] on 7th December, 1968, following observations by the BRB that there had been an absence of any undertaking by the St Andrews Town Council, the official closure notices were posted.'[47]

The last train ran on Saturday 4 January 1969, the official closure date being Monday 6 January – the same day as the Waverley Route closed. The dramatic events on the latter, at Hawick and Newcastleton on the 5th and 6th,[48] overshadowed a low-key farewell in north-east Fife, as reported by the *Courier*: 'There were lively scenes to mark the last journey from Leuchars to St Andrews at 11.07 pm, but no enthusiasm . . . As the empty train drew out of St Andrews on its way to the depot in Dundee, passengers joined in singing "Auld Lang Syne" and sent up three cheers for the St Andrews railway staff.'[49]

The Leven arguments

In September 1967 a deputation from Fife County Council had travelled to London to meet the Minister of Transport and argue the case for the threatened Leven, Newport-on-Tay and St Andrews branches.

In October the railway trade unions were, as standard practice, supplied with a memorandum setting out the details of the proposed Leven closure, including the impact on staffing.[50] This indicated that Leven station (handling passengers and parcels, but not freight) had no fewer than seven staff: two clerks, three leading porters and two signalmen. A 'basic railway' would have needed only a third or less of that number. Nor did Leven need a signal box and double-track over the last 1¼ miles from East Fife Central Junction on the 'main line' to Methil. And even the 4¼ miles of double-track from East Fife Central to Thornton Junction would eventually represent over-provision, as freight traffic dwindled.

The unions were also supplied with additional financial detail which stated that while the direct earnings of the service were only £8,510 annually, the 'contributory gross revenue' – presumably reflecting a lot of through travel from Leven to Edinburgh – was no less than £46,530. BR's 'expected loss in total revenue' was £23,200, i.e., only 32% of the contributory revenue was forecast to be lost – a questionable assumption, given the poor bus–train interchange at Kirkcaldy which ensued. Estimated direct expenses totalled £53,179.

The number of passengers booked at Leven station in the year ended August 1967 totalled 18,659 (with 559 season tickets issued), but the public Heads of Information which accompanied the staff memorandum put this in starker terms: during the week ending 13 May the average daily number of passengers alighting from northbound trains at Leven on Monday to Friday was only 81 – spread across 12 trains. Numbers were better during the holiday season, with the average during the week ending 15 July being 145 on Monday to Friday, and 491 on Saturday 15 July, the memo noting that the latter was the start of the Glasgow Fair holiday period and therefore represented 'maximum peak travel'.

Overall, these were highly discouraging numbers, demonstrating – in the words of John Yellowlees[51] – 'the long dark shadow cast by the Forth Road Bridge', which by this time had also led to the Kirkcaldy–Edinburgh local service frequency being cut.

However, the TUCCS would have to reach conclusions on hardship, and this included consideration of the relative costs and journey times of the proposed replacement service compared to the train. The rail Cheap Day Return of 12s from Leven to Edinburgh would be matched by a new Combined Rail Cheap Day / Bus Return, while a through bus return cost 10s 6d. The rail journey time of between 62 and 78 minutes would be replaced by a combined bus / rail journey (changing at Kirkcaldy) of 93 minutes, or a through bus taking 95 minutes – not a realistic commuting journey time.

On the bus front, the 13 September 1968 meeting of the TUCCS had to deal with a robust complaint echoing the concerns voiced by East Neuk campaigners in 1964–65 about the quality of bus / rail connections at Leven. Professor Dr W.H.J. Childs of Heriot-Watt University – supported by Sir John Gilmour MP – had written to complain that, ironically as a result of newly improved rail services between Leven and Edinburgh, connectional allowances between train and bus at Leven were now unsatisfactory.[52]

In his original June 1968 letter, Childs referred to 'little co-ordination between British Railways and Alexander & Sons (Fife) Ltd', with the result that out of eight theoretical southbound connectional opportunities at Leven, there were only three 'reasonable' connections of 10 minutes. For journeys from Edinburgh, the situation was much worse, with connectional allowances 'either impossibly small or unacceptibly [sic] large': indeed, out of 20 theoretical connectional opportunities (there were two bus stop options in this direction) only four fell within the range 10–15 minutes, with the worst being 35 minutes.

Correspondence involving Childs, the TUCCS and BR continued through June, July and August, reaching no satisfactory conclusion, essentially because bus-to-bus connections took timetable-planning priority at

Leven. As Sir John Gilmour noted ominously in his letter of 25 June to the TUCCS: 'From what Dr. Childs has told me, fewer and fewer people are using the train because of the long delays between train and bus, and this must have an effect on the possible closing of the line between Leven and Thornton.'

Childs's last letter to the TUCCS prior to its 13 September meeting drew a fundamental conclusion from the exchanges between the rail and bus companies: 'It is particularly alarming that both parties to the agreement made with the Minister of Transport [at the time of the East of Fife line closure] appear to have conveniently forgotten its existence when changes in service times are made. It is left to a member of the travelling public to draw the attention of your committee when a deterioration of conditions has set in, before any effort to co-ordinate is made.'

How long the MoT agreement remained in force – in theory or in practice – is not known, but such concerns about bus–rail integration remain all too persistent 50 years later.

In late 1968, BR applied to the MoT – as part of the new regime under Section 39(4) of the 1968 Transport Act – for 1969 grant aid in respect of the Leven service.[53] The projected earnings were effectively the same – £7,000 – as cited to the NUR, but costs had leapt from £56,640 to £93,000. The latter represented a calculation of the long-run costs of maintaining the service, as opposed to the short-term saving from withdrawing it. The contrast between such bottom-line figures (particularly the full allocation of track and signalling costs, plus interest and administration) would cause consternation among campaigners in the few remaining closure cases before the decade ended, notably in respect of the Waverley Route.[54]

The public hearing was held on 15 January 1969 in Leven, with the TUCCS Chairman, E.W. Craig, stating that the annual receipts for the line were given by BR as £7,230, while the estimated direct expenses were £56,640 – both being different figures from those supplied to the NUR (and BR presumably not having advised the larger grant-aid figure). In an echo of forceful arguments that would be made for re-opening the Levenmouth line four decades later, David Reid, the Fife County Council Traffic Officer, pointed out that the area was one of five special development districts in Scotland. He also queried the financial information provided by BR: 'This attempt to open up the validity of the figures produced was ruled out of order by Craig, the chairman, who also rejected any idea that British Rail had [in 1965] given any guarantees about the future of Leven station.'[55]

But the minister had implied a guarantee in his conditional consent to the Leven–St Andrews closure. Here was the TUCCS sticking rigidly to the narrow remit it was given by the 1962 Transport Act – doubtless to the relief of BR and the MoT. Another body with even less sympathy for rail users facing hardship – perhaps unsurprisingly – is referenced in a powerful description of the public hearing proceedings by Hajducki, Jodeluk and Simpson:

> The last witness, James Tweedie, commercial manager of the Scottish Bus Group, gave the show away when he admitted very candidly that, 'Bus services had been built up over the years to serve Fife and beyond and had not been designed as road–rail interconnecting services. Their primary purpose had been the service of the communities.' And, in view of the fact that the so-called connecting services had already been routed away from Leven station and the company's unwillingness to provide better connections if the Leven line was to close, it appeared that the 'service of the communities' effectively meant that this bore a direct relation to the profits of the nationalized Scottish Bus Group and little to the environmental and social benefits which an integrated transport system would have brought to the country. Its privatized successors have been no better in either of these respects.[56]

The TUCCS annual report for 1969 records the verdict reached on Leven in language blandly familiar from the Beeching era – far removed from the practical difficulties which would be faced by former rail users in terms of, *inter alia*, the longer journey times, increased costs and lack of shelter at bus stops which had been cited by objectors at the hearing: 'After carefully considering all the written and oral objections the Committee concluded that, in the event of the passenger train services being discontinued, any hardship which may be caused to the existing users of the stations at Sinclairtown, Dysart, Thornton Junction, Cameron Bridge and Leven would be alleviated by the proposed alternative transport arrangements.'[57]

The MoT verdict was advised to the BRB in a 12 June 1969 letter: unsurprisingly, the minister accepted the TUCCS verdict on alleviation of hardship, so the line to Leven would close, subject to 'minor alterations [being made] to three existing bus services to improve connecting facilities'.[58] Professor Childs could have been excused a rueful response to the latter, and those who had warned that the closure of the East of Fife line in 1965 would lead, perhaps inexorably, to the loss of Leven, could say: 'I told you so.'

The public notices announcing the closure decision made reference to the replacement bus services, including special mention of the bus–train connection which 'has also been arranged from Crail to Edinburgh, via Leven and Kirkcaldy': this would depart Crail at 6.17 a.m. and, with a change of buses at Leven and a change from bus to train (not immediately adjacent) at Kirkcaldy, would reach Edinburgh Waverley at 8.55 a.m. The intrepid public transport user from Crail now faced a journey of two hours 38 minutes (with two changes) compared to the through rail journey of one hour 56 minutes on the 6.49 a.m. train from Crail to Edinburgh in 1965. Such was the price of progress.

The line closed on Monday 6 October and, according to the *East Fife Mail* two days later, 'the broken clock on the platform at Leven station signalled on Saturday evening that time had despairingly run out . . . for at 8.25 pm the last passenger train left from a dark and dejected platform on its ultimate journey to Thornton.'

It is hard to disagree with Hajducki, Jodeluk and Simpson's sentiment about the loss of one rail facility after another: 'In the space of barely five years, East Fife had regressed by more than a century back to the era of the horse and trap and a time when the only railheads had been the newly opened but distant stations at Kirkcaldy, Cupar and Leuchars. The government had spoken and the trains had vanished.'[59]

Was the fate of St Andrews and, in particular, Leven, effectively predetermined by the closure in 1965 of the East of Fife route linking the two towns? As David Prescott has pointed out,[60] the closure of the East Neuk section would have looked a lot different if it had been presented as a single proposal for axing Thornton to Leuchars. The through route seems to have had (relatively speaking) a surprisingly good ratio of receipts to costs – although the 11-mile section from Crail to St Andrews was poorly patronised compared to the 17 miles west of Crail. There was plenty of scope to cut costs further by infrastructure rationalisation and de-staffing of stations.

On the demand side, it clearly could have been developed as a scenic route attracting the 'Land Cruise' market, which had lost its core, circular tour with the probably inevitable demise of the Callander–Crianlarich section in 1965 (see Chapter 11) – potentially followed by later opportunities to develop the emerging charter train market, as well as the standard service for local users and holidaymakers. But whether the changing pattern of holidaymaking (with domestic resorts being ditched for the warmer attractions of Spain) and the inexorable growth of car ownership would have allowed a through route reprieved in 1965 to survive the 1968–69 cull of Fife and Forth estuary railways is anyone's guess.

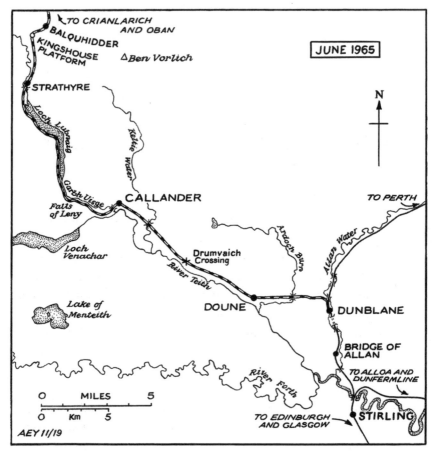

For most of its life, Callander was an intermediate station on the through line to Oban, serving as a passenger terminus only from 1858 (when the first trains ran from Dunblane) until the opening of the railway as far as Glenoglehead in 1870, and then briefly – in 1965 – when a landslide in Glenogle closed (a month earlier than planned) the doomed railway north of Callander. The sparsely populated railway corridor to Oban uniquely had no fewer than six crossing loops at locations without a passenger station; Drumvaich Crossing, mid-way between Doune and Callander, survived until the Dunblane–Callander closure. (Alan Young)

11

The baby and the bathwater: Callander

In the 1840s early railway speculators had their eyes on Oban, with its ferry and fishing traffic, and on the wider hinterland of Argyll for its presumed mineral wealth. In 1845, the Scottish Grand Junction Railway was proposed to run from the weaving village of Callander (expected to be connected in due course at Dunblane to the planned Scottish Central main line from Greenhill on the Edinburgh & Glasgow Railway) across the Highland boundary at the Pass of Leny, then through Glenogle and Glen Dochart to Crianlarich, continuing via Glen Lochy, Loch Awe and the Pass of Brander to Oban.

But late that year the bubble of 'Railway Mania' began to burst when the Bank of England put up interest rates. The Grand Junction scheme was abandoned, as was the planned Dunblane, Doune and Callander Railway; however, the Scottish Central scheme survived, reaching Dunblane (and Gleneagles) in 1848.

The Dunblane–Callander proposal was revived in 1856 and the 11¼-mile railway opened to traffic in 1858. With an initial train service of only two trains a day in winter, but five in summer, the focus on developing tourist traffic was immediately apparent.[1] Callander was again seen as a launching pad for a route to the West Coast – but 71 miles of mostly challenging terrain (and precious little intermediate population) made for a tough engineering task. The Callander & Oban Railway secured parliamentary approval in 1865, but the line did not reach Oban until 1880. Nominally independent, it was operated by Scotland's biggest railway company, the Caledonian, until 1923.

A tourist route from beginning to end

Oban was already a thriving town of some 3,000 people and the centre of an established network of steamer services, but the trains brought many more visitors, and in its halcyon years the Oban line and tourism prospered together, often in conjunction with other modes of transport. The apotheosis of tourist rail travel was reached in 1914 with the advent of the Pullman car *Maid of Morven*, described thus by John Thomas: 'This unique vehicle was a combined observation, lounge and kitchen car . . . The internal decoration, after the Sheraton period, was lavish; the walls were panelled in finely figured pearwood, and there were marquetry pilasters with details after Pergolesi.'[2]

While the experience 50 years later would not be quite so sublime, rail travellers through Callander could still experience the delights of an observation car. In 1957 BR had begun attaching to summer trains to Oban a car which had been built for the London & North Eastern Railway's luxurious streamlined *Coronation* express service introduced in 1937 at the height of competition between the ECML and WCML for prestige travel between London and Edinburgh / Glasgow.

But despite this encouraging development, all was not well with the passenger train service. John Thomas offers a brutal verdict on the railway in its last years: 'Anyone who travelled the line in the long, crowded trains of summer Saturdays in the '50s would have concluded that the C & O was a vital, prosperous concern. Weekdays told a different story, and in winter the trains were left almost empty. At times the three-coach 6 a.m. from Stirling ran all the way with three passengers or less.'[3]

Despite its passenger woes, in the late 1950s the Dunblane–Oban line was still very much a multi-purpose railway, central to the economic life of the corridor it served, in 1958 carrying substantial quantities of non-passenger traffic: 90,000 tonnes of freight (primarily aluminium-related traffic for the Kinlochleven smelter near Ballachulish, coal, general merchandise and livestock), 200,000 bags of mail and 160,000 parcels.[4] However, the singling of the Dunblane–Doune double-track section in 1955 was a straw in the wind (and a good illustration of Beeching's later blind spot about 'fixed' costs). As BR's finances deteriorated further and Beeching became involved in the future of the rail industry in 1960, the prospects for the eastern half of the C&O looked steadily worse – not least through the availability (since 1897) of a chord line from Crianlarich (Upper) station to the C&O, allowing faster journeys from Glasgow to Oban via the West Highland Line.

Beeching spells out the future

The Beeching Report maps published on 27 March 1963 showed that the

Dunblane–Oban line fell within the lowest density category for both passengers (0 to 5,000 per week) and freight (0 to 5,000 tons per week). North of Dunblane, the only station short of Oban which was not in the lowest station receipts category (£0 to £5,000 per annum) was Callander, at £5,000 to £25,000 per annum.

Seen from today's perspective, it seems surprising that this small non-industrial town fell into the medium category for freight (5,000 to 25,000 tons per annum), but the Callander goods depot served a wide catchment area, and in 1963 BR was still handling a broad range of everyday freight commodities, not least domestic coal: at the time 34 million tonnes was consumed annually in the UK, compared to only one million tonnes today.[5] Domestic coal remained the backbone of BR wagonload freight services until the early 1980s.

For the general public, however, the heart of the issue was Map No. 9, 'Proposed withdrawal of passenger train services': this showed that the news was worse than expected for Callander, as the entire 40 miles of the Dunblane to Crianlarich (Lower) section were proposed for closure, with Oban trains diverted via the West Highland Line to Crianlarich (Upper).

In February 1964, BR management (in Inverness, surprisingly) circulated to staff – in advance of the formal proposal to close Dunblane–Crianlarich – both the Heads of Information supplied to the TUCCS and a separate paper setting out revised staffing arrangements and proposed revised passenger, parcels and freight services.

The memo for staff [6] detailed the number of passengers 'booked' at each station between Dunblane and Oban in 1963, but, as usual in closure proposals, excluded inbound traffic. Predictably, Oban saw the most – at 26,257 for the year – but Callander (population only 1,627) came a significant second at 10,724, and Doune (866 residents) third at 4,284. The Heads of Information set out the number of passengers using individual trains 'on representative days' but what the latter represented was not clarified. Passengers alighting at / departing from Callander per train were typically in the low double figures, and single figures in the case of Doune. There were exceptions, such as late afternoon summer departures from Callander, typically joined by around 50 passengers – and the special case of the 6.50 a.m. from Stirling on winter Mondays to Fridays, joined by 106 passengers at Dunblane and 31 at Doune, with a total of 148 alighting at Callander: the vast majority of them pupils at McLaren High School. That was truly a trainload.

The BR memo detailed no fewer than 21 staff employed between Doune and Callander (inclusive), of whom 11 were signalmen working at the Doune and Drumvaich crossing loops and the two Callander boxes. This was a labour-intensive operation more appropriate to a past era than the challenging present of intense road competition.

By the summer of 1964, with closure threatened, some aspects of the railway looked distinctly rundown. Returning by rail to Edinburgh from a Scout camp in Killin, I can recall the train drawing into Balquhidder station – by then an unstaffed halt – and seeing a platform overtaken by that ubiquitous sign of dereliction, rosebay willow herb. John Thomas evokes the same station as a symbol of the line's decline: 'Travellers in passing trains saw a broken, grass-grown platform, and peeling buildings with open doors revealing papers scattered over the floors of former offices.'[7]

By that time, the Monday to Friday train service essentially comprised – in winter – three through trains from Oban to Edinburgh / Glasgow supplemented by five local trains from Callander to Edinburgh and / or Glasgow, all but one loco-hauled, with inevitable cost implications. Strangely, the service was significantly better in the Down direction, with four Oban trains and seven locals. In contrast to the tourist-oriented 1858 timetable, in summer the Callander local service dropped to four trains daily, albeit augmented to five on Saturdays (plus the three or four through trains from / to Oban).

The service was irregular – an interval of anything from 40 minutes to 2 hours 48 minutes between Callander departures – but offered relatively fast journey times: 34 minutes to Stirling, compared to 50 minutes on the competing bus; 92 minutes against 130 minutes to Glasgow; and 117 minutes against 160 minutes to Edinburgh. Day return and weekly season tickets were competitive with the bus, being generally only a few pennies more expensive, such as 4s 6d against 4s 5d for a Callander–Stirling day return.[8]

Objectors object, and BR prepares its arguments for the TUCCS

With the TUCCS public hearing scheduled for 18 November 1964 in Callander, BR prepared its customary internal Brief for Liaison Officer.[9] This provided synopses of the 121 objections, covering the closure of the Dunblane–Crianlarich section and four intermediate stations on lines which would remain open: Bridge of Allan, Loch Awe, Falls of Cruachan and Ach-na-Cloich. BR summarised the principal grounds of objection in terms of:

- the effect on the education of pupils attending McLaren High School in Callander
- the inadequacy of the proposed alternative bus and train services
- the general condition of roads in the district
- the lack of bus–rail co-ordination at Crianlarich and Stirling
- the effect on the tourist trade, 'with specific reference to Callander'
- the loss of an efficient parcels service by passenger train

BR noted two key flows south of Callander: around 140 school children daily from Dunblane and Doune to Callander, and about 50 daily commuters between Callander, Doune and Stirling / Edinburgh / Glasgow. Thirty-one objections came from people residing east and south of Callander who were concerned about the impact on the education of the schoolchildren, including extra-mural activities outside school hours. BR proposed a new bus service from Dunblane, 'duplicated as necessary', which would extend the journey time for Dunblane pupils by about 15 minutes each way.

No fewer than nine aspects of the inadequacy of bus facilities were cited among 55 objections, unexpectedly including three objecting to the 'absence of smoking facilities' on buses. As regards travel sickness, BR reported that Mrs Dorothy Mahoney had 'tried all the various tablets on the market to no avail. In the absence of a train service it would appear that it would be necessary for her to invest either in a motor car, cycle or pony and trap.'

Connoisseurs of quality public transport would not have been reassured by BR's comments that 'buses with automatically operated doors *usually* preserve the heat . . . Toilet facilities *of a sort* can usually be made available at stopping places en route . . . It is agreed that mothers with children are handicapped but there is *always* a helping hand when difficulty with luggage is encountered [emphases added].'

A four-page objection from the Town Clerk of Callander raised a wide range of issues, not least the impact on tourism, including reference to BR's *Six Lochs* excursion train (see Chapter 10) bringing in as many as 1,000 people a day to Callander at weekends; indicative of the area's scenic quality was its later designation as part of Scotland's first National Park. In 1961 the *Six Lochs* operated every Sunday out of Glasgow from 21 May to 27 August, and on another 25 local holidays it ran from origins as diverse as Gourock, Grangemouth and Strathaven.[10] The Town Clerk also painted the bigger picture: 'During 1963, 23,000 excursionists visited the town. While it is impossible to isolate precisely the business such people bring to the town from the total volume of tourist business, it seems reasonable to suppose that each tourist on average may be expected to spend about a pound on such things as a meal, refreshments, souvenirs, postcards, cigarettes and sweets. This proposed closure represents a potential loss to the town of from £15,000 to £25,000 annually. This we claim is a considerable hardship.'[11]

He wished 'to protest on behalf of the diesel excursionists themselves' – and rightly so, as the official notices of proposed closure would only have been posted at stations offering regular timetabled services over the Dunblane–Crianlarich line, a category which applied to few of the originating stations of the excursion trains. He also cited some specific examples of 'potential hardship to citizens of Callander', one of which was rather stretching the definition of both hardship and citizens: local funeral undertakers were in the habit of having coffins sent by passenger train from Glasgow 'at necessarily short notice. There is no road service in operation which can be depended on to perform this service so rapidly and so reliably.'

A more conventional concern related to two young people who commuted between Callander and Dunblane: 'The two girls concerned are Miss Dorothy Drummond and Miss Irene Cameron who have to start work in Dunblane at about 8.30 a.m. At present they are admirably served by 7.52 a.m. ex-Callander in the morning and the 5.35 p.m. ex-Dunblane in the evening. If the trains are taken off they will have to catch the 7.7 a.m. bus from Callander for Stirling, leave Stirling at 8.1 a.m., finally reaching Dunblane at 8.22 a.m. . . . On return they would have to have their employer's permission to leave work early to catch the 4.50 p.m. bus ex-Dunblane to change at Doune in order to catch the bus from Stirling reaching Callander at 5.50 p.m.'

Such personal inconvenience or hardship would be the lot of tens of thousands of former rail passengers across the country. A less personalised – but no less convincing – objection was submitted in a five-page letter sent from his Beith, Ayrshire address by the SRDA Honorary Secretary, Tom Hart. Citing the scenic attractions of the line for tourists from England, Hart argued that the closure notice should have been published in the leading British newspapers, so that English tourists could have objected, had they so desired. He also raised an important issue for all tourist routes threatened with closure, specifically in terms of the passenger numbers and revenue attributed to the lines concerned: 'No mention is made of the passenger traffic arising from excursion and charter trains which pass over this route. On most railway routes, such traffic is normally light in relation to the traffic arising from the regular trains but the Callander line is exceptional in that its scenic attractiveness plus its utility as a link in the circular excursion route from Glasgow to Glasgow [but see page 163 for the full range of origin points in 1964] via Crianlarich, Killin, Callander, and Stirling gives rise to a very substantial amount of excursion and charter traffic. This traffic is thought to be in the region of at least 20,000 passenger journeys per year.'[12]

The BR brief sought to downplay the impact of closure in terms of travel between Glasgow, Doune and Callander, pointing out that in addition to proposed new bus services, an hourly frequency already operated between Stirling and Callander, compared to eight or nine trains. But it over-reached by claiming that 'no great hardship would ensue if the train service were withdrawn in that a rail / bus arrangement [interchange at Stirling] would provide for an almost parallel service and with, in many cases, entirely comparable times.'

It then suggested – in apparent contradiction – that the average extended journey time 'seldom exceeds' 15 minutes for Callander. However, in the case of the three through trains from Glasgow (as opposed to those involving a change of train at Stirling) between 7.55 a.m. and 6.05 p.m., the journey times post-closure would deteriorate by 24, 25 and 28 minutes. There were only two through trains a day from Edinburgh to Callander, and after closure these journeys would be extended by eight and 38 minutes. Overall – given the half-mile walk between the railway and bus stations in Stirling – it was not an enticing prospect.

The brief also included 'Supplementary Details (not supplied to T.U.C.C.)', including a table which underscored the extent to which rail was losing out to bus and car competition: the number of passengers booked at Callander had declined by 29% between 1960 and 1963, and season tickets by 27%.

The TUCCS and MoT reach their verdicts – and the line closes

The TUCCS Annual Report for 1964[13] records that at the public hearing on 18 November, 'a considerable number of objectors appeared to further their written representations', and 'after carefully considering all the objections, the Committee agreed that, until such time as the desirable major road improvements in the area have been completed, serious hardship would be experienced by the present rail users [between Dunblane and Crianlarich] if the service were discontinued in view of the existing road conditions coupled with the fact that that there is heavy tourist traffic during the Summer months. Some suggestions were made whereby this hardship may be alleviated in certain instances.'

While 'hardship' was the TUCCS's sole criterion, there were wider regional development issues at play, which – in theory – could have an impact on the future of threatened lines. The 27 May meeting of the SEPB was attended by no fewer than 30 individuals representing 14 government departments. Gordon Stewart, Scottish Region's Assistant General Manager, might have felt isolated as the sole BR representative, but – as a consistent advocate of closures – he had little to worry about on this occasion. The SEPB's verdict on Dunblane–Crianlarich was only marginally short of BR's wishes: 'It was agreed to approve the majority view of the sub-committee not to oppose closure subject to retention of the track from Dunblane to Callander which might be required to serve long term growth in the Stirling area.'[14]

Two months later, C.P. Scott-Malden ('An Under Secretary, Ministry of Transport') wrote to the BRB in London, advising – with a drearily familiar form of words for closure decisions – that 'the Minister has considered the reports of the Consultative Committee and all other relevant factors including the views of the Scottish Economic Planning Council on the implications of the proposals. He has noted the Committee's view that the closures would cause hardship to present users of most of the stations involved, particularly those between Dunblane and Crianlarich.'

Yes, duly noted, but the MoT conclusion was that 'if certain additional bus services are provided, any remaining hardship would be insufficient to justify the retention of the service'. Accordingly, the minister had given consent to closure of the entire line. Of the SEPB's suggested retention of the track from Dunblane to Callander, there was not a mention.

The date of closure was to be 1 November 1965, but an 'Act of God' intervened to bring an abrupt end to the Dunblane–Crianlarich train service: in the early hours of 27 September a landslip blocked the line in Glenogle. For the last time, a coffin would play a small but symbolic part in the twilight of the railway, as described by John Thomas: 'In the middle of the night the railway staff arranged for the remains of Roderick Walker, a former Glasgow policeman, to be transferred with his funeral party, bound for the South Uist steamer at Oban, from the Night Mail (12.30 a.m. from Stirling), which was held at Balquhidder; this was despatched by road to Oban, where the *Claymore* [ferry] was kept waiting.'[15]

A full inspection revealed that the landslide was more serious than originally thought, and a decision was taken to abandon the train service between Callander and Crianlarich immediately. A now DMU-operated service continued to link Glasgow and Callander until Saturday 30 October (there was no Sunday service), when the last passenger train ran. The daily freight train to Callander from Alloa Yard (one of the white elephants of the 1955 Modernisation Plan) had already been withdrawn, so that was the end of the town's railway after 107 years of service.

Should Callander have been saved – or protected for future reinstatement?

I have a nostalgic attachment to that scenic line of route from Callander to Crianlarich by Loch Lubnaig, Glen Ogle and Killin Junction to Strath Fillan. But it was clearly difficult to justify the retention of a through railway in such a sparsely populated corridor – which no longer even has a bus service west of Killin – particularly when the consequent diversion of Glasgow–Oban trains to the shorter route via the West Highland Line brought 20-minute quicker journeys for through travellers from Glasgow. But Dunblane to Callander should have been a different proposition. One can readily envisage a drastic cut in costs to create a 'basic railway'. The DMU running time from Dunblane to Callander was only 19 minutes, enabling an up-to-hourly service to be provided over a single-track 'long siding' with 'One Train Working'.

All four signal boxes and all crossing loops extant at the time of closure[16] could have been eliminated – although it would have been sensible to retain a loop at Callander to accommodate charter trains – with perhaps only a couple of ticket-issuing / parcel-handling jobs retained at Callander station. In its most drastic version that would have represented an overall reduction of ground operating staff of 85% or more compared to the last days of the through-route service – a classic demonstration of Beeching's 'blind spot'.

In October 1966 an 'in confidence' memorandum was circulated to the SEPB, including comments by the SDD on 'certain formation lengths and station sites for which the Railways Board are seeking Ministry of Transport approval to [sic] disposal'. The SDD's Planning Division – echoing SEPB advice the previous year, before closure – recommended that 'the Dunblane–Callander section (including the station sites at Doune and Callander) be retained' since: 'In view of the growth potential of the Falkirk – Stirling – Grangemouth Area and the demand for good quality residential areas in, and on the periphery of, the Central Belt, expansion could take place in this direction as far as Callander in which case a commuter line would be a decided asset.'[17]

The memo also cited what may or may not have been a contrary view from Callander Town Council, which wished to use 'part of the formation of this line for development'. But in any event the 27 October SEPB meeting – at St Andrew's House, with the ultimately infamous 'Gorgeous George' Pottinger[18] in the chair – 'agreed that in view of the possible use of the line as a commuter line the formation from Dunblane to Callander would be retained'.

No evidence has been found that the MoT imposed any such embargo on route disposal, and if they did, how long it was maintained. What is now indisputable is that there have been many breaches of the 11-mile former railway formation over the last six decades. The likelihood of re-opening is addressed in Chapter 15.

12

A right royal scandal: Ballater

Once the railway had reached Aberdeen from the south in 1850, the tentacles of what would become the GNOSR system were soon spreading across the North East. The first branch line, from Aberdeen 17 miles west to Banchory in Deeside, opened in 1853, and was eventually completed by a further 26 miles to the village of Ballater, near Balmoral Castle and Braemar, in 1866. Queen Victoria had been visiting Deeside since 1851, and the new railway became an integral part of royal travels. It is said that Ballater was the destination of more crowned heads and royalty than any other station in Europe.

The easternmost section of the single-track Deeside Line hosted part of the famed Aberdeen suburban service – 'the Subbies' – which began operation to Culter in 1894, stimulating population growth around Cults, Culter and Park, with double-track progressively extended from Aberdeen through Culter to Park between 1884 and 1899, and new stations opened at Holburn Street and Pitfodels.[1] But this fast and intensive service (and the latter two stations) succumbed to road competition as early as 1937, and the Aberdeen–Park section was singled in 1951.

A unique experiment

As we have seen, the late 1950s briefly saw a resurgence of patronage on Scottish branch lines following the replacement of steam by DMUs (predominantly) and railbuses – while the Deeside Line played host to a unique traction experiment. In 1954, the Electricity Consultative Council for the North of Scotland recommended that experiments should be made with battery railcars on one or more branch lines, in part reflecting the statutory duty of the North of Scotland Hydro Electric Board (NOSHEB) to aid economic development in the Highlands.[2] BR was initially less than enthusiastic

195

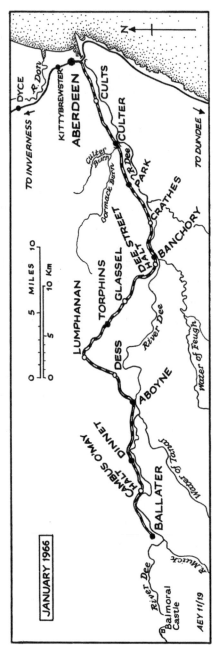

The first 17 miles of the Deeside Line from Aberdeen to Banchory (opened in 1853) closely followed the course of the River Dee. Beyond Banchory, however, the line promoters decided to take a sweep to the north through Lumphanan to reach Aboyne (a further 15 miles), thereby avoiding two bridges over the Dee. This was claimed to offer substantial cost savings but added two miles to the through journey and saddled the Deeside Line with its steepest gradients. From Aboyne (opened in 1859) the railway ran close to the Dee throughout its final 11-mile section to Ballater, opened in 1866. (Alan Young)

about the project and an early attempt to deploy such a vehicle on the Crieff branch came to nothing. However, the British Transport Commission and NOSHEB reached agreement in 1957 to introduce a battery railcar – converted from a two-car DMU by BR at its Cowlairs Works – the following year on the Deeside Line.

The new unit proved to be the first replacement of steam traction in the North East, arriving in Aberdeen in early 1958, then entering regular service on the Deeside Line on 21 April that year, followed a couple of months later by DMUs, together displacing steam from regular passenger services on the branch.[3] Batteries were partially recharged during the day, taking advantage of train lay-over times of up to 1½ hours at the Aberdeen and Ballater termini. The battery railcar was popular with passengers, due to the absence of vibration and its very low noise levels – and to coincide with its introduction, the daily train service was doubled from three trains each way to six.

The BR 'Report on the progress of diesel schemes in the Scottish Region'[4] issued in 1960 does not indicate whether the Deeside Line fell into the category of route (like Fraserburgh and Peterhead) where dieselisation was 'designed to reduce costs in areas known to have little to offer in the way of potential traffic', or if it was expected to stimulate new business as well as cutting costs. In practice, however, the combination of battery railcar and DMU replacing steam yielded a substantial 64.9% increase in receipts in the 12 months ended March 1959 compared to March 1958. In the second year of battery railcar / DMU operation (over nine months to December 1959), receipts increased again – perhaps inevitably, more modestly – by 11.5% compared to the equivalent first nine months of 'non-steam' operation.

Beeching's verdict – and the media reaction

The likely fate of the Deeside Line was starkly portrayed in Map 9 of the Beeching Report published on 27 March 1963. Together with every other railway in north-east Scotland, bar the main line from the south to Aberdeen and the Aberdeen–Inverness route, the branch to Ballater was shown – appropriately – in black, denoting 'All passenger services to be withdrawn'. The line and its stations were listed in the lengthy appendix to the report setting out the full closure programme, but that was not the only mention.

The Deeside Line was one of four Scottish railways featured in Beeching's case studies, and together with the Crieff / Comrie branch represented the only two out of the 10 routes on which revenue exceeded both 'movement'

197

and 'terminal' costs. This reflected the fact that these services boasted the lowest movement costs per train-mile – 2s 6d in the case of Deeside and 2s 4d for Comrie / Crieff, compared to the other routes ranging from 3s 1d (a DMU operation) to 7s 7d (steam haulage). Part of the explanation for the low Deeside cost may lie in the partial use of the battery railcar – one keen observer, David Murray-Smith, commenting on 'its smooth and silent running' and noting that 'it appears to have had operating costs similar to those of two-coach DMUs'[5] – but its appearance on the line was in reality intermittent, due to a variety of technical problems from late 1960 onwards.[6] The low cost per train-mile may, as suggested by David Prescott,[7] reflect a relatively long route with some quick turn-rounds at the termini, allowing hourly costs (e.g., train crew) to be spread over a lot of miles.

It was only once 'direct track and signalling expenses' were brought into the equation that withdrawal of the services to Ballater and Comrie / Crieff became 'financially justified'. And the Deeside figures would be at the heart of the controversy – over the next three years – as to the actual losses the line was incurring, and to what extent these could be reduced.

Virtually the entire front page and editorial page of the *P&J* of 28 March were taken up with reactions to the Beeching Report – little wonder, as its circulation area included no fewer than 14 rail services threatened with closure. The main headline – 'DOWN WITH BEECHING! – says North-east' – jockeyed for attention with 10 other headlines on the front page. 'Town and country explode in anger', 'Death-blow for tourism', and 'Shock after shock' summed up the sentiments. The editorial, noting that Labour's Harold Wilson had the previous day talked of 'the disintegration of the British transport system', commented: 'We have, of course, the assurance of the Minister of Transport and the Secretary of State for Scotland that rail services will not be withdrawn without ensuring that adequate alternative means of transport are available. But how adequate is adequate?'[8]

The paper reported the reaction of MPs throughout the north of the country – and rail users in the West Aberdeenshire constituency would read that their MP, Lieutenant-Colonel Alex Forbes Hendry (a 'Unionist', as was the common description of Conservatives then), had mixed views on the work of the BRB chairman: '[He] described the Beeching Report as a brilliant analysis of a situation which exists at the present time of a railway system which is trying to run on Victorian lines. The report used no imagination in trying to consider how the services in the remote parts of the country could be brought up to date.'

A swift and imaginative response – but BR erects a brick wall

A bold plan to avoid closure was announced only a day after Beeching had unveiled his report. On 29 March 1963, the *P&J* reported, under the headline 'Deeside tourist body wants to take over railway', that Hendry had already submitted the Deeside Tourist Association's proposal to the Minister of Transport – and 'if there is a favourable response, Deeside's example might well be followed by other areas with outstanding tourist attractions'. That was to prove a forlorn hope on both counts, but the MP for West Aberdeenshire was enthusiastic: '"I myself know the line,"' Mr Hendry tells the Minister, "and I am a regular passenger. Many of my constituents," Mr Hendry continues, "are so convinced that this line could be run profitably that I have been asked as a matter of urgency to inquire whether British Railways, who are unable to run the line, would be prepared to hand it over to the local community, with the redundant rolling stock, to be run as a local enterprise."'[9]

The subsequent progress of the closure proposal process is – unusually for a railway history book – described and analysed in much detail in A. Derek Farr's *Stories of Royal Deeside's Railway*, published in 1971. Farr, in his chapter on 'Anatomy of a Closure', places the fate of the line to Ballater in a much wider context: 'The story of the closure of the Deeside Line is in effect the story also of the closure of most small branch railway lines, as well as being the story of how indifference and bad management of nationally organised bodies is tending to act against the best interests of local communities.'[10]

He writes that a 13 May Aboyne meeting of eight campaigning organisations (including local authorities) agreed to appoint a firm of management consultants to look into the running of the line, with a view to suggesting economies, and – surprisingly – that 'the District Traffic Superintendent of British Railways agreed to co-operate by supplying the necessary information'. Kinord Associates of Aberdeen were appointed to undertake the work, and their report would prove to be a revelation.

In November 1963, BR gave notice of its proposal to close the Deeside Line, citing 'Estimated Receipts' of £14,370 and 'Estimated Direct Costs' of £50,080 – with the MoT subsequently clarifying in a memo to the SEPC that 'this does not include the cost of maintaining the track to freight standards though it is the Board's intention to close the line completely following withdrawal of the passenger service'.[11] But as we shall see, although the evident gap between revenue and expenditure was enormous, the line was saddled with infrastructure and staffing well beyond what was required for a fit-for-purpose passenger service. However, BR looked to be on stronger ground on passenger numbers: 'On Mondays to Fridays throughout the year a total of 250–300 passengers travel in each direction [on 5 or 6 trains]. On Saturdays, the total is 230 in winter, but holiday and tourist travel in summer increases this to 420 between Aberdeen and Ballater and 310 in the opposite direction.'[12]

The MoT memo referred to an average of 20–30 passengers per train on winter weekdays (in evident contradiction to the BR figures above) and 40–60 on summer weekdays ('excluding excursion services'). Perhaps not many observers could have foreseen it, but the latter reference reminds us that a surviving Deeside Line today would have been a major attractor of special charter trains from Central Scotland and beyond, a market which began to expand in the 1970s and 1980s and now includes the luxury land-cruise *Royal Scotsman*.

BR's Heads of Information conceded that 'the interval between trains averages 2½ hours, with an overall range of 1½–4¼ hours'. The latter statistic was not impressive, and observers might also have pointed out that the absence of any 'short workings' from Aberdeen to Banchory limited BR's ability to generate more leisure and shopping traffic over the 17 miles of the line closest to the city.

The discrepancy between rail and replacement bus journey times was substantial in the case of the two principal stations on the line: Aberdeen to Banchory would be extended from 32 to 48 minutes, and Aberdeen to Ballater from 82 to 110 minutes.[13] And these bald statistics could not convey the negative transformation of the *quality* of public service provided. Unlike the situation on other – generally shorter – routes proposed for closure, the connectivity and frequency of alternative bus services listed in the Heads of Information was a mish-mash:

> Messrs. W. Alexander & Sons (Northern) Ltd. operate several bus services in the area. Between Aberdeen and Ballater the service via the A.93 road serves all points except Glassel, Torphins and Lumphanan, and consists of 5 buses daily in each direction at intervals varying from one to five hours.
>
> In addition, there is a bus service between Aberdeen and Banchory, which, including the above services, gives an hourly frequency

for most of the day. The service is further supplemented over the section between Aberdeen and Culter where buses operate at very frequent intervals on the Dyce-Culter route.

Glassel, Torphins and Lumphanan have a separate service to Aberdeen but, as this operates over roads at least two miles north of the A.93 road there is no direct bus connection between these three places and any other point on the branch line. On Mondays to Fridays there are five buses in each direction at intervals of 1¾–4 hours. One bus less runs each way on Saturdays.

Messrs. Strachan's Deeside Service also operates between Aberdeen and Ballater via Banchory and Aboyne, and provides 7 buses in each direction on Mondays to Fridays and 8 on Saturdays, with a service interval of one to three hours. As this service runs on the south bank of the Dee between Aberdeen and Banchory, and certain buses also keep south of the river between Banchory and Ballater, it does not provide an alternative to all the points served by rail.[14]

As in the case of Fraserburgh, the contrast with the simplicity of the rail timetable – and its scope for enhancement – could hardly have been greater. And few Ballater rail passengers – contemplating 110 minutes on the bus, perhaps longer in wintry conditions – would have been consoled by BR's advice that 'W. Alexander (Northern) Ltd. Intend to ask the authority of the Traffic Commissioners to run an additional bus service leaving Ballater at 7.0 a.m. for Aberdeen. This bus would operate on withdrawal of the train service.'

Official objections to BR's proposal having been lodged with the TUCCS, the original proposed closure date of 2 March 1964 was postponed, pending a TUCCS hearing. In the meantime, internal discussions on the Deeside closure were held within BR. Following the public announcement of the proposed closure, BR issued (in November 1963) a memorandum to inform the consultation process between management and staff.[15] The minutes of a Sectional Council meeting on 31 January 1964 in Glasgow note that the staff side commented that 'not enough had been done to develop the potential passenger traffic in the summer from tourists', but Mr Methven from management responded bluntly: 'The facts were that most of the tourists travelled by road by private car, and by bus tours and it was a very difficult thing to compete against this. Apart from tourists the position was that the traffic was just not there.'[16]

This defeatist posture was evident in meetings across Scotland to discuss closures, and it was not the only time that the supposedly conclusive phrase, 'the traffic was just not there', was recorded in consultation minutes. Management's disingenuous attitude was on display again a month later at another management / staff meeting in Glasgow to discuss closures: 'Mr. Bell [staff side] stated that to have 8 signal cabins in 43 miles was too heavy and some savings in this connection could be made. Mr. Ferguson replying stated that any staff saving which could be made would have no real effect on the ultimate costs.' And there it was left. BR was not exactly facing an inquisition from the trade unions – but that was certainly not true of other interested parties. . .

A devastating critique

The independent report on the railway was produced in two instalments in January and March 1964, and the line's historian, A.D. Farr, has commented that 'few such documents can have been produced in recent years which revealed so much official apathy and plain bad management on the part of a public concern'. BR does not emerge well from his description of the subsequent manoeuvring: 'From the start it appeared that the British Railways Board felt that they had something to hide, for on instructions from the Board in London the previous offer to co-operate was refuted and all requests for a breakdown of expenditure were refused. In subsequent attempts to justify this *volte face* it was explained that the original offer was made in the belief that the object of the exercise was to examine the possibility of local interests taking over the line. From the minutes of the relevant meeting it is abundantly clear that no such confusion existed when the offer of co-operation was made.'

The only official figures available to the campaigners and their consultants were those supplied by BR within the Heads of Information, provided as a matter of course when there were objections to closures, and – unusually in this case – the data contained in the Beeching Report's table of 10 case studies illustrating the assessments made of the annual revenue and expenses for a variety of threatened passenger services. And, fuelling suspicions of a conspiracy, there was a significant difference between the two sets of figures.

BALLATER AND BALLACHULISH

The unique battery railcar (seen here approaching Ferryhill Junction, heading west) had its first day of regular operation on 21 April 1958, and when it left Aberdeen at 9.40 a.m. every seat was occupied. *David Murray-Smith*

Aboyne station was rebuilt in 1896 in distinctive style, with two turrets and a canopy over the station entrance – seen here in August 1959. Fortunately the building has survived. *David Murray-Smith*

One of the unique selling points of DMU (and in this case battery railcar) services, was the opportunity to share the driver's view ahead: in this case an impressive gantry of semaphore signals at Ferryhill Junction on a Ballater-bound journey on 7 May 1960. *David Murray-Smith*

The delightfully-situated Cambus O'May Halt, overlooking the River Dee, was intended to serve anglers, tourists, a nearby hunting lodge and the modest local population: seen here on 18 September 1960. *David Murray-Smith*

Multiple tracks of the main line to the south at Ferryhill Junction foreground a westbound Royal Train hauled by a pair of NBL Type 2s in the last years of the Deeside Line. *Norris Forrest / Transport Treasury*

A short branch line diverged west of Culter station to serve the Culter Paper Mill, which had its own saddle-tank loco, seen here in October 1961. *David Murray-Smith*

Dee Street Halt was more convenient for the town centre than Banchory station, but passengers would pray for good weather, as the halt did not boast even a 'bus shelter'! *Norris Forrest / Transport Treasury*

A head for heights was useful climbing the wooden staircase to Dee Street Halt. The halt had a working life of just five years, closing with the rest of the line in 1966. *David Murray-Smith*

It's the last summer of Deeside Line operation, in 1965, but at the time this photo of the Ballater terminus was taken the railway's future still hung in the balance. The author is worrying whether he and his father will manage to catch the Aberdeen-bound train! *Frank Spaven*

A demolition train is seen here at Aboyne station – both platforms littered with chair screws which had fixed the metal chairs (carrying the rails) to the track's wooden sleepers. *Norris Forrest / Transport Treasury*

Tank engine No. 55208 (one of a class introduced by the Caledonian Railway in 1900) hauls the 3.48 p.m. Ballachulish–Oban train at Ballachulish Ferry on 26 May 1958. *WAC Smith / Transport Treasury*

The lengthy 'running in' board at Connel Ferry, seen here in 1964, demonstrates the station's wide catchment once it became a junction in 1903. *Norman Turnbull*

Too much traction: a Birmingham Type 2 of 1,250 horse power prepares to depart from Ballachulish on 18 May 1964 with just two coaches in tow. *Norman Turnbull*

This Easter 1966 view of the railway estate at Ballachulish captures a 'Mary Celeste' period just two weeks after the line's 26 March closure. *Frank Spaven*

Three years after its 1966 closure, the timber-built North Connel halt is looking decidedly the worse for wear. In the background is the distinctive Connel Ferry Bridge. *David Spaven*

While the Beeching Report's 'Total Expenses' of £50,080 was the same as the 'Total Direct Costs' in the Heads of Information, Beeching's 'Estimated Receipts' of £21,370 were significantly higher than the figure of £14,370 in the subsequent Heads of Information. There was a simple explanation, which was in the Beeching Report (and which the TUCCS received 'confidentially'): BR estimated that £7,000 of the line's £21,980 contributory revenue to the rest of the network would be lost on closure.

But, bizarrely, BR did nothing to assuage the understandable concerns of those who had not read the Beeching Report in full: 'On enquiring into this discrepancy the investigator was told that "no amplification or explanations of cost or revenue figures will be given".'[17] David Prescott sees a wider lesson in the Deeside example: 'I think this sums up the whole Beeching / Marples position across the country. There was an edict from top to bottom that the closure programme will be implemented, and the data collection was to support the closure programme, not to inform it, and as such would not stand detailed scrutiny. It was only the Minister who was, very occasionally, going to cut across this edict – as happened with the East Suffolk and Central Wales lines. It was a centrally-driven, and no doubt controlled, plan, and in the end it was all about politics – nothing else.'[18]

BR's stonewalling attitude made headlines in the Tory-supporting *Daily Mail* on 6 February 1964 – 'Marples faces row over Royal line closure' – with the paper reporting that the West Aberdeenshire MP, A.F. Hendry, had written to the Minister of Transport, 'demanding that figures justifying closure of the Aberdeen–Ballater line should be sent to consultants working for local opponents of the plan'. It was reported that BR had refused to give answers to a list of detailed financial questions, and: 'They say that they are under no obligation to do so and that anyway objections to closure can only be made on grounds of hardship.'[19]

BR would not budge, but despite this setback the consultants produced a detailed examination of the line, although Farr does not indicate how the various component costs were estimated in the absence of official data. Presumably, however, trade union and other sources could provide indicative labour costs (a key component) and other figures.

The critique of staffing (and the related issue of signalling and signal boxes) was perhaps the most powerful criticism of the way the line was run – and is a recurring, central theme in this book. Despite operating only six passenger trains daily in each direction (and a freight train three times a week), 'the line boasted a staff of four stationmasters, thirty-seven other station staff, sixteen signalmen, two level crossing keepers, twenty-four permanent way men and nine and a half train crew – a total of 92½ men, or one man for every three passengers each day if one accepts the Beeching report's survey figures . . . The competing bus company had no resident staff at all on Deeside.'[20]

The signalling resources on the line (generating operating and maintenance costs) were vastly in excess of what was needed. The single-track branch from Ferryhill Junction to Ballater was controlled by no fewer than eight staffed crossing loops / block posts,[21] the consultants pointing out that the short block sections were appropriate for a timetable involving one train for every five miles – but the actual maximum passenger train density on the 42¾-mile line at any one time was only two.

However, unlike de-staffing stations (which was a relatively easy option, with effectively only industrial relations' difficulties to be overcome), the more dramatic savings in annual maintenance / operating costs offered by infrastructure rationalisation would all involve capital expenditure at a time when BR was in financial difficulty. And in the 1960s, once a route had formally been proposed for closure, it made sense for BR to avoid what might be abortive expenditure.

The critique of fare structure was less clear-cut than other aspects of running the railway; as found in the Heads of Information for other Scottish branch lines, BR's 2nd class Day Returns were competitive, generally being within a few pennies of the bus return fare (and sometimes actually the same price or cheaper). It was the Ordinary Returns which stung the passenger: 22s for Aberdeen–Ballater, compared to 8s 10d on the bus (and 9s for the rail Day Return).

The consultants' critique of management techniques were said by Farr to be 'general criticisms applying to the railways as a whole'. The rationalisations recommended suggested that the consultants had – or had access to – significant intelligence on, and understanding of, the practical scope for railway economies. Their thinking pre-dated by some two years the ground-breaking 'basic railway' concept which BR Eastern Region General Manager Gerry Fiennes and colleagues began developing in 1966. Farr summarises as follows:

> The proposals made to relieve the financial loss were that the stations should all be run as un-manned halts with tickets issued on the train, on the lines of the bus service. This alone would effect a labour saving of not less than £20,000 pa. The line should be divided

into two sections only for signalling purposes . . . This would mean a labour saving of around £8,250 pa, as well as a maintenance cost reduction of 75% on signalling equipment. Level crossings could be replaced by automatic raising barriers operated by the trains, and this would also save £1,000 pa, in crossing keeper wages. The train crew manning could be reduced to give 80% driver utilisation (which would still be less than any of the bus services in the area) and so save some £2,500 pa in labour costs. Cost of track maintenance could probably be reduced by using fewer men (and subsequently was, the number being reduced from twenty-four to thirteen later that year), and minor maintenance jobs 'farmed out' to local contractors. Finally of course, a realistic and competitive fare structure was necessary. These recommendations would have saved some £30,000 pa, or more.[22]

David Prescott strongly endorses the thrust of the key recommended rationalisations, with only one significant caveat: '80% driver utilisation was unrealistic in 1964 – and it still is today! Two signalling sections would indeed have sufficed, but two signal boxes and three block sections – with crossing loops at Banchory and Aboyne, and One Train Working from the latter to Ballater – would have facilitated additional short workings to cater for greater demand between Banchory and Aberdeen. The analysis shows how badly poor management let down the communities that the railway served – and the lessons still apply today, with the grossly inflated costs now being charged by Network Rail to re-open or build new stations and lines greatly restricting the number of communities that can be reconnected with the railway, thereby repairing some of the damage inflicted in the 1960s.'[23]

BR's feathers are ruffled

Having digested the consultants' report, the local MP, Hendry, wrote personally to Beeching on 11 June to challenge BR's position. Being unaware that the TUCC would be supplied confidentially with details of contributory revenue (and a cost breakdown) he asked Beeching 'to kindly rectify this omission, so that the T.U.C.C. may have the proper facts before them when they come to consider your proposals'. Citing the consultants' estimate that at least £30,000 of costs could be saved annually, he also noted that 'even before the publication of your Report, there was a good deal of criticism locally about the extravagant way in which this line was worked, and it was well known that, within the organisation, very substantial savings could be made. This was borne out by various railway men at differing levels, who, naturally, must remain anonymous.'[24]

Hendry argued that BR's refusal to release any information to the consultants created the impression that 'your Board's case would not stand up to critical examination'. He urged Beeching to read the consultants' report, and he expressed the hope that 'you will find it conforms to the principles of efficient business management which you have applied so successfully elsewhere'.

A few days later, an alarmed Mr Haygreen at the BRB wrote to Gordon Stewart, Scottish Region's Assistant General Manager, enclosing the letter to Beeching and the consultant's report, and requesting comments, 'particularly on the cost at which it is suggested we could operate the service': 'It would appear that what was originally understood to be an enquiry into the possibility of local interests taking over the line, in the event of abandoning it, has developed by accident or design into an attack on the case we have made for withdrawing the passenger service.'

Stewart went to town on this, producing a four-page letter responding to some – but far from all – the points raised by the consultants and the MP, as described in an attached five-page summary. Noting that 'the full cost pattern in this case' was supplied in the Beeching Report, he was able to launch a scathing response by latching on to what *seems* to have been a basic error made by the consultants: 'Now that the Consultants' report is available, I think we read in it every justification for not providing further figures. No very logical use has been made of those figures in their possession and in suggesting that a station staff saving of £20,000 per annum can be made from allocated terminal expenses of £9,250 [in the Beeching Report table] there is a measure of the lack of understanding of our figures.'

It is hard to believe that the consultants could really have made such a simple mistake – were they also taking account of *freight* terminal expenses, or using some other definition different to BR's? Regardless, it was enough for Gordon Stewart. 'I therefore see no purpose in making fuller details available or in discussing the matter with the Deeside Railway Preservation Committee,' he responded to Haygreen. The consultants also seem to have made a mistake on staff numbers, over-estimating these by 15 – but this did not significantly undermine a core argument, and it was a bit rich for BR to criticise this when they had denied access to the official figures.

The last thing Scottish Region wanted was a light shone on the undoubted scope for economies in the way that BR ran the Deeside Line. Stewart had his key excuse, and he sought to further rubbish the opposition with sneering comments such as: 'contains little of helpful substance', 'too trite to carry conviction' and 'the consultants have misled themselves'. He indicated that he 'would not propose to deal with every point made in the report' – this was something of an understatement: of more than 30 points raised, only three were answered fully or properly, two were partly answered, some seven were unconvincing responses, and all the rest – around 20 – were completely ignored. Among the latter were: fares policy; better promotion of the line; decentralised management; sale of surplus buildings; and investigation of the scope to change Board of Trade regulations in order to achieve operational economies.

One of the consultant's points which was effectively ignored related to bus–rail co-ordination: 'The Alexander Bus Company on Deeside have indicated that British Railways do not seem interested in planning joint agreements on schedules with the object of improving load factors on both rail and bus services. Yet both are nationalised concerns whose policies should be the same – improved transport at less cost. Neither concerns can operate really profitably on Deeside.' Stewart's response certainly deserves the epithet 'trite': 'A rather mysterious co-ordination between bus and rail is suggested as benefiting rail. It is self-evident that the two methods are competitive so long as both are continued.'

On the key issue of signalling costs, where the consultants had suggested cutting back from eight signal boxes (and nine block sections) to only two block sections, with a crossing loop at the half-way point, the BR response invoked a phoney argument to discredit a sound idea: 'Our present service involves crossings at Culter (4 miles), Park (11 miles), Banchory (17 miles), Lumphanan (27 miles). A selection of one crossing place whether at mid point or elsewhere would produce a rigid timetable which would not meet the needs of this branch.' Stewart should have been more careful in his scathing criticism of the consultants' suggested mistakes: Culter was *seven* miles from Aberdeen, and the station *four* miles west of the city (Cults) had lost its crossing loop in 1953. What the BR man conveniently omitted to mention was that no train made more than one crossing on the line, and some made none. With a fast journey time of 72 minutes (by closing the smaller stations, see below) there would be sufficient flexibility to accommodate an enhanced regular train service and occasional tourist charters, with only two

– or perhaps more robustly, three – block sections. That really would have been an effective way to 'meet the needs of this branch', as Stewart had so disingenuously put it.

One further potential economy (and associated service enhancement) which is not mentioned in Farr's book – and presumably therefore was not suggested by the consultants – would have been the closure of half a dozen or so of the least-used stations, whose daily passenger totals, at most, barely reached double figures (leaving the eight busiest stations open). The fastest train in the 1963–64 timetable – the 8.03 p.m. battery railcar service from Ballater – omitted these stops, and took only 72 minutes for the journey to Aberdeen.[25] If this had become the standard transit time – competing more effectively with the private car – then two DMUs would have been able to provide a 1½-hourly service frequency from end to end (perhaps eight trains a day, compared to the six in 1963), supplemented by a further DMU operating a more frequent Banchory–Aberdeen service, where the demand was highest.

As well as the pressing need for cost-cutting, what was equally clear at the time was the need to boost the revenue side of the equation, Farr adding that 'a positive "selling campaign" could have attracted greatly increased custom to the line, which had received virtually no publicity since nationalisation'. There can be no doubt that if the line had survived, it would now be one of the 'Great Scenic Rail Journeys' promoted by ScotRail, attracting travellers from afar, as well as providing a vital commuter service (particularly from Banchory and stations east thereof to Aberdeen), and relieving congestion on the road system. But, sadly, it was not to be.

The objectors and the TUCCS

A week before the public hearing in Aberdeen on 23 September 1964, BR produced its customary Brief for Liaison Officer.[26] This clarified that while there had been 314 objections, 280 of these had been received 'on a stencilled form'. The objectors' case – much of which had become a familiar litany across closure proposals in the mid 1960s – was summed up as follows: 'The principal grounds of objection relate to the inadequacy of the alternative bus service with regard to speed, frequency, comfort and facilities; to the lack of bus services between the Torphins / Lumphanan area and Aboyne / Banchory; to the lack of bus / rail co-ordination at Aberdeen; to the bad conditions of the roads in the area in winter; and to the effect of the closure on tourism and employment.'

The brief tried to 'spin' the deterioration in journey times by bus – 'It is true that bus journey times are longer than rail, but not unreasonably so' – and sought to minimise six different aspects of 'lack of comfort and facilities' on buses, including that recurring plug in closure cases for the use of 'KWELLS' to tackle travel sickness. One is tempted to wonder if BR managers were on commission to promote these. However, there was a rare unqualified admission of unflattering contrasts to the train: 'It must be acknowledged that reading and writing are difficult on a bus.'

In the accompanying 'Heads of Information: Supplementary Details (not supplied to T.U.C.C.)', information was supplied in tabular form, '*to give some idea* [emphasis added] of bookings and receipts at Ballater'. During a period – 1960 to 1963 – when UK car ownership grew by 33% (from 4.9 million to 6.5 million vehicles),[27] a 9 per cent growth in rail patronage at Ballater (excluding season tickets) looks remarkably healthy, particularly as the 1960 start-point post-dated by a year the immediate surge of patronage associated with the introduction of DMU / battery railcar operation. However, it may be that part of the growth at Ballater reflected the impact of bookings and receipts re-allocated to the terminus as a result of de-staffing four smaller stations during this period.

Ballater at the time had a population of only 1,302, and four further stations served populations between 1,000 and 2,500, the rest being measured in the hundreds or less. The total patronage of the line can be roughly calculated by reference to the BR brief's comment that on Mondays to Fridays in winter 'we carry an average of 46 passengers per train': as the Saturdays and summer situations were not greatly different, this suggests (for 12 trains a day, operating six days a week) that total patronage was of the order of 170,000 annually – no mean achievement for a railway serving only very small towns and villages.

In terms of facts and figures – and lines of argument – BR was now well prepared for the 23 September public hearing in Aberdeen, the TUCCS significantly less so, and the objectors at a decided disadvantage. However, the TUCCS were supplied confidentially with the standard 'Amplification of Financial Information' (effectively a summary of the entry in Table 1 of the Beeching Report), including the impressive movement cost of only 2s 6d per train-mile.

The proceedings of the public hearing did not want for publicity, with a melodramatic claim giving the *P&J* its headline for the following day's story: '100-year setback if Deeside line axed.' This was only one of many blunt warnings given at the 4½-hour session, reported the newspaper: 'In a last-ditch stand to try to save the line, claimed to be "one of the most beautiful train journeys in Britain," objector after objector, representative of almost every public body in the area, went into the witness box and told of the hardship which would be caused to individual travellers, the blow that would be dealt to the expanding tourist trade and to potential industry if the Beeching axe fell on it.'[28]

Some of the most insightful comments were made by Mr W.A. Colclough, Aberdeen's Director of Planning, in his capacity as Chairman of Aboyne and District Citizens' Association: 'There would be a great increase in commuting to and from Aberdeen in the next 10–20 years, he forecast, and he instanced a development planned by Aberdeen County Council which envisaged the doubling of the present population of Lower Deeside, from Culter to the city boundary, to 16,000 ... Mr Colclough also pointed out that as car traffic increased, more and more restrictions would be placed on parking in the centre of Aberdeen ... America, he reminded the committee, was now seeing how wrong it was for them to let their public transport run down and take off their railway connections. And he added: "For goodness sake let us not fall into the same trap!"'

But fall into the same trap we did – in part aided by myopic railway managers such as Gordon Stewart, who was in typically dismissive form at the hearing. Having pointed out that BR had had to withdraw Sunday services due to lack of patronage, he could not resist remarking sarcastically on the success of development in rail-less Braemar, Spittal of Glenshee and Tomintoul: 'One also reads about the thousands of people visiting Deeside on Sundays. One wonders how they get there, because they cannot go by train.' Demonstrating an attitude almost of contempt for some of his customer base – and ignoring the absence of a more frequent service for commuters between Banchory and Aberdeen – he commented: 'It appears that the bulk of the daily passengers use three of the trains, and on the others our only patrons are retired people or tourists.'

In defence of Gordon Stewart, Rae Montgomery – who met him on several occasions and found Stewart to be 'a most amenable man' – argues that 'his attitude to the consultant's report may have been insupportable, but railwaymen were proud people and didn't like to be told by outsiders how to run their railway!'

There was to be no succour for campaigners from the key bodies advising the Minister of Transport on wider strategic issues. In a paper to the SEPC

11 June 1965 meeting in St Andrew's House, the SEPB declared itself sat-isfied that there were 'no strong economic planning grounds' for opposing closure. But rail advocates could have drawn a sliver of comfort from the SEPB's caveat that 'retention of the track from Aberdeen to Banchory would be desirable to safeguard possible future growth requirements (of both com-muter and industrial traffic) in the Aberdeen area'.[29]

The TUCCS concludes – and the government gives its verdict

The TUCCS annual report for 1964 records that reference was made at the public hearing to the consultants' report for the Deeside Railway Preservation Society – but passes no comment on this. The TUCCS conclusion was far from clear-cut: 'Some members of the Committee were of the view that, providing a limited stop bus was introduced to cater for workers travelling to and from Aberdeen and provision made for a bus service from Aboyne to Banchory following the course of the present rail system, at times suitable to allow the residents to fulfil business commitments at the terminal points, the hardship, which would result from the withdrawal of the service, could be alleviated. An equal number of the members were of the opinion, however, that even if the additional bus service were provided, the serious hardship which would be experienced by all the users of the present train service would not be ameliorated.'[30]

What the annual report did not mention, as pointed out by journalist, writer and rail supporter Gordon Casely,[31] was that the TUCCS 'wielded the axe' on the casting vote of chairman Sir John Greig Dunbar, one-time Lord Provost of Edinburgh. In practice, however, even a majority – or unanimity – of the TUCCS opposing closure was no guarantee that the minister would refuse consent. But at least BR and bus operators were no longer – post-1962 – part of the committee.

On 31 August 1965 the MoT wrote to the BRB detailing the minis-ter's decision on the Deeside Line across four pages of text, with the core message in a single paragraph: 'The Minister has considered the report of the Consultative Committee and all other relevant factors including the views of the Scottish Economic Planning Council on the implications of the proposal. He accepts the view of half the members of the Committee that having regard to the bus services at present being provided no appreci-able hardship would arise from the closure if certain additional bus services were provided. He has therefore decided to give his consent to the closure subject to the conditions mentioned below which, inter alia, require the provision of additional bus services meeting the particular needs to which the Consultative Committee referred.'[32]

A dozen extra bus departures were stipulated over various sections of the route, with Farr recording that these were approved by the traffic commissioners on 26 November in Aberdeen, and, strikingly, that 'it was admitted that the Deeside bus routes were "being run at a substantial loss".' One might argue that the transfer of (some) rail passengers would improve the bus economics, but the bigger issue was the lack of transparency about rail and bus operational finances, and the neglected scope for greater co-ordination of the two modes.

An altogether grander form of transport made its last appearance on Deeside in the summer of 1965, taking the Queen to and from Ballater (for Balmoral). The line's future was still in the balance during her holiday journey north on the Royal Train, but by the time she returned to London on 15 October 1965, she would have known that this would be her last journey on the Deeside Line. Perhaps appropriately, the final Royal Train from Ballater was hauled by two of the notorious NBL Type 2s (see Chapter 9). Evidently it was standard practice by this time on the Deeside Line not only to double-head the Royal Train (this applied, and continues to apply, everywhere on the rail network) but also to stable a spare Type 2 at Banchory as an insurance policy – testimony to the lack of confidence in the reliability of the NBLs.[33] As late as 1962, when Kittybrewster shed had a diesel allocation of 20 Type 2s (and five English Electric Type 1s) – the best part of two years after diesels had arrived *en masse* in Aberdeen – it had still been the practice for Royal Trains to and from Ballater (and fish specials from Fraserburgh and Peterhead) to be worked by steam power.[34]

Following the closure decision, the Minister of Transport declined an invitation to visit the area in February to sample winter travel conditions, and no reply was forthcoming to the local MP's question: 'In the event of the railway line being closed, is it the intention of the Minister to direct the bus operators to provide shelter and lavatories at stopping places comparable to those provided by the railway?' In an editorial column on 19 October 1965, the *P&J* wrote that the minister 'has not made the merest pretence of answering the people who argue that there are ways of running the line more economically'.[35]

The final correspondence between the local MP and the government before closure involved a new Minister of Transport, Barbara Castle, who wrote in a letter to him, as recorded by Farr: 'I can see no reason for disagreeing with his [her predecessor's] conclusion that the further retention of this service at a cost of some £100,000 a year to the tax-payer could not possibly be justified.' This massively increased figure for the line's losses inevitably served to make local anger even greater, and in a letter to the MoT the MP wrote:

> I simply cannot understand how the track maintenance cost is £71,240 per annum [the figure quoted by the ministry]. Presumably that includes the wages of the man who is required to walk from Banchory station to Banchory Dee St. Halt twice a day to light and extinguish a paraffin lamp a few yards from a powerful electric street light, and other insanities of that kind. Even at that, however, I find the figure incredible, and I should be more than grateful if you would kindly give some kind of breakdown of the figure . . . I feel certain that Dr. Beeching did not just think of a number. But, without some sort of breakdown, I'm afraid that is the impression locally.[36]

The explanation for the big difference between, on the one hand, the £100,000 quoted, and on the other hand, the inferred loss of £35,710 in the BR Heads of Information, almost certainly lies – at least in part – with the first figure being a calculation of long-run costs of maintaining the whole line (including all the track costs, rather than only the marginal element for passenger traffic) as opposed to the short-term saving from withdrawing the passenger service on the assumption that freight continued and took its share of track and signalling costs. But evidently no breakdown of the former figure was ever supplied, and it seems reasonable to assume that it did not take any account of the wide variety of potential economies suggested by the campaigners' consultants and (half-heartedly) by the trade unions.

Reflecting on the closure saga, Gordon Casely, who travelled on three separate final trains – in the last week of passenger services, on the last goods train and on the demolition train – comments that 'I still mourn the loss, five decades later' and poses the question: 'Could the Deeside Line have been saved? Given the atmosphere of resignation that prevailed everywhere in the early 1960s, it would have been touch-and-go – though as matters turns out, it certainly wasn't for lack of trying. A few brave spirited citizens tried to rally support . . . I well remember how robust campaigning by Deeside stalwarts such as John Harrower at Dinnet and Cllr Jim Robbie in Lumphanan proved no match against apathy and indifference.'[37]

Casely, an active campaigner against closure, has less kind words for two other individuals, one of whom was prominent in the campaign: 'Hendry MP was an utterly useless individual, and vies with the then provost of Ballater, William Anderson, as having let the line die. John Harrower, a natural conservative and ardent line campaigner, would only use either name by almost spitting it out.'[38]

Whatever the strengths and weaknesses of individuals, they were all mere Davids against Goliath. Hendry – who would be unseated at the general election only five weeks after the line's closure, and replaced by James Davidson (Liberal), an MP 'who left no stone unturned that couldn't be turned over in his efforts to save the line'[39] – finally wrote to Beeching's successor as BRB chairman, Stanley Raymond, to explore the scope for a private takeover. Raymond's response included the killer condition that 'there could be no question of selling the track or land between Banchory and Aberdeen' (implying that it would be protected for the future). The P&J reported on 15 February 1966 that the provost of Ballater had made the obvious comment that 'keeping the section between Aberdeen and Banchory will kill any hope of a private company taking over the line. No private company would operate only between Ballater and Banchory.' BR had finished off the opposition, after nearly three years of struggle, and would in due course dispose of the Aberdeen–Banchory section which there had been 'no question of selling'.

Closure and (eventual) dismantling

The final passenger train on Deeside ran on Saturday 26 February 1966. On the following Monday it was the lead story in the P&J, with the 'END OF ROYAL LINE' headline jostling for attention with 'Cheers of excited throngs' and 'Last trains give Ballater station its busiest day'. One aspect of the report gave pause for thought: 'In all the excitement at the Ballater terminus of the branch, scene of so many Royal arrivals and departures, there was a touch of irony, summed up by a veteran railman now retired. Ruefully he declared as he surveyed the milling throng: "Just half of all this when the line was still running and it would not be closing tonight."'[40]

This was a not unfamiliar theme during the last rites of axed branch lines. Communities often had great emotional attachment to 'their' railway, and motorists appreciated its availability when the car was being repaired at the local garage or during extreme winter weather – but when it came to using the railway regularly, too many folk were voting with their feet rather than taking note of the 'use it or lose it' exhortation. Yes, the finger could be pointed at BR for various failures, but car owners had to shoulder some of the blame too. Prioritising personal convenience too often undermined a precious public asset – one of the downsides of the burgeoning consumerism of the late 1950s and early 1960s.

Meantime, the Deeside Line had a lingering death. Freight to Ballater lasted only until July, when the terminus was cut back to Culter, where a paper mill continued to generate traffic for the railway, but this truncated freight service in turn ceased on 30 December 1966. Regular steam-hauled services on Deeside had ended in 1961, but BR added a nostalgic touch to the last day's proceedings. The very last freight train was specially hauled by B1 No. 61180 in those twilight days of steam in Scotland – it would be withdrawn the following year – and the train also carried enthusiasts in four brake vans, with Farr recording:

> Among those awaiting the train on Culter station was George Watson, who at eighty-eight could look back on a lifetime of railway service which included twenty-seven years on Deeside. During this time he was for seventeen years stationmaster at Glassel and served on all the Deeside stations except Dess. He was in charge of the signal box at Dinnet when the Czar of Russia travelled along the line in 1896, and later the same year helped Queen Victoria into her carriage at Ballater.
>
> After a little shunting the train collected some wagons of timber [wood for the railway workshops at Inverurie and sleepers for Derby][41] and set off for Aberdeen, carrying the same load that the line was built to carry 113 years previously – tourists and timber.

It is hard to disagree with the verdict in Farr's concluding paragraph of *Stories of Royal Deeside's Railway*: 'It is almost certain that the Deeside Line need not have closed. Since that sad day social factors have been taken into account in considering closures, and subsidies made available for some lines. It has also been reported that the Ipswich–Lowestoft branch line [Gerry Fiennes's test-bed for the 'basic railway'] is being re-signalled and re-organised to effect a cut of running costs from £100,000 a year to £10,000. It could have happened on Deeside, but all that is left now is a weed-overgrown and decaying track bed, vandal-damaged buildings, and an inadequate and congested alternative by road.'

And what was travel along Deeside like without trains? Those with no access to a car had to get used to sub-standard public transport, and after some years the ministerial stipulations on bus services could be quietly forgotten. The last word on the daily transport reality can be left to Farr:

> The bus services, rather than being doubled were in fact halved, while conductors were taken off the buses and the collection of fares by the driver consequently slowed up the whole service. Buses were found to be so cold in winter as to cause considerable discomfort to passengers, while most of the villages had no bus shelter. The buses could not carry dogs or perambulators and even the passenger's luggage was at the mercy of the bus crews, and was liable to be left behind if they refused to carry it. The timing of the buses was utterly unrealistic, for example a hospital appointment in Aberdeen at 2 pm, meant that someone from Torphins had to catch a bus at 9 am. In Aberdeen, although the bus terminal is just opposite the station, no railway porters are allowed to carry luggage to or from the station and buses. Finally the closure coincided with the imposition of severe car parking restrictions in the city and the consequent increase in the number of commuters forced onto the inadequate public transport system.

Some remnants of the railway were soon up for disposal. In March 1967, Dow Bros. wrote to BR[42] quoting a price of £8,952 for demolition of 50 structures at 16 stations, ranging from £60 for 'Platforms only' at Dee Street Halt (in fact, there was only one platform, and little more, at this low-cost station opened as recently as 1961)[43] to £970 for no fewer than seven structures at Ballater – although thankfully not the fine station building, which survives to this day. One wonders what logic lay behind this planned wanton destruction of at least 10 station buildings which could have found productive alternative uses?

As reported by Farr, the last throw of the die was a second bid (in 1969) for the line to be taken over by private enterprise. Gordon Casely writes: 'My own contribution was a small enterprise which attempted to attract business capital into a Deeside Line Project, and we took as our example the then Border Union Railway Company, the commercial organisation then attempting to reopen the 106-mile Waverley route from Edinburgh to Carlisle. We failed of course. Privatisation hadn't been invented, and our raw lack both of business experience and entrepreneurial skills showed through. There was the additional factor that hard work and enthusiasm, however well meant, are little match against communal apathy. All we gained was a 16-week delay in demolition of the line to allow us to come up with cash and a business case.'[44]

Nearly 2½ years after a 1966 general embargo on disposal of assets on closed lines, the MoT relented and gave BR the go-ahead to dispose of the redundant track, signalling and route formation. BR then, in December 1969, invited bids for two contracts to recover the redundant assets – two being required because a land slip at Lumphanan prevented a recovery train from proceeding further west. Among the various categories of items identified across the two contracts were 91,347 yards of track 'as scrap', 12,392 yards of serviceable rails and 50 underbridges.[45]

The Chief Civil Engineer in Glasgow estimated in December 1969 that the entire project would yield a net credit of £74,169. BR conducted nine bidding contractors on a site visit the following month, and in February 1970 the £135,000 offer by Arnott Young of Dalmuir to purchase 44 miles of track 'in situ' (and to undertake other contract works, including return to BR of serviceable material) was accepted by BR, subject to the work commencing in two weeks and being completed with 10 months.[46]

The Deeside Line's last commercial role was, ironically, to yield a profit for BR.

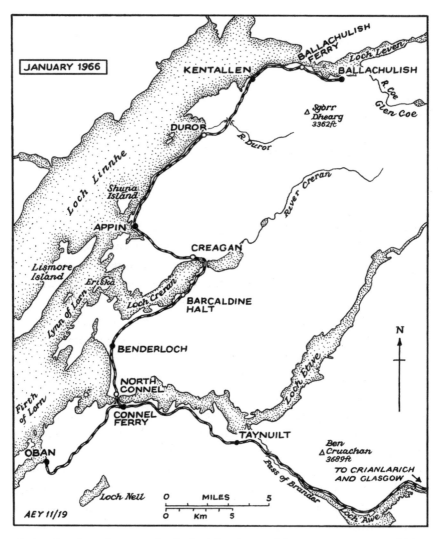

The heavily indented Lorn coastline by Loch Linnhe – and the expensive structures which a railway would require to bridge two sea lochs – provides part of the explanation for the very late arrival of the railway at Ballachulish, in 1903 (the last line to open in the Highlands). Bridging Loch Leven to create a through route to Fort William – as happened with the A82 road bridge in 1975 – would have been no small task, but without such a strategic role this branch serving only small villages was doomed to disappear in the 1960s' cull of rural railways. (Alan Young)

13

No strategic vision: Ballachulish

Once the Callander & Oban Railway (C&O) reached the west coast port in 1880, there followed decades of jockeying for position between different companies – notably the C&O and the West Highland Railway – who were keen to take a railway to Fort William and indeed up the Great Glen to Inverness.

The C&O promised a railway from Connel Ferry, on the Oban line, to Ballachulish – then bridging Loch Leven to reach Fort William from the south. This proposal lost out to the West Highland's scheme to approach Fort William via Rannoch Moor and Glen Spean, but when the rival Highland Railway (based in Inverness) and North British Railway (operator of the West Highland Line) agreed not to promote any railway in the Great Glen for 10 years, the C&O scheme was revived in a different guise. Its proposed line from Connel Ferry to Ballachulish, then bridging Loch Leven to reach Fort William, was opposed by a proposed West Highland extension south from Fort William (also bridging Loch Leven). However, 'the North British encountered opposition at Fort William, where a railway extension would create a further barrier at the lochside [the existing railway from Glasgow cut off much of the town from Loch Linnhe]. Hostility was also encountered at Ballachulish where there was an objection to the bridge from shipping interests.'[1]

Two Acts of Parliament were passed on 7 August 1896 to allow for a West Highland branch from Fort William to the north side of Loch Leven opposite Ballachulish, and a C&O branch to Ballachulish – but the bridge was not sanctioned, and the line south from Fort William was never built.[2] The 27¾-mile Ballachulish branch began operations in 1903, as the last railway to be built in the Highlands. Perhaps surprisingly, though, the idea of a railway bridging Loch Leven would resurface 60 years later.

The Ballachulish–Oban train service revolutionised transport in the area, where journeys had previously been very slow via a mix of steamer / ferry / circuitous road routes along the heavily indented coastline. The opening in 1907 of the hydro-electric-powered aluminium smelter at nearby Kinlochleven substantially boosted freight traffic at Ballachulish, with trains bringing in the alumina raw material and taking out the finished product. But the new main road built through Glencoe in the early 1930s offered an easier and more direct passenger route to the south, adding to the general trend of rail services being undermined by the rise of the car, bus and lorry.

The writing seemed to be on the wall when the Beeching Report was published in March 1963: Map 3 of 'Passenger traffic station receipts' revealed that every station on the branch fell into the lowest revenue category (less than £5,000 per annum); unsurprisingly, the service was listed for withdrawal. But not everyone assumed that meant the end of the railway through Benderloch and Appin . . .

A bold bid to change West Highland railway geography

The Ballachulish line's status as a terminating branch always constrained its potential, as the Victorians must have guessed when pressing the case for bridging Loch Leven to create a through route to Fort William. But the idea did not die, being resurrected in a little-known episode just as Dr Beeching was preparing to launch his report. On 21 March 1963, R.A. Fasken,[3] Secretary of the Advisory Panel on the Highlands and Islands, wrote to its Chairman, Lord Cameron:

> Possible Ballachulish–Fort William Railway Link
>
> I have been in touch with Messrs. Sutherland (Road Engineer) and Spaven [my father] of S.D.D. about estimated costs of this 12-mile link and the financial effect if such a link replaced the present 63 miles of Crianlarich–Rannoch–Spean Bridge–Fort William West Highland line.
>
> I do not think I can do better than send you the enclosed copies of their reports. Sutherland's estimate is £1.44m. including signalling and telegraphic communications for the 12 miles; Spaven's is £1.2m. In addition, Sutherland estimates that the additional cost of a single track rail bridge and viaduct, associated with a 24 foot

carriageway road bridge (which would cost £0.5m), would be £0.15m., i.e. a total of £1.59m. for 12-mile track and bridge.

From various sources, Spaven estimates that single-track maintenance costs [are] between £2–3,000 per mile. Given the new link and the abandonment of the Crianlarich–Fort William West Highland railway, there would be a net saving of 51 miles or, in maintenance cost, anything from £100–150,000 per annum. The lower figure of £100,000 would be sufficient to serve a loan of £1.58m. at 6 per cent. over 50 years.

This might well be an interesting exercise for the Transport Group if British Railways could be persuaded to consider this proposal seriously and give a reasoned answer to our prima facie case.[4]

Hopes for a constructive response from BR to a subsequent letter from Fasken were misplaced. Scottish Region's Assistant General Manager, Gordon Stewart, politely but firmly scotched the concept in his 23 July 1963 reply: 'As I think you know, this idea has been floated from time to time, but has not been developed because of the difficult terrain and limited potential of the route and, especially, because of the high capital cost involved . . . even from the studies which our Engineers have made of the project "on paper" it would appear that the capital cost would be upwards of £3 million. Taking also into account operational costs of the Ballachulish line and the new extension, plus interest on capital, and setting against this the savings from the closure of the Rannoch Moor section, the indications are that we would still incur a working deficit of around £100,000 a year.'

It is striking that Stewart made no mention of the *current* deficit – this was possibly an implicit admission that the reduced mileage of a reconfigured rail network would yield a significantly lower operating and maintenance cost, not least through avoiding the exposed and isolated section across Rannoch Moor. But no figures were offered by BR to allow objective analysis of the case for investment, and Stewart briskly concluded that rationalisation and making best use of existing facilities was the way forward and 'we see in the Beeching Reshaping Plan a more efficient and certainly less expensive way of keeping communication to Fort William and Oban'. He was, however, correct in his assessment of the difficulty of the terrain along the hilly / mountainous coast from Loch Leven to Fort William – but plenty of other Highland railways had overcome such challenges, Spaven having cited in his report the cost of the 1954 diversion of the Kyle line at Lochluichart to facilitate a hydro-electric construction scheme.

It was also reasonable for Stewart to include in the calculation of net maintenance cost savings the cost of maintaining the Ballachulish line – if one assumes it would otherwise be closed as part of the Beeching programme. Based on that assumption, the net mileage saving would be 23 miles (rather than 51), i.e., the removal of 63 miles via Rannoch plus the addition of the 28 miles of the Ballachulish branch and the 12 miles of the new extension. But, in a sense, this was a detail – where was the strategic vision to secure long-term savings and create one of Britain's most scenic through rail routes (albeit while closing another one of different character)?

Fasken did not give up, however, mentioning in a 25 July letter to Lord Cameron that a colleague 'would be prepared to float this "new line" idea in an article in the Glasgow Herald'. But in the fixation and furore over the rail closure programme, pressing for new railway construction in a rural area proved to be a lost cause. This visionary concept – which I suspect originated with my father – became no more than one of the 'what ifs?' of Scottish railway history.

Beeching's proposed closure goes out to staff consultation

A memorandum issued by BR (from Inverness) in November 1963, as part of the consultation between management and staff, advised that notices of proposed closure of the line would be posted at stations on 25 November 1963. As usual, 'the stations affected' were deemed to be only those directly served by those trains proposed for withdrawal. So, for the Ballachulish branch, on which the number of passengers (excluding schoolchildren) virtually doubled from winter to summer, a substantial proportion of users may well have been unaware of the statutory process by which they could formally lodge an objection with the body – the TUCCS – which (in theory) had a significant bearing on the fate of the railway.

The BR memo provided figures on 'passengers booked' at the line's stations in 1962, excluding passengers booked at other stations such as Oban (in particular), Glasgow and Edinburgh. The bald numbers were not impressive: only Benderloch, Appin, Ballachulish Ferry and Ballachulish reached four figures, the largest being 3,943 at the latter. The Heads of Information stated: 'Between 110 and 200 passengers [across three trains] use the service daily in each direction throughout the year. The figures include about 70 children travelling to and from school in Oban.' Even allowing for the fact that the passenger trains were only allocated marginal costs over and above those required to provide a freight service, it is little surprise that the financial information provided in the Heads of Information revealed that expenditure on passenger services was nearly three times the level of revenue: £39,550 'Estimated Direct Costs' and £13,850 'Estimated Receipts'. A single sentence advised that the 'camping coach' facility at Creagan would be discontinued. Given the sublime views across Loch Linnhe to Morvern, it is little wonder that BR also (at least until the 1962 season) had coaches at three other locations on the Ballachulish branch: Appin, Benderloch and Kentallen.

Perhaps the most striking aspect of the Heads of Information – and very different from the circumstances on the other branches considered in this book – was the statement that 'no alternative road facilities exist at present between Connel Ferry and Ballachulish', i.e., there was no bus service.

A consultation meeting between management and staff on the line's closure took place on 30 December 1963 in Perth (hardly convenient for Ballachulish, by any mode of transport!), and Arthur Leith, chairman of the staff side, offered some straight talking: 'It is accepted that finance should play a part in the discussions and it is requested that the financial information given should be broken down to give a clear picture of all the factors taken into account.'[5] It was explained to the staff side what the sources of estimated receipts and direct costs were, 'but they would not accept this and could only conclude that the figures quoted were conjectural rather than factual'. Requests for proper breakdowns of financial information to be supplied to staff and the public (and BR's resistance to providing them) had been a recurring feature of closure proposals throughout the country – but one player in the closure process (the TUCCS) would be allowed a little extra detail.

Public consultation

The Brief for Liaison Officer for the 7 October 1964 hearing in Oban reveals that there were only 24 objections to the withdrawal of passenger train services, but one of these was submitted on behalf of Ballachulish Branch Rail Users, representing the views of 1,115 petition signatories residing in the area.[6] The principal grounds for objection were: the inadequacy of the bus as a replacement; the poor condition of roads along the rail corridor; and the loss of speedy and reliable transport for urgent and perishable goods.

The BR Heads of Information had provided no details of replacement bus services, as none were then in operation, but the internal brief noted that the proposed service would take 110 minutes from Ballachulish to Oban, compared to 96 by train – with the road detour around Loch Creran being a contributory factor. Commenting on points raised about travel sickness on buses, the BR brief conceded that 'travel sickness can admittedly be distressing but this malady is susceptible to attack by placebo, nostrum or orthodox medicine'. Neither the dictionary definition of nostrum ('an idea for solving a problem, especially one that is not very good'),[7] nor the need to take medicine, were votes of confidence in the quality of the proposed replacement bus service.

Section 4 of the brief incorporated the confidential 'Amplification of financial information' supplied to the TUCCS. What use the committee was able (or willing) to make of the additional information is unclear, but the high cost (6s 5d) per train-mile demonstrated that loco-hauled operation was an expensive business. The Beeching Report's 10 case studies identified five of nine non-steam (DMU / diesel loco / diesel railbus / battery railcar) examples as costing less than 4s per train-mile – and only 2s 4d in the case of the Comrie branch and 2s 6d for the Deeside Line. The 'balance of track and signalling costs', i.e., those attributable to Ballachulish freight train operation (£53,710), dwarfed the cost attributable to passenger operations (£11,780), and demonstrated that when freight services were withdrawn (and switched to Fort William) then the mis-match between revenue and expenditure would be monumental – for an unrationalised railway.

The TUCC verdict – but a long wait for the ministerial decision

No record of the proceedings of the public hearing held on 7 October 1964 in Oban has been found in the National Records of Scotland, but the TUCCS's annual report for 1964 states: 'The Committee were of the view that considerable hardship would be experienced by all users in the event of the passenger train service being withdrawn until such time as certain road improvements were carried out which would facilitate the operation of a reliable bus service.'

The TUCCS views on Ballachulish were submitted to the minister on 6 November, but more than 15 months elapsed before the MoT announced consent to closure, reflecting the requirements to alleviate the considerable hardship flagged up by the TUCC: conversion of the Connel Ferry Bridge to a toll-free road crossing (a long-mooted move which may have persuaded some locals to support rail closure); additional passing places on single-track sections of the A828 (which is now two-lane throughout) and temporary upgrading of the Barcaldine Bridge (pending its ultimate bypassing) to enable safe passage of buses; and the provision of an entirely new bus service from Oban to Ballachulish.

In the meantime, the writing already seemed to be on the wall, as Nigel Welbourn's diary recording a trip on 30 August 1965 illustrates: 'Went on line from Oban to Ballachulish. The carriage was in a disgusting state. Pictures had been turned back to front and drawn on, paint had been put on the seats which had been slashed. Signal posts were brown with rust and the track was overgrown with a grass-like plant. On first sight it looked as if the line was already closed.'[8]

The 21 February 1966 letter of consent from the MoT to the BRB imposed various conditions, including transfer of the Connel Ferry Bridge and the Creagan Bridge to the highway authority (the latter opening up the prospect of shorter road journeys), and the provision of bus services at 'approximately' the same time as the trains.

A supplementary memorandum was issued by BR to staff in March 1966, spelling out the posts to be eliminated following complete closure later that month (general freight services having been withdrawn the previous year). A total of 26 posts (excluding civil engineering staff) was listed, including one station assistant and one signalman at each of the four crossing loops / block posts. At Ballachulish, six train crew were to go, and at Connel Ferry – where it was proposed to close both the east and west signal boxes (creating a 13-mile block section from Oban to Taynuilt) – eight posts were to be withdrawn. The only good news was: 'Negotiations are at present proceeding with Shell Mex and B.P. Ltd. to erect an oil storage plant on the site of the former goods sidings at Connel ferry station to be worked as private siding, access would be by token controlled ground frame and would not interfere with the closing of the two signal boxes named.' This facility would survive as a rail-served location until the early 1990s, but has been supplied entirely by road haulage (from Grangemouth) since then.

Back in 1966, the last train to Ballachulish ran on 26 March and was the lead story in the next edition of the *Oban Times* on 31 March: 'A CHAPTER OF RAILWAY HISTORY IS CLOSED.' The 9.35 p.m. train had pulled out of Oban with nearly 100 passengers on board, 'to the accompaniment of a send-off so exuberant than one might easily have supposed the line was being opened rather than closed'. Not everyone shared the hilarity, with Baillie William Currie (a railway employee himself) reported as saying that he was 'horrified to hear of these scenes, adding: "After all, there are many families being deprived of a reasonable living through the withdrawal of these services and wondering whether they were going to be thrown on the scrap-heap or have to go to other parts of Scotland."'

One of the crowd watching the train depart was in reflective mood. Peter Macinnes, 79, a retired railway joiner, had witnessed the first train to use the line in 1903, the first train of any description he had ever seen: 'The railway made a big difference to life north of the [Connel] bridge and it is rather sad to think that this is the last train that will use it.' From then on, the Ballachulish branch would only be memories.

Was there an alternative to closure?

Latterly there were only three passenger trains a day in each direction on the branch (four on Saturdays), and no freight traffic. None of the Up and Down trains crossed on the branch, so all four crossing loops / block posts[9] and their staffed signal boxes – at Benderloch, Appin, Kentallen and Ballachulish – were effectively unnecessary for the normal timetabled service. However, it would appear that BR had substantially reduced staffing since the original closure proposal; nevertheless, the remaining 26 (excluding Permanent Way staff) were a large number to support only six trains a day over 27¾ miles of railway.

Even an enhanced service of five trains each way – better geared to the tourist market – could have been accommodated with none of these crossing loops, on the basis of a 'long siding' of single-track from Connel Ferry and no signalling on the branch, with only 'One Train Working' permitted at any time. But this would have been deemed too drastic even in the 1960s, and – had the minister refused consent, and BR then proceeded to rationalise infrastructure and operations to create a 'basic railway' – then perhaps one loop would have been retained at Appin, the half-way point of the line. This in turn would have been a useful asset when the tourist charter train market began to expand in the 1970s and 1980s.

In his unique memoir of working on the construction of the line, Duncan Kennedy had no doubts about the attractiveness to tourists: 'The natural features of the landscape – the rugged line of the coast that compelled the railway to its devious course, the encroaching sea at Connel and Loch Creran

– these created difficulties for those who planned the line, adding to the cost of works and providing problems for the engineers. But for the traveller with an eye for rural beauty they had a value of their own . . . If those who originally pioneered the line had only had in mind the opening up of the country for the benefit of the stranger who wished to come and view the beauty of the Highlands, they could hardly have found in all the land a region more richly endowed.'[10]

The practice – until the very end of service – of using 1,250hp main line diesels to haul two or three passenger coaches presumably reflected historical operational synergies of inter-working locomotives on passenger and freight services, but after the withdrawal of freight in 1965 it was a commercial nonsense. There were few steep gradients on the branch, and more cost-effective DMU operation would also have enabled BR to tap better the tourist market through marketing the views available from the glass-fronted, non-smoking and First Class sections at either end of the train. Admittedly, operating a single DMU at a remote location would have been challenging, requiring a DMU 'circuit' on the Oban–Glasgow run to allow swapping round for maintenance – but such an arrangement had worked for Fraserburgh to St Combs between 1959 and 1965.

Infrastructure rationalisation, using DMUs and de-staffing all the stations would certainly have improved the economics, although the railway's nine stations served only villages and townships, all of which had a population of less than 1,000 – other than Ballachulish, which peaked at around 1,800 in the late 19th century but had declined substantially by the time of the closure of the railway.[11] Unlike the equally thinly populated Mallaig line, Ballachulish had no compensating wider strategic role, such as interchange with important ferry services.

In light of the lengths of railway solum later used for the inevitable upgrade of the parallel A828 – including the partial demolition and rebuilding of the Creagan Bridge to carry the road, thereby eliminating a significant detour – it is hard to see how the line could ever have been a viable (in the widest sense of the word) proposition as only a branch railway. However, as part of a re-orientated through rail route from Glasgow (and Oban) to Fort William – closing the line from Crianlarich to Fort William via Rannoch Moor – it would have constituted one of the most attractive stretches of railway in the entire British Isles.

Table 2: Key features of the 10 detailed case studies

LINE (& YEAR OF CLOSURE)	ROUTE / SERVICE CHARACTERISTICS						FINANCES	TUCCS PROCESS
	Mileage[1]	Track & signalling significantly rationalised?	Most stations de-staffed?[2]	Service converted to DMU / railbus?	Trains pd (in each direction) Mon–Fri	Total passengers per day (Mon–Fri in winter)[3]	Receipts / Direct Costs ratio[4]	Number of objections to TUCCS
Peebles (1962)	34½	No	No	*Yes*	7 / 8	301	c.20–35%[5]	not known
Crieff / Comrie (1964)	14¾	No	Yes	*Yes*	10[6]	150–200	10%	25
Peterhead (1965)	13¼	No	Yes	No	3 / 4	60	4%	11
Crail (1965)	28¼	No	No	*Mostly*	5	640–800	52%	119
Fraserburgh (1965)	40¾	No	Yes	No	5	536	24%	33[7]
Callander (1965)	11¼	No	No	No	8 / 11		n/a[8]	
Ballater (1966)	43¼	No	Yes	*Yes*	6	500–600	29%	34[9]
Ballachulish (1966)	34	No	No	No	3	220–400	35%	24[10]
St Andrews (1969)	5	**Yes**	No	*Yes*	20 / 22	712	50%	23[11]
Leven (1969)	6	No	No	*Yes*	8 / 10	222	16%	45

1. route mileage over which passenger services were withdrawn completely – in most cases trains operated over a longer distance, typically from a main line 'hub' rather than the actual junction with the main line.
2. excluding signalmen.
3. the numbers (from BR Heads of Information documents) are not definitively comparable, as different counting conventions seem to have been used at different times.
4. the ratios of 'Receipts' to 'Direct Costs' of the service have been calculated from the basic data supplied in BR's Heads of Information documents – it should be noted that the BR Receipts figures generally did not include contributory revenue, which was very significant in some cases: for example, more than six times direct receipts in the case of Crieff / Comrie.
5. a pre-1962 Transport Act closure, with financial information supplied by BR in different format from post-1962 withdrawals; in October 1961 BR stated that the line was 'earning approximately £30,000 per annum whereas the costs are in the region of £60,000' (page 110), but other comments by BR (pages 106 and 112) confusingly imply that these were either only terminal and movement costs, or just movement costs, in both cases excluding track and signalling. The overall Receipts to Direct Costs ratio may therefore have been anything in the range 20–35% (for the basis of this calculation see endnote 20 on page 258).
6. 10 trains per day Gleneagles–Crieff; 3 trains per day Crieff–Comrie.
7. excluding petitions / objections on behalf of others.
8. not available – BR data relates to the entire Edinburgh / Glasgow–Oban via Callander service.
9. excluding petitions / objections on behalf of others.
10. *ditto.*
11. *ditto.*

14

What lessons can we learn?

What might be called the brutal butchery of the Beeching era and its immediate aftermath stripped Scotland of all its traditional branch lines. Such a drastic end-game was not inevitable, as I sought to demonstrate in Part One's overview of the birth, life and death of the country's branch lines, and in Part Two's case studies. Together these allow us to draw a number of conclusions on the headlong rush to close railways in the 1960s – and to learn lessons, some of which may still be valid in the 21st century.

It would be invidious to try to judge which was the worst closure of the case studies. It depends on one's criteria – not only those set out in Table 2, but also the level of population cut off, the quality of replacement bus services, the potential for rail service development, the underlying economics of a rationalised railway operation, etc. However, of those lines which had realistic prospects of surviving, the Dunblane–Callander section stands out as the most glaring case of a missed opportunity to transform finances through three key measures: track and signalling rationalisation, de-staffing of stations and conversion to DMU operation (falling, respectively, within Beeching's route cost categorisation into 'Track and Signalling', 'Terminals' and 'Movement').

It is easier to conclude which were the more justified closures: the sparsely populated Ballachulish corridor and the circuitous railway to Peterhead. Perhaps the biggest surprise to emerge from the research and analysis is the East of Fife line through Crail – very much a rural railway, but with substantial scope for cost reduction and opportunities for service improvement to further enhance what was already a manageable revenue-to-cost ratio.

Overall, the broad thrust of our Scottish analysis sits comfortably with Faulkner and Austin's history of rail closures across Britain, which concludes with no fewer than 18 over-riding lessons to be learned. Among those which have particular resonance in the context of Scotland's branch lines are:

There has never been a good understanding of the costs of lines and services, or of the residual liabilities which may mean that cost escapement will be years behind the running of the last train.

In short, do not trust the statistics. At best, they tell only half the story; at worst, they can be manipulated to support any argument.

The speed of closure gave little time for reflection or consideration of alternatives.

Much planning for reduction of the network was carried out in great secrecy and requests for public information were routinely denied. Governments, the BTC and the BR board, in its early days, failed to deal with the (accurate) charge from campaigners that closures were implemented without any attempt to reduce costs or raise revenue, and that information on which decisions were based was flawed.

The combination of secrecy, limited data and the lack of accountability meant that lines were lost which were making a positive economic contribution and many were closed prematurely.[1]

However, while several dozen branch lines have survived in England and Wales – an interesting contrast with Scotland, and one which has yet to be explored by railway historians – it is important to seek to draw conclusions specific to the experience north of the border.

The summary of key features of the detailed case studies in Table 2 shows wide variations in some aspects of the different routes – including length (ranging from five to 43¼ miles) and service frequency (from three to 20 / 22 trains daily) – but one common characteristic stands out above all, and therefore comes first among our 11 principal conclusions:

1. The scope for infrastructure rationalisation was ignored

The almost complete absence within the official closure process of any consideration of the scope for infrastructure rationalisation, as part of an alternative strategy based largely on making economies, is quite remarkable. On many occasions, campaigners or local trade union branches raised with BR the scope to make savings through the likes of track singling, elimination of surplus crossing loops and closure of the smallest stations (and de-staffing some of the remaining ones) – but the standard management response was either to ignore such arguments or to sweep them aside as a wholly inadequate response to heavy losses. The consistency of such responses points to control by central diktat.

In the one case identified where local BR management initially agreed to co-operate with a move to explore the scope for different ways of running a railway – the Deeside Line – the district traffic superintendent was quickly slapped down, and BR erected a brick wall around its doctrinaire 'closure or bust' approach. Rae Montgomery concludes: 'The fundamental obstacles to any sensibly thought-out economies in operating were the Government's hell-bent determination to reduce the BR network and BRB HQ's overweening compliance.'[2] And the latter attribute applied no less to BR Scottish Region HQ.

No 'smoking gun' has been found, but Beeching's strange (apparent) conviction, as expressed in his 1963 report, that 'high system cost' was 'fixed' and 'unavoidable' – despite the long history of rail infrastructure being altered over time – suggests that a decision was taken at government / BRB level that the whole closure programme was to be implemented as quickly as possible (and within a timescale shorter than one which would realise most of the operating / maintenance economies from an alternative strategy). It would appear, therefore, that this blatant hole in his report was not so much 'Beeching's blind spot' as 'Beeching's blind eye'. As David Prescott suggests, this could reasonably be described as an establishment stitch-up.[3]

2. Opportunities for service development / promotion to increase revenue were rejected

The corollary of Beeching's rejection of such economies was a similarly widespread dismissal of the opportunities for service development / promotion to increase revenue. Whether it was speeding up the Peebles service to reflect the traction power of DMUs compared to steam, accelerating trains to Ballater, Crieff and Fraserburgh through closure of the smaller stations, or bringing Land Cruise trains to the East of Fife line, the BR response was always the same: 'The traffic was just not there' (or similar). While the context on all routes was traffic being lost to the roads – reinforced by a widespread assumption that local rail services outwith the conurbations were in irreversible decline – there was plenty of evidence that the introduction of fast, frequent, regular-interval services could arrest the decline and even turn the tide (exemplified by the DMU-operated timetable from Edinburgh to Dunfermline and Kirkcaldy introduced in 1960, albeit that this was an outer-suburban rather than rural service).

Ironically, there could be beneficial synergies between cost reduction *and* service improvement, as in the case of closure of smaller stations and perhaps most obviously through the conversion to DMU operation. BR did introduce DMUs for all or most services on just over half the case-study lines, but there were some important omissions – notably Callander and Fraserburgh – which saddled such routes with higher costs (and without the tourist-friendly panoramic views from the front and rear of the DMUs).

A related, subsidiary, conclusion, which partly pre-dates Beeching's arrival at BR – and applies to only one of the case studies in Part Two – is that BR made a fundamental error in not replacing unreliable railbuses with DMUs. Once the inherent problems had been identified in 1958–59, the opportunity should have been taken to substitute the more capacious and operationally flexible single-car DMUs. That would not have been enough to save the long and sparsely populated Speyside Line, but – together with infrastructure rationalisation – would have substantially improved the Gleneagles–Crieff prospects. Instead, we are left with that damning but accurate verdict on the impact of railbuses on British branch lines: 'Too little, too light and too late.'

3. *BR's secrecy and defensiveness – in response to campaigner and trade union doubts about the estimation of costs and revenues – spoke volumes*

Financial losses on branch operations lay at the heart of the drive for closures throughout the history of the railway from the 1920s until the late 1980s. But the controversy over this crucial question reached its apotheosis in the Beeching era, characterised by campaigner and trade union doubts, and BR secrecy and defensiveness, about the estimation of costs and revenues of threatened services.

There was a cavalier attitude to financial estimates throughout BR – to take four examples explored in this book, aspects of the data for the Crail, Crieff, first Kilmacolm and Leven closure proposals are confusing and / or unconvincing. As David Prescott has commented: 'The figures, at best, are volatile and are probably not representative or reflective of the real revenues – so not a basis on which to make far-reaching decisions.' This follows on from Gerry Fiennes' verdict in 1967 that when the Marples / Beeching axis began to define their territorial ambitions for branch lines, 'they laid it down in general that rural railways did not pay, which was true; and could never pay, which was false'.

4. Holiday / tourist lines were particularly disadvantaged by BR's revenue attribution

Research suggests that holiday / tourist lines were particularly disadvantaged by BR's revenue attribution conventions, evidently not getting the financial credit for at least three types of traffic: inbound tickets not 'booked' on the line itself; charter train / Land Cruise revenue; and receipts from Local Runabout and Freedom of Scotland tickets. To add insult to injury, the key traffic survey for the Beeching Report took place in April, which worked significantly against holiday locations. It is therefore likely that in up to six of the post-1962 case study routes the overall financial health of the train service was under-stated due to the uncredited value of holiday traffic: Ballachulish, Ballater, Callander, Crail, Crieff / Comrie and St Andrews.

5. Some routes showed a relatively healthy relationship of revenue to costs

An important discovery has been that, even on the basis of the limited (and perhaps dubious) figures supplied by BR for Heads of Information, few of the lines analysed were what might be described as basket cases. The ratio of published receipts to costs may have been only 4% for the miserable Peterhead service, but some routes showed a relatively healthy relationship of revenue to costs. The East of Fife service through Crail registered a remarkable 52% ratio figure. In this and the other detailed case studies there was clearly an opportunity to further improve their ratios through a combination of cost-cutting and service improvement, providing the taxpayer with better value for money in return for an enhanced rail contribution to local and regional economic, social and environmental welfare.

6. The prevailing political culture and popular context in the 1960s had a major impact on the closure process

Looking back 60-odd years, it is easy to lose sight of the impact of the prevailing political culture and popular context in the 1960s, the feeling within government – and much more widely – that cheap fuel for motoring was a permanent fixture and therefore the demand for travel by rail would inevitably continue to fall. But this was not a monolithic view which went unchallenged at the time: one thinks of the vision of the SRDA, campaigning at national level, and the wisdom of individual campaigners such as the Chairman of Aboyne and District Citizens' Association who cited the downside of the roads-dominated American transport experience and warned against falling into the same trap. However, such concerns were swept aside in the ultimately futile rush to eliminate BR's losses through quick closures.

And we should not forget that very different approaches to rail strategy were adopted in mainland Europe, where nothing like the drastic Beeching cuts was inflicted on the rail networks of countries such as Austria, Germany and Switzerland, where greater strategic state direction and / or state railway companies were in place long before Britain.

7. The BR closure proposal procedure and the associated TUCC process were geared to minimising objections from passengers

A striking aspect of the closure process is how few formal objections to closure were submitted to the TUCCS: of the eight detailed case studies where the figures are known, all bar one (Crail) registered fewer than 50 individual objections. While the archive material has not yielded a great deal of intelligence on the quantum of regular (daily or weekly) passengers, all nine case-study routes for which the total weekly patronage data is available – bar one – generated between 1,000 and 5,000 single journeys per week in winter (and usually more in summer), the one exception being the Peterhead branch (low hundreds). We can therefore reasonably conclude that in all cases – including the Crail example of as many as 119 objectors – only a very small proportion of rail users took advantage of the statutory objection procedure. Why was that?

A degree of effort would have been involved in those pre-computer days, but, for a service which was valued, producing a short letter of objection does not seem much to ask. However, were some passengers simply cynical about any likely benefit from objecting? As we have seen, *The Social Consequences of Rail Closures* study found that many former rail users felt that closure policy had been determined years before the actual decisions were announced. There were widespread concerns about the role and proceedings of the TUCCs specifically, such that 'many people felt that better and more

acceptable decisions could have been reached had the procedure incorporated more open and comprehensive public discussion of the consequences
likely to arise at the time of closure and also in the years following it'.[4]

With regard to the *visibility* of the opportunity to object to the TUCCS,
tourist / holiday routes were once again at a disadvantage. The 1962 Transport
Act only required BR to publish notices of the proposed withdrawal in two
local newspapers and to post notices at the stations affected during two successive weeks – so, for example, the Crieff / Comrie proposal would register
neither in Edinburgh nor Glasgow, as there were no through trains from
either of these cities.

Overall, we may therefore conclude that the BR closure proposal notifica-
tion procedure and the associated TUCC process were geared to minimising
objections from passengers, and hence reducing the political pressure to
reprieve. This is unsurprising, given that in 1961, as we have seen, 'officials
were already working to ensure that the Transport Bill would reduce the role
of the consultative committees in order to speed things up and quieten them
down'. Individual hardship as determined by the TUCC was (in theory)
the only determinant of the strength of case against closure – although, in
practice, politics was key – and this meant that the quantum of evidence as
discussed at TUCC hearings was likely to have significantly underplayed the
overall value of the rail service to users, not to mention the wider economic,
environmental and social benefits.

8. The TUCCS completely failed to challenge the BR position

That alternative strategies – instead of closure – were rarely implemented
must in part be attributed to the lack of challenge from the TUCCS. All
the TUCCs across Britain had a narrowly drawn remit relating only to
individual hardship, but BR did supply them confidentially with additional
financial detail – including contributory revenue and a breakdown of costs
into movement, terminals and track and signalling.

While definitive conclusions are difficult to reach in the absence of detailed
records of most of the post-1962-Transport Act TUCCS's deliberations on
individual closures, there is no evidence of BR data ever being challenged or
alternative approaches to operation being suggested for consideration. One
might ask why the TUCCs were given additional financial information if no
practical use was then made of it? That sentence perhaps contains its own
answer.

9. *There were too many half-hearted campaigns against closure*

Of the nine railways in Scotland which were 'Beeching reprieves', by far the most dramatic were the Far North and Kyle lines. Vigorous grassroots and high-level campaigning (exemplified by the 'MacPuff' movement) – as opposed to just formal objections to the TUCCS – were combined with particular political sensitivities to save no fewer than 232 miles of rural railway. The Highlands had long been 'a special case', and branch lines in other parts of Scotland could not hope to provoke the same level of public outrage at closure proposals, but my research points to half-hearted opposition by campaigners and / or trade unions being a contributory factor to the demise of some 50% of the case-study lines.

The lack of central support from the NUR left individual routes vulnerable to the lottery of local union branch officials' capability and / or commitment. Of the eight main case-study lines where BR management / staff consultation meeting records have been found (all 10, bar Callander and Leven), in only the Ballachulish, Crail, Fraserburgh and St Andrews examples does there seem to have been a combination of union zeal and strong public opposition, but of course that still was not enough to avoid the axe.

10. *Scotland needlessly lost a significant number of rail routes*

The end-result of the foregoing factors – and given that this book has analysed in detail a reasonable sample of the scores of services withdrawn north of the border in the 1960s – is that we can now argue that Scotland needlessly lost a significant number of rail routes. With sensible strategies for cost reduction and appropriate service improvement, losses would have been substantially reduced, while the wider societal benefits of the retained railway would have been appreciably enhanced.

Of the 10 routes dissected in greatest detail we can conclude that only two in their entirety did not justify retention, rationalisation and development: Ballachulish, which as a dead-end branch line had no realistic future, and Peterhead, which was seriously disadvantaged by its circuitous route to Aberdeen. Three others would have been cost-effective prospects if cut back to their core markets: Callander–Dunblane, Crieff–Gleneagles and Peebles–Edinburgh. These three, and four of the other five routes, were arguably capable of being managed progressively such that, at minimum, revenue would exceed 50% of costs, and in some cases break-even might just have been possible.

Possibly the only exception is the Thornton–Leven stub, which survived from 1965 to 1969, but appears to have been grievously wounded by the loss of the through service to Crail and St Andrews and by the subsequent – poor to non-existent – bus–rail interchange arrangements at Leven. And a wider point is made by David Prescott: 'The idea that passengers would be encouraged to change from a Scottish Bus Group rail-replacement bus into the remaining train service was doomed to fail because SBG would try hard to keep them on the bus.'[5]

11. Central and local government largely failed to provide strategic protection of former rail corridors

My final conclusion relates to the aftermath of closure. While in a number of cases the MoT imposed embargos on disposal of the solum, in due course these were either formally abandoned or quietly forgotten. In the widespread absence of strategic (ideally statutory) protection of former rail corridors by government – and given BR's never-ending need to improve its finances by selling off land and property – the large majority of the routes examined in this book sooner or later fell prey to *ad hoc* breaches and fragmentation of the solums by housing, industrial development, roads, etc. As Rae Montgomery suggests: 'Whenever lines and their branch appendages were to be closed, as a minimum directive the solums should have been held in a "public land asset bank" so that, instead of being sold off in penny lots, the nation at large would be enabled to benefit. They could have been used as wayleaves for fibre optic cables, water and power lines, cycleways and footpaths (as some were), but with the proviso that wherever there was a perceived likelihood of future rail reinstatement, short or long term, all works would have to be installed in such a way that such reinstatement would not in any way be impeded.'[6]

The failure to adopt such a visionary strategy was to have significant implications for future re-opening prospects: in the case of the Borders Railway the lack of protection of the old Waverley Route solum added some 40% to the costs of re-opening,[7] and it was only political factors (as opposed to 'the business case') which ensured that the line was partially re-opened.

One of the few closed routes in Scotland where the solum was fully protected for possible future rail re-use was Airdrie–Bathgate, following closure of this freight-only line in 1982 – apparently in the belief that it might re-open for freight, although in practice it would prove to be a passenger re-opening. In a far-sighted initiative, BR transferred the solum to Railway Paths Ltd. – the ownership arm of Sustrans, the cycling and walking path charity – but with a claw-back clause making provision for relocation of the path should rail re-opening be required.[8] If only such vision had been the norm 20 years earlier.

Of the 10 most detailed case-study routes in this book, just two – Fraserburgh and Peterhead – have benefited from strategic vision along their entire length – with both corridors re-made as walking / cycling routes. This was largely driven by the upper-tier local authority, Grampian Regional Council, which had powers over transport and strategic planning – but all the regional councils were abolished in 1996, swept away in a cost-cutting (and gerrymandering) initiative by the Conservative government and replaced by a fragmented pattern of generally much smaller, single-tier councils.

Are there lessons for the future?

We now live in a very different Britain and a very different Scotland to those which saw the last branch lines north of the border disappear more than 50 years ago. The closure of individual routes – to help reduce the subsidy requirement for the national rail system – has been off the agenda for more than three decades, and the demands of the 'climate emergency' (a striking contrast to the limited environmental awareness of the 1960s) suggest that further line re-openings are likely to be at the heart of future transport investment programmes. Chapter 15 investigates how many of this book's cases may benefit.

Of the 11 conclusions reached above, two appear to have continuing resonance despite the transformation in political attitudes to railways. In a perverse way, 'the scope for infrastructure rationalisation was ignored' applies to the new Borders Railway. While the amount of double-track railway was cut back to the absolute minimum (leaving no spare capacity) and bridges spanning the single-track railway were not 'future-proofed' for doubling, the road construction elements (10 kilometres in total) of the rail scheme were all gold-plated. The new dual-lane road access to the village of Fountainhall (population 200), for example, resembles a slip-road off the M8, yet the railway it crosses (serving a population in excess of 50,000 in the Borders) is only single-track. Most of the stations have multiple lines of industrial fencing and vast quantities of carbon-intensive concrete, while the apotheosis of wasteful expenditure can be found at Stow station: following the opening of the railway a village which previously had no CCTV cameras now has 40. Clearly, railway stations are very dangerous places – unlike the A7 through Stow, of course.

We can also see evidence today of 'secrecy and defensiveness' over estimation of the costs and revenues of new routes. Unpublished research[9] shows that the cost of new stations doubled post-privatisation and doubled again in the 2000s. Since then, over the decade to 2017, new station costs did not only double, but trebled to the current £8–£10 million price tag for an average two-platform station – with no apparent change in the size / quality of station and facilities provided for the rail traveller. And the Scottish Government has obfuscated in the face of modern station re-openings which, as we shall see in the next chapter, have routinely generated patronage far in excess of the official forecasts.

15

Branch line renaissance ahead?

By the 1980s – after the global shock of the 1973 oil crisis – it had become clear that road transport was not the panacea assumed in the 1960s.

Concerns about the environment, road congestion, changing patterns of urban development, local economic regeneration and social mobility fuelled pressure for rail solutions. The growing pace of rail re-openings reached a modern peak in 1987, under the entrepreneurial stewardship of BR's new Provincial Sector, later Regional Railways, working with local government to cost-effectively expand the reach of rail services. That year, 26 new stations opened across Britain, three of them in Scotland. The previous year, the freight-only Edinburgh–Bathgate line (and three stations) had re-opened to passenger traffic, and the results were spectacular: passenger journeys of 264,000 per annum were predicted, but by 1989 usage had already exceeded 1 million.

Subsequent route re-openings similarly made a nonsense of official forecasts. The Hamilton to Larkhall line re-opened in 2005, 'and by 2008 trains were carrying around 40% more passengers than predicted'.[1] The Stirling–Alloa railway which re-opened in 2008 quickly delivered 180% more passengers than forecast, while the apotheosis of forecasting failure came in the first year of the Borders Railway (opened in 2015) when the three stations within the Borders – Stow, Galashiels and Tweedbank – saw, respectively, 313%, 330% and 681% more passengers than officially predicted.[2]

No fewer than 89 passenger stations have opened / re-opened north of the border since 1970. Fifty-two of these were on existing passenger service routes, while 37 were on routes opened / re-opened to passenger traffic having previously been abandoned or carrying only freight traffic. There has been no central government or rail industry plan to achieve this – progress has come usually as a result of local or regional initiatives by local authorities and rail campaigners, aided by forward-thinking rail managers. But due credit should go the devolved government in Scotland where the rail network has benefited (until recently) from a more determined policy towards rail re-openings than south of the border, including funding contributions towards the construction of new stations and new routes.

The fundamental aim underlying the Beeching Report – that the rail network could be shrunk down to a profitable core, rather than expanded – was finally consigned to the dustbin of history some years after the infamous Serpell Report of 1983. And now the wider economic, social and environmental benefits of a growing rail system are encapsulated in the substantial public subsidy for the ScotRail franchise, incurring a (pre-Covid impact) cost of more than £7 billion over 10 years. This is seen as a positive investment – quite the opposite of the Marples / Beeching thinking that the railway could and should be profit-making.

As yet, none of the route re-openings in Scotland has involved what one might describe as a traditional branch line: all are effectively part of the 'Greater Glasgow' or 'Greater Edinburgh' commuter networks. However, in 2019 long-time rail campaigners were surprised but delighted by a Scottish Government announcement that the Thornton–Levenmouth line would be re-opened for passenger (and possibly also freight) traffic. Might that be just the first re-opening of a number of the branch lines featured in this book?

In its planned submission to Transport Scotland (the Scottish Government agency) on the latter's 'Strategic Transport Projects Review 2' process, the sustainable transport alliance Transform Scotland intended to argue that all mainland communities with more than 10,000 population should be served by rail.[3] That would add a dozen new railway routes to the network, including those to Fraserburgh / Peterhead, Levenmouth, Penicuik and St Andrews. And in early 2021, the Scottish Green Party went even further in its 'Rail for All' briefing[4] (based on a report by David Prescott and me), arguing the case for returning rail to all towns with over 5,000 population – but, where this proved not to be feasible, ensuring that they were part of an integrated national 'ScotRail coach network'.

Of the 30 most populous towns in Scotland with no rail service,[5] 10 are located on former rail routes examined in some detail in this book. Their populations range from 6,910 in Kelso to 30,530 in the contiguous Methil, Leven and Buckhaven settlements to be served by the re-opened Levenmouth line. At the opposite extreme among the case-study routes is Ballachulish, with only 640 residents: the village is not even among the

450 most populous settlements in Scotland. Given the wide variations in population, one would therefore expect future rail re-opening prospects to vary from 'very strong' to 'extremely unlikely'.

But population is not the only factor – distance from the existing rail network, the quality of current bus–rail interchange, the extent of local road congestion and economic / social factors all come into play on the 'demand' side. And on the 'supply' side, there is considerable variation in the extent of loss of line-of-route or station locations to other land uses (such as housing and roads) and / or major structures such as bridges over rivers and roads which have been demolished. In most cases the land has been sold off and has suffered significant breaches, which render potentially prohibitive the cost of re-opening in relation to the likely benefits. Railways – with their signalled, guided tracks and dedicated corridors – are expensive to construct, operate and maintain, and, as Beeching rightly concluded, as a guiding principle: 'We should expect the provision of railways to be limited to routes over which it is possible to develop dense flows of traffic, of the kinds which lend themselves to movement in trainload quantities and which, in part at least, benefit from the speed and reliability which the railways are capable of achieving.'[6]

In the 1960s, reprieving and rationalising a line which struggled to meet such exacting criteria – but nevertheless could have performed a valuable ongoing economic, environmental and social function – would have been one thing. To now re-create such infrastructure – after half a century of loss to alternative land uses – is an altogether more challenging and costly exercise.

However, the declaration of a 'climate emergency' by First Minister Nicola Sturgeon in 2019 can be expected to have a transformative impact on the prospects for rail re-openings, after decades where road building has been the preferred priority of governments of all political hues, both Scottish and UK. The prospects for the lines whose closure stories have been examined in this book are now briefly considered, in broad order of likelihood.

But a big caveat has to be made: we now face a global shock far worse than the 1973 oil crisis. There is enormous uncertainty about the levels of public investment which will be available for new transport infrastructure, and the long-term impact of the Covid pandemic on local, regional, national and international travel habits cannot be predicted with any confidence. Within Scotland, travel patterns may change, especially with the possibility of home-working reducing centralised office work and thus reducing the regular peak flows of traffic and people on public transport. While geographical travel patterns may remain broadly the same, the numbers travelling may not expand as they have been doing – and may fall – and ongoing 'social distancing' would have an impact on rail economics. However, there remains the urgent and growing need to address the climate emergency, for which rail transport should always be a key solution.

The strongest prospects

As far back as the early 1990s determined efforts were being made to press the case for passenger rail services to be reinstated to the adjacent towns of **Leven, Methil and Buckhaven**. Sadly, these were unsuccessful, but over the last decade the LevenMouth Rail Campaign (LMRC)[7] has vigorously argued for rail reinstatement as a key agent of economic regeneration in this often-forgotten corner of Scotland. With a population of over 30,000, the three towns constitute by far the largest continuous built-up area north of the border without a rail service.

After years of foot dragging by the Scottish Government and its Transport Scotland agency, Cabinet Secretary Michael Matheson announced in 2019 that the line would be re-opened for passenger (and potentially freight) services, with 2023 now the target year for trains to begin running. It is estimated that the project, which also includes improved bus services and walking and cycling facilities, will cost around £70 million.

Crucially, the whole route has remained the 'mothballed' operational property of Railtrack, later Network Rail, since the last freight trains ran to Methil power station in the early 1990s and to Cameron Bridge distillery later that decade. And from 2012 to 2015 there was a short-lived re-opening to Earlseat open-cast coal facility, a mile east of Thornton Junction. Unlike the Borders Railway, which required the Waverley Railway (Scotland) Act 2006, this new rail link will therefore not need any such Act of the Scottish Parliament. Passenger stations will be provided at Cameron Bridge (serving as a park-and-ride facility for the surrounding area) and at Levenmouth itself, close to the town's modern bus station. There is, in addition, potential for a freight railhead at Diageo's Cameron Bridge distillery (the largest grain distillery in Europe), which would also serve its major bottling plant at nearby Bandeath.

Following the opening of the Borders Railway in 2015, the dubious honour of being further from the rail network than any other towns of their size in Britain shifted from Galashiels and Hawick to **Peterhead** (30 miles) and

Fraserburgh (40 miles).[8] With a population of over 19,000, Peterhead is the second largest town in Scotland without a rail service – and is now Britain's top fishing port.[9] Fraserburgh is the 11th largest town without trains and has a population of just over 13,000.

There is an intensive bus service between Peterhead and Aberdeen (some services running via Ellon, discussed below) but inevitably buses are affected by city traffic congestion and can struggle to offer the service quality and speed of a train. Peterhead's railway, which closed in 1965, suffered from its circuitous route to Aberdeen via Maud, and a more logical routing for any future railway would be to follow broadly the alignment of the former line from Ellon to Cruden Bay and Boddam (closed completely in 1948), extended onwards the few miles to Peterhead. Even this more direct route (around 27 miles) would stretch the limits of a potential lower-cost 'TramTrain' operation (vehicles capable of street-running, but also equipped to run on 'heavy rail' tracks)[10] – and in any case a 'heavy rail' solution, while expensive, would open up the prospect of rail winning long-distance fish traffic from Peterhead to southern and continental markets.

Conceivably, given a new rail routing to Peterhead, the best way to reconnect Fraserburgh to the rail system would be to extend the Peterhead line along the coast via St Combs – thereby providing a valuable local link over and above the connection to Aberdeen, rather than following the original alignment from Ellon via Maud and Strichen.

In recent times, however, official studies of rail re-opening feasibility have focused on an initial 13-mile route to **Ellon**, which could act as an effective railhead for both Peterhead and Fraserburgh. Ellon's population is over 10,000, and it is the 13th largest town in Scotland without a rail service. The most recent consultancy study[11] in 2017 for Nestrans (the regional transport partnership) examined three different options, with varying degrees of infrastructure provision. Estimated costs ranged from £283 million through £311 million to £381 million: equating (albeit without allowing for inflation) to *nearly double to treble the cost per mile of the Borders Railway*, despite the latter having suffered many more breaches of the solum than the line to Ellon, which is now a walkway and cycle path. The consultants concluded: 'All options deliver "poor value for money" with costs outweighing benefits.'

In the two most expensive options, the consultants included the cost of redoubling the ¾-mile single-track section of main line railway through two tunnels between Aberdeen station and Kittybrewster. Astonishingly, they failed to examine the alternative of a TramTrain operation, with street-running cutting capital costs and generating extra revenue from additional city centre stops. Questions should also be asked of the seemingly exorbitant capital cost estimates – and one can only wonder if the lessons of the forecasting failure for the Borders stations were taken on board.

Other good cases

The closure of the railway to **St Andrews** was controversial, but the loss of trains has not constrained its development as a global attraction for golfing holidays and university education. The town's population is now nearly 18,000 and it is the third largest in Scotland without a rail service. St Andrews has long enjoyed a vigorous rail campaign by *StARLink*, which was launched in 1989 'with a view to reconnecting the town to the rail system in the interests of convenience for travellers, the alleviation of traffic congestion and reduction of car-generated pollution'.[12] As the StARLink website notes: 'The town's infrastructure cannot cope with the increasing pressures placed upon it, not only from visitors and tourists, but also from students and commuters.' The arguments for rail are therefore very much focused on congestion and environmental pressures – in contrast to those which have been mobilised for Levenmouth rail reinstatement, based largely on economic and social deprivation.

As Faulkner and Austin point out, it was to be many years after the St Andrews rail closure before a proper bus–rail interchange was provided at Leuchars station, but the situation is now very different from 1969: 'It has to be admitted that, even without its railway, access to St Andrews by public transport is good . . . during the day no fewer than nine buses an hour connect Leuchars station with St Andrews. Through ticketing is available and the bus station at St Andrews sells national rail tickets. A busy taxi rank and a large car park with a ramped footbridge at Leuchars have transformed the position at the time of closure. The station has now been renamed Leuchars for St Andrews and the bus connections are shown in the railway timetable.'[13]

St Andrews bus station also provides real-time rail information for train arrival and departure times at Leuchars station, and the interchange arrangements at the station can reasonably be described as among the best in Scotland – admittedly not the greatest accolade by European standards.

Significant sections of the former rail route have been lost to development, suggesting that a TramTrain solution (through to Dundee and beyond) is the most realistic option, but there is still strong advocacy for a strategic 'heavy rail' route running towards Edinburgh (rather than Dundee), helping to maintain St Andrew's place 'on the world stage'. Yet we cannot be certain how far the demand for international educational and leisure travel will recover from the pandemic – which, let us not forget, was spread globally by the availability of cheap mass-transport by air. My view is that TramTrain would best help solve St Andrews' congestion and environmental problems – and that other towns in Scotland have more pressing needs for a return of 'heavy rail'.

Penicuik may have lost its trains a very long time ago, but – with a population of 16,000 – it is now the sixth largest town in Scotland without a train service. Edinburgh's growth as a financial, government and service centre has stimulated substantial house building across Midlothian, but only the eastern extremity around Eskbank, Newtongrange and Gorebridge is currently served by train – providing a safe and sustainable alternative to increasingly congested roads.

An embryonic campaign for reconnecting Penicuik to the rail network has recently emerged and will doubtless have to decide whether TramTrain or 'heavy rail' solutions are best for the town and its hinterland. Significant sections of the circuitous former rail route from the Penicuik terminus (not well sited in relation to the current spread of the town) via Bonnyrigg to Eskbank (and onwards to Edinburgh) have been lost to development, but much of the solum of the former Glencorse branch line (which terminated only a couple of miles north of Penicuik and remained open for freight to Bilston Glen colliery until 1991) has been preserved as a walking / cycling right of way. With street-running from Penicuik to Glencorse / Bilston Glen, TramTrains could then follow the segregated former 'heavy rail' route as far as Danderhall, before turning off to run along the A7 corridor past the Edinburgh Royal Infirmary to Cameron Toll, then joining the Edinburgh South Suburban Line and / or continuing direct on-street to the city centre.

In the absence of a re-opened railway to Peebles (see below), one or more stations on a TramTrain route from Penicuik could act as a park-and-ride railhead for the Borders town – but the speed of rail transit to Edinburgh (partly determined by the number of intermediate stops) would be a critical determinant of how many motorists (and bus users) might switch from road to rail.

Although the corridor served by the Deeside Line to **Ballater** was not heavily populated, the railway punched above its weight – and could have done so much better with proper promotion of its scenic attractions. Subsequent housing development within the Aberdeen commuter catchment has changed the balance within the corridor: west of Banchory, population is still sparse (just under 3,000 in Aboyne, and around 1,500 in Ballater itself); but both Banchory and Peterculter now have over 7,500 residents, while the population of the Culter and Cults suburbs has continued to grow.

Unsurprisingly, therefore, road congestion, and air quality and road safety problems have also grown. For traffic heading into the city centre, the Aberdeen Western Peripheral Route – completed at an astronomical cost of around £1 billion – is an irrelevance, but a re-opened railway could offer significant benefits. A TramTrain operation from **Banchory** to Aberdeen could readily avoid the Deeside Way walking and cycling route on the former single-track solum west of Park. East of Park the former double-track line-of-route potentially has space for both a single-track railway and a walking / cycling path (albeit that such 'shared space' is not always popular with walkers, due to conflicts with speeding cyclists). TramTrain's routing flexibility would also ease difficulties on a short, constrained stretch of corridor near the main line junction at Ferryhill.

The axing of the **Kilmacolm** branch was a shocking late closure, but the Paisley Canal to Glasgow section has gone from strength to strength since re-opening in 1990 (and subsequent electrification), and meantime the combined population of Bridge of Weir, Houston and Kilmacolm has grown to more than 15,000. The former double-track formation would allow both a single-track (electrified) railway and the current walking / cycling path to be accommodated – putting right the serious injustice of the 1983 closure.

Long shots

Like many towns within the commuting orbit of Edinburgh, **Peebles** has grown significantly in the last 50 years and now has a population of around 9,000. Much of the rail solum has been lost in the town itself and in the built-up areas of Midlothian through which it passed. This constraint – and the large number of level crossings which bedevilled the railway – suggests that while a 'heavy rail' return is highly unlikely, TramTrain operation as a 10-mile extension of a line to Penicuik could be feasible. Due to their superior braking capability (from a maximum speed of 62mph), TramTrain routes can incorporate level crossings, whereas there is a presumption against these for new 'heavy rail' lines.

A TramTrain route would involve street-running within Peebles and then broadly following the alignment of the old railway to the southern edge of Penicuik, where a new alignment could lead down to the town centre and street-running on the initial section towards Edinburgh. A legitimate question is the extent to which a 62mph TramTrain – rather than the 75–90mph of a typical 'heavy rail' regional train – could hope to compete with the bus and, in particular, the car. However, it is unlikely that more than one intermediate stop (at Eddleston) would be justified between the outskirts of Peebles and Penicuik – and north of Penicuik the frequency of stops would have to be carefully considered in order to ensure that rail's speed advantage was not lost.

The railway through **Kelso** which closed in 1964 offered a miserable service and was overloaded with unnecessary infrastructure costs. The site of the town's poorly located station, south of the River Tweed, is now obliterated by development, but much of the 11½-mile solum to St Boswells (including the imposing Roxburgh Viaduct) remains unbreached. Kelso is a significant centre but its 6,000 population is less than half the size of Hawick – so might a reinstated railway from Tweedbank to Hawick, with park-and-ride and bus interchange at St Boswells, be the most realistic option? Or could there be a strategic case for rebuilding a further 22 miles through Cornhill / Coldstream to Tweedmouth and Berwick on the ECML, in part as a diversionary route?

A 'two-pronged' rail solution south of Tweedbank could see hourly train services to both Hawick and Kelso, thereby creating a combined half-hourly frequency at St Boswells – but in such a scenario, car drivers from the Kelso area might prefer to 'railhead' at the latter and not use 'the branch', significantly undermining its utility. However, Kelso is a more affluent town than Hawick, and has a greater satellite population – and therefore could be expected to generate more rail trips per head.

Callander now has a population of just over 3,000 and was an extremely popular tourist and visitor centre prior to the Covid outbreak. David Prescott, who lives in nearby Dunblane, undertook a reconnaissance of the corridor in 2019 and concluded that the impact of large sections of the solum of old railway having been built over in Dunblane, Doune and east Callander would be to push the cost of a reinstated 'heavy rail' route up to – very broadly – around £500 million. This is significantly more than the cost of the Borders Railway, which is nearly three times as long and serves a substantially bigger population.

His conclusion is that the most realistic rail option would be a TramTrain operation, thus avoiding much of the heavy engineering needed to get round the breaches of the old line in Dunblane, Doune and Callander. It is still not a cheap option – with capital costs (excluding the TramTrains themselves) possibly of the order of £300–£350 million. And a service potentially linking Stirling, Stirling University, Bridge of Allan, Dunblane, Doune and Callander would probably need ongoing financial support as well.

One can only rue the short-sighted failure of central and local government to take on board the 1966 recommendation of the SDD's Planning Division to protect the Dunblane–Callander solum for a potential future commuter line. But – unless there is substantial population growth in the area (which seems unlikely in a National Park area) – Callander would be well behind a significant number of larger towns in Scotland in the queue for rail investment funds.

On a car-facilitated foot survey of key points along the former Gleneagles–**Crieff** railway in 2019, David Prescott and I identified around a dozen breaches of the alignment through removal of bridges, embankments and cuttings, absorption into fields, building works, etc. – the most serious being obliteration by the dual-carriageway A9 only a few hundred yards from Gleneagles station, infill or removal of former road bridges, and a range of obstructions north of the former River Earn crossing, in particular at, and on the approach to, the former Crieff station site.

It is clear that a railway from Gleneagles to Crieff could not be reinstated without major capital expenditure on the infrastructure, quite possibly on a new alignment in places – and with a population of under 8,000 (and a limited surrounding catchment), there would not be sufficient demand or wider benefits to justify creating a modern railway when other significantly larger towns are likely to have much stronger claims.

However, an option would be to explore creation of a new TramTrain alignment of around 18 miles from Crieff to Perth, along the A85 corridor via Methven, Almondbank and the substantial housing developments on the west side of the city.

The **East Neuk** towns remain highly popular with visitors, but unlike the situation when the railway closed in 1965 these are not generally folk spending a week or two's summer holiday in Lundin Links, Largo, Elie, St Monance, Pittenweem, Anstruther or Crail – but rather day-trippers and second-homers, the overwhelming majority travelling by car.

Regrettable as the loss of the railway has been, it is difficult to see conventional trains ever returning. Much of the former rail solum has been ploughed into fields, and in Leven the entire line-of-route through the station which closed in 1969 has been built over. A 'heavy rail' line from the East Neuk to the site of the planned new Levenmouth station (well to the south of the original Leven station) could not be constructed without massive dislocation.

From the wider public transport perspective, there would appear to be two potential alternatives for the future. By far the lowest cost option would be to ensure that the new Levenmouth station is provided with a safe, direct walking route to the modern bus station, around 200 metres distant. And to optimise the convenience of through bus–rail journeys, the bus service to the East Neuk towns and St Andrews could become part of an integrated national 'ScotRail coach network', with connecting services and through ticketing to provide an extremely high quality of service, as applies in the much-admired system in Switzerland.

Alternatively, might Tram Train work for the East Neuk, with its half-dozen small towns (Anstruther the largest, with a population of 5,000) spaced out over a 17-mile corridor, followed by a further 11 miles to St Andrews? And to improve rail's penetration west of Levenmouth, a new alignment could run directly through Methil, Buckhaven, East Wemyss, Dysart, Sinclairtown and Kirkcaldy town centre, terminating at the town's railway station.

Only in unforeseen circumstances

The inclusion of the **Ballachulish** line in this book's case studies was less a reflection of the case for a reprieve in 1966 than a reminder of the lack of strategic vision – for a re-orientated West Highland rail network – earlier that decade. The branch only ever served villages, and Ballachulish now has a population of just 640. Without a through rail link from Oban to Fort William across Loch Leven, this coastal corridor by Loch Linnhe is simply not 'railway country'. And significant sections of the former railway solum have been taken over to improve the A828, also allowing bus journeys to be speeded up. It is hard to conceive of any circumstances in which trains will once again cross the Connel Ferry bridge and thread their way through the sublime scenery of Benderloch, Appin and Kentallen to the village in the shadow of the slate quarries. But this is the sole 'no-hoper' for branch line renaissance in the dozen routes we have dissected.

Closing thoughts

The first railways in Scotland providing both passenger and freight services were opened for business in the early 1830s, and scores of branch lines followed over the next seven decades – but by 1969 they had virtually all lost their passenger trains.

This book has argued that during the 1960s we needlessly lost a significant number of rail routes which could have made a cost-effective ongoing contribution to economic, social and environmental welfare across the country. Beeching may simply have been doing the bidding of the government, but his failure to exploit the widespread scope for infrastructure rationalisation – short of complete closure – on 'the best of the branch lines' now looks unforgiveable.

Beeching died in 1985, at a time when the revival of railways well beyond the core inter-city network was already under way. One wonders what he made of this positive development, so different from his pessimistic outlook of 1963. And if he is now looking down from the Great Guillotine in the Sky, does he have any regrets about his 'blind spot', or rather the 'blind eye' he turned to the obvious alternatives to closure?

The closures remedy within *The Reshaping of British Railways* report was, in part, an establishment stitch-up – for which dozens of Scottish towns paid, and are still paying, the penalty. However, while Glenburnie Junction to St Fort will never see trains again, the fact that we are now contemplating a possible branch-line renaissance in Scotland demonstrates that much has changed for the better in the six decades since Dr Beeching wrote his drastic prescription.

Notes

Foreword

1   BRB, *The Reshaping of British Railways*.
2   Fiennes, G., *I Tried to Run a Railway*.
3   Spaven, D., *Waverley Route: the life, death and rebirth of the Borders Railway*.
4   Spaven, D., *Highland Survivor: the story of the Far North Line*.
5   Vallance, H.A., *British Branch Lines*, BT Batsford, 1965, p. 7.
6   St John Thomas, D., *The Country Railway*.
7   https://www.lexico.com/definition/branch_line [Last accessed on 15 May 2020.]
8   Drummond, A., *A Quite Impossible Proposal: How Not to Build a Railway*, Birlinn, 2020.
9   https://www.transporttreasury.co.uk/ [Last accessed on 3 July 2020.]

Glossary and list of abbreviations

1   https://en.wikipedia.org/wiki/Bogie#:~:text=A%20bogie%20in%20the%20 UK,to%20an%20entire%20railway%20carriage. [Last accessed on 14 June 2020.]
2   https://en.wikipedia.org/wiki/Passenger_rail_terminology [Last accessed on 14 June 2020.]
3   https://en.wikipedia.org/wiki/Permanent_way_(history) [Last accessed on 15 May 2020.]
4   https://railcar.co.uk/type/ [Last accessed on 14 June 2020.]
5   https://en.wikipedia.org/wiki/Rolling_stock [Last accessed on 19 June 2020.]
6   Hall, S., *Modern Signalling Handbook*, Ian Allan Publishing, Third Edition 2001, p. 66.
7   Shunters were under 800hp; Type 1s 800–1,000hp; Types 3s 1,500–1,999hp; Type 4s 2,000–2,999hp and Type 5s over 3,000hp. See: https://en.wikipedia. org/wiki/British_Rail_locomotive_and_multiple_unit_numbering_and_ classification [Last accessed on 15 June 2020.]

Chapter 1

1   Wolmar, C., *Fire & Steam*, p. 122.
2   Ransom, P.J.G., *Iron Road*, p. 66.
3   St John Thomas, *The Country Railway*, p. 16.
4   Ibid., p. 15.
5   Thomas, J.A. and Turnock, D., *A Regional History of the Railways of Great Britain, Volume 15 North of Scotland*, p. 22.
6   Ibid., p. 17.
7   Ibid., p. 18.
8   Ibid., p. 19.
9   Ibid., p. 86.
10 26 January 2021 review in *The Times* by Laura Freeman of: Elborough, T., *Through the Looking Glasses*, Little,Brown, 2021
11 Smith, M., *British Railway Bridges & Viaducts*, Ian Allan, 1994.
12 St John Thomas, *The Country Railway*, p. 52.
13 Clough, D.N., *Dr Beeching's Remedy*, p. 14.
14 St John Thomas, *The Country Railway*, p. 53.
15 Clough, *Dr Beeching's Remedy*, p. 14.
16 In discussion with the author in 2020.
17 Clough, *Dr Beeching's Remedy*, p. 17.
18 In discussion with the author in 2020.
19 Clough, *Dr Beeching's Remedy*, p. 17.
20 Wolmar, *Fire & Steam*, p. 197.
21 'A headshunt is a single siding, usually located at the end of a Yard or set of loops. They are typically provided to allow locomotives to run round trains, or to provide space for shunting within the Yard to occur without blocking main lines.' See: https://www.simsig.co.uk/Wiki/Show?page=usertrack:glossary:headshunt [Last accessed on 15 May 2020.]
22 St John Thomas, *The Country Railway*, p. 74.
23 https://www.railwaysarchive.co.uk/documents/HMG_Act_Light1896.pdf [Last accessed on 15 May 2020.]
24 Malcolm, E.H., *The Cromarty & Dingwall Light Railway*, Cromarty Courthouse, 1993.
25 Wolmar, *Fire & Steam*, p. 195.
26 Ransom, *Iron Road*, p. 119.
27 Fasken, D. and Spaven, D., *The Insider Rail Guide: Aberdeen to Elgin & Inverness*, Kessock Books, 2017.
28 Ransom, *Iron Road*, p. 123.
29 Bonavia, M.R., *The History of the LNER, the First Years 1922–3*, Allen and Unwin, 1982.
30 St John Thomas, *The Country Railway*, p. 55.
31 Wolmar, *Fire & Steam*, p. 228.
32 St John Thomas, *The Country Railway*, p. 106.

33 Ibid., p. 198.

34 Betjeman, J. (BBC Home Service, 1940) in *Trains and buttered toast*, John Murray, 2007.

35 https://www.scottishreview.net/KennethRoyInveramsay531a.html [Last accessed on 1 July 2020.]

36 Mackenzie, R.F., *A Search for Scotland*, Collins, 1989.

37 Roy, K., *In Case of Any News: A Diary of Living and Dying*, ICS Books, 2019.

38 I was tickled to discover, only recently, that my great-grandfather's first two names – James Cruickshank – echoed the much-admired Hearts and Scotland goalkeeper of the 1960s and 1970s. I also like to think that I am (distantly) related to Aberdeen-born Denis Law.

39 Ransom, *Iron Road*, p. 116.

40 Plowden, W., *The Motor Car and Politics*, Pelican Books, 1971.

41 St John Thomas, *The Country Railway*, pp. 147–149.

42 Ransom, *Iron Road*, p. 161.

43 Vallance, H.A., *The Great North of Scotland Railway*, David St John Thomas Publisher, 1991 edition, pp. 174–175.

44 Thomas, J.A., *A Regional History of the Railways of Great Britain, Volume 6 Scotland: the Lowlands and the Borders*, p. 83.

45 Data from an NBR traffic notebook covering the years 1921 to 1928 (therefore running into the LNER period), as advised by Andrew Boyd.

46 Wolmar, *Fire & Steam*, p. 252.

47 Barclay, G., *If Hitler comes*, Birlinn, 2013, p. 81.

48 Noble, S., *The Vanished Railways of Old Western Dunbartonshire*, The History Press, 2010.

49 Spaven, *The Railway Atlas of Scotland*, p. 153.

50 Excluding the withdrawal of Uplawmoor–Ardrossan boat trains in 1939.

51 Wolmar, *Fire & Steam*, pp. 266–267.

52 Acworth, W.M. *Scottish Railways*, Murray, 1890 – in Mellor, R.E.H. (ed.), *The Railways of Scotland: Papers of Andrew C. O'Dell*, Centre for Scottish Studies, Aberdeen (undated), p. 5.

Chapter 2

1 Faulkner, R. and Austin, C., *Holding the Line: How Britain's Railways Were Saved*, Oxford Publishing Co., 2012, p. 17.

2 Mullay, A.J., *Scottish Region: A History 1948–1973*, pp. 17 and 22.

3 Simmons, J. and Biddle, D. (eds.), *The Oxford Companion to British Railway History*, Oxford University Press, 2003, p. 421.

4 Wolmar, *Fire & Steam*, p. 273.

5 Ibid., p. 275.

6 St John Thomas, *The Country Railway*, pp. 77 and 200.

7 Faulkner and Austin, *Holding the Line*, pp. 17–19.

8 National Records of Scotland, ref. RCC 1/14.

9   Mullay, *Scottish Region*, p. 66.

10   National Archives, Kew, ref. AN97/21 (courtesy of Robert Drysdale).

11   Ibid.

12   Clough, *Dr Beeching's Remedy*, p. 59.

13   National Records of Scotland, ref. RCC 2/5.

14   Smith, R., *The Making of Scotland*, Canongate, 2001, p. 747.

15   *Edinburgh Evening News*, 14 October 2019 (courtesy of John Yellowlees).

16   http://www.disused-stations.org.uk/p/penicuik/index.shtml [Last accessed on 15 May 2020.]

17   Hurst, J., *The Glencorse Branch*, The Oakwood Press, 1999, p. 55.

18   In discussion with the author in 2020.

19   Courtesy of Louis Wall, via John Yellowlees.

20   Mullay, *Scottish Region*, p. 50.

21   Clough, *Dr Beeching's Remedy*, p. 46.

22   In discussion with the author in 2020.

23   Loft, *Last Trains*, p. 33.

24   Wolmar, *Fire & Steam*, p. 274.

25   Jones, R., *Beeching: the inside track*, Mortons Media Group Ltd., 2012, pp. 64–65.

26   (via Wikipedia) *Tufnell, R.M., The British Railcar: AEC to HST, David & Charles, 1984, pp. 26–27.*

27   Wolmar, *Fire & Steam*, p. 276.

28   Ransom, *Iron Road*, p. 212.

29   O'Dell, A.C., and Richards, P.S., *Railways and Geography*, Hutchison University Library, second (revised) edition, 1971.

30   *The Railways of Scotland: Papers of Andrew C. O'Dell*, REH Mellor (ed), Centre for Scottish Studies, Aberdeen University, 1983, p. 4.

31   Ibid., p. 29.

32   (via Wikipedia) *Cooke, B.W.C. (ed.), 'B.R. Lightweight Diesel Trains', in The Railway Magazine, June 1954.*

33   Peacock, W. (ed.), *Border Railway Portfolio*, Cheviot Publications, 1982.

34   https://www.railcar.co.uk/topic/the-edinburgh-dmu-story/ [Last accessed on 15 May 2020.]

35   http://www.railwaysarchive.co.uk/docsummary.php?docID=23 [Last accessed on 15 May 2020.]

36   Clough, *Dr Beeching's Remedy*, p. 88.

37   British Transport Commission, *Modernisation and Re-equipment of British Railways*, BTC, 1955, p. 6.

38   Ibid., p. 31.

39   Ibid., p. 20.

40   Ibid., pp. 32–33.

41   In discussion with the author in 2020.

42   Gourvish, T., *British Railways 1948–73: a Business History*, Cambridge University Press, 1986.

43 Loft, *Last Trains*, p. 83.
44 'Some signal boxes are equipped with an intermediate block section, or IBS. This normally takes the place of an old absolute block section [the length of track between two block posts on which only one train is allowed in each direction – or in the case of single-track lines to ensure that the line between crossing loops can only be occupied by one train at any one time] and is commonly found where former absolute block sections and their associated signal boxes have been removed. Essentially an intermediate block section allows two block sections, and therefore two trains, to be on the same line but controlled by the same signal box.' See: https://en.wikipedia.org/wiki/Absolute_block_signalling [Last accessed on 15 May 2020.]
45 In discussion with the author.
46 Loft, *Last Trains*, p. 95.
47 National Records of Scotland, ref BR/RSR/18/18 (Appendices 18 and 19).
48 In discussion with the author in 2020.
49 Modern Records Centre, University of Warwick, ref. MSS.127/NU/MV8/3/159.
50 National Records of Scotland, ref. DD 17/1107.
51 Mullay, *Scottish Region*, p. 78.
52 BRB, *The Reshaping of British Railways*, p.16. Within a section on 'Stopping-Train Services', what became known as the Beeching Report quotes steam loco-hauled train movements costs of 'about 15s. 0.d. per train mile' and in the case of DMUs, '4s. 0d – 6s. 0d. per train-mile, according to density of traffic'.
53 Wolmar, *Fire & Steam*, p. 281.
54 Hardy, R.H.N., *Beeching: Champion of the Railway?* Ian Allan Ltd., 1989, p. 32.
55 https://api.parliament.uk/historic-hansard/commons/1960/oct/26/british-railways [Last accessed on 15 May 2020.]
56 In discussion with the author in 2020.
57 Bradley, S., *The railways: nation, network and people*, Profile Books, 2015, p. 411.
58 Loft, *Last Trains,* p. 154.
59 In discussion with the author in 2020.
60 Faulkner and Austin, *Holding the Line*, p. 7.
61 BRB, *The Reshaping of British Railways*, p. 7. 'Sundries' were less-than-wagonload freight consignments aggregated together to create wagonloads – as distinct from generally smaller 'parcels' typically conveyed in passenger trains.
62 Wolmar, *Fire & Steam*, p. 280.
63 Ransom, *Iron Road*, p. 225.
64 Loft, *Last Trains*, p. 12.
65 Hart, T., 'Scottish Railway Development Association', in *The Railway Magazine, February 1963.*

Chapter 3

1   BRB, *The Reshaping of British Railways*, p. 10.
2   Ibid., p. 2.
3   Ibid., p. 4.
4   Clough, *Dr Beeching's Remedy*, p. 118.
5   Loft, *Last Trains*, p. 294.
6   In discussion with the author in 2020.
7   Loft, *Last Trains*, p. 298.
8   Faulkner and Austin, *Holding the Line*, p. 5.
9   In discussion with the author in 2020.
10   In discussion with the author in 2020.
11   Hillman, M. and Whalley, A., *The Social Consequences of Rail Closures*, Policy Studies Institute, 1980, p. 24
12   Ibid., p. 25.
13   Faulkner and Austin, *Holding the Line*, pp. 21–22.
14   Ibid., p. 33.
15   BRB, *The Reshaping of British Railways*, p. 16.
16   Of the 11 out of 12 case study routes in Part Two of this book which were single-track when Beeching joined BR in 1961 (only the Kilmacolm line was double-track), just St Andrews enjoyed a service frequency equivalent to hourly or better (albeit this was irregular-interval). And all Scotland's lengthy single-track routes, in Galloway (to Stranraer) and the Highlands (to Oban, Fort William, Mallaig, Kyle and Wick/Thurso), had no more than a handful of trains in each direction daily. Source: BRB, 'Passenger Services Scotland' timetable, 12 September 1960 to 11 June 1961 (author's collection).
17   The use of specialist track machines (rather than large teams of Permanent Way 'gangers') to correct irregularities in the horizontal alignment (line) and vertical irregularities (surface) of the track. See: https://en.wikipedia.org/wiki/Track_(rail_transport). [Last accessed on 15 May 2020.]
18   The Permanent Way Institution, *British Railway Track*, Fourth Edition 1971, chapter IV, p. 153.
19   In discussion with the author in 2019.
20   Across four wholly DMU-operated services analysed in the Beeching Report's 10 case studies (pp. 100–101 of the report), the average share of operating/maintenance (running) costs was: Movement 44%, Track & Signalling 36%, Terminals 20%.
21   In discussion with the author in 2020.
22   BRB, *The Reshaping of British Railways*, pp. 100–101.
23   Ibid., p. 17.
24   Loft, *Last Trains*, p. 191.
25   BRB, *The Reshaping of British Railways*, p. 18.
26   Loft, *Last Trains*, p. 99.
27   BRB, *The Reshaping of British Railways*, pp. 18 and 16.

28 In discussion with the author in 2020.

29 Loft, *Last Trains*, p. 190.

30 Alexander, F. and Nicoll, E.S., *The Register of Scottish Signal Boxes*, self-published, 1990 (courtesy of A. Boyd).

31 Joy, S., *The Train That Ran Away*, Ian Allan Ltd., 1973, p. 62.

32 Loft, *Last Trains*, p. 60.

33 Ibid., p. 59.

34 Fiennes, *I Tried to Run a Railway*, p. 114.

35 Hardy, *Beeching*, pp. 102–103.

36 Clough, *Dr Beeching's Remedy*, p. 116.

37 https://en.wikipedia.org/wiki/Level_crossings_in_the_United_Kingdom [Last accessed on 15 May 2020.]

38 Spaven, *Waverley* Route, p. 91.

39 Faulkner and Austin, *Holding the Line*, p. 33.

40 Ibid.

41 In discussion with the author in 2020.

42 Hardy, *Beeching*, p. 75.

43 Loft, *Last Trains*, p. 192.

44 In discussion with the author in 2020.

45 Bagwell, P.S., *The Railwaymen Volume 2: The Beeching Era and After*, George Allen & Unwin, 1982, p. 134

46 Ibid., p. 143.

47 In discussion with the author in 2020.

48 Loft, *Last Trains*, p. 164.

49 Ibid., p. 287.

50 National Records of Scotland, ref. RCC 2/11.

51 Spaven, *Highland Survivor*, pp. 92–93.

52 Loft, *Last Trains*, p. 213.

53 Spaven, *Waverley* Route, p. 69.

54 National Records of Scotland, ref. RCC 9/4.

55 Ironically, the minister had refused consent to closure in 1964.

56 An unusual single-platform station – on a double-track railway – used only for excursion train arrivals for Hibernian FC football matches, the last such train having run in June 1964, see: https://www.railscot.co.uk/locations/E/Easter_Road_Park_Halt/ [Last accessed on 15 May 2020.]

57 Having survived since the 1964 withdrawal of the Lanark–Muirkirk service which served it, and no race-meeting excursion train having run since then.

58 Loft, *Last Trains*, p. 187.

59 Hillman and Whalley, *The Social Consequences of Rail Closures*, p. 78.

60 Spaven, *Waverley* Route, p. 129.

61 Ibid., pp. 92–93.

62 Ibid., p. 55.

63 Spaven, *Highland Survivor*, p. 51.

64 Ibid., p. 52.

65   Ibid., p. 52.

66   Spaven, *Waverley Route*, p. 32.

67   The SCDI was established (as the Scottish Development Council) in 1931 with a mission to 'examine and consider impartially the industrial, commercial and economic problems with which the country is faced' and to promote appropriate solutions. It created the first industrial estate in Scotland (at Hillington) in 1938, and it had been in the forefront of attracting overseas manufacturing investment to Scotland from the late 1940s to the 1960s. It is still an important player on the Scottish scene.

68   Spaven, *Highland Survivor*, chapter 9.

69   Ibid., pp. 114–115.

70   National Records of Scotland, ref. SEP 17/5.

71   The precise number of line closure proposals is in part dependent on definitions, e.g., whether or not to include the closure of short stretches of track leading to main line termini closed in Glasgow, Edinburgh and Dundee. Also, there are discrepancies between the Beeching Report text ('Part 1') and 'Part 2' (maps), as in the case of the proposed future (or not) of the Dalry–Kilmarnock and Glasgow–Kilmarnock (via Barrhead) lines.

72   'Stone Cold', in the *Scottish Review*, 23 December 2020: https://www.scottishreview.net/SRAnthologyDec2020.html [Last accessed on 5 January 2021.]

73   The figure of 42 closures referred to in the *P&J* is thought to refer to those lines where all passenger services were to be withdrawn, as opposed to the grand total of 50+, which included lines where only local stopping services were to be withdrawn.

74   *P&J*, microfiche archive at Aberdeen Central Library.

75   Faulkner and Austin, *Holding the Line*, p. 41.

76   https://hansard.parliament.uk/Commons/1963-04-30/debates/4a00b735-ea47-492e-affd-1e700cd980f8/Railways [Last accessed on 15 May 2020.]

77   https://en.wikipedia.org/wiki/Tom_Fraser [Last accessed on 15 May 2020.]

78   National Records of Scotland, ref. RCC 9/4.

79   SRDA, 'Scottish Railways – the next five years', 1964 (courtesy of T. Hart).

80   Faulkner and Austin, *Holding the Line*, p. 41.

81   National Records of Scotland, ref. RCC 2/14.

82   Loft, *Last Trains*, p. 246.

83   Jones, *Beeching*, p. 69.

84   BRB, *The Reshaping of British Railways*, p. 15.

85   National Records of Scotland (Ibid.).

86   The precise number is in part dependent on definitions, as a number of closure proposals were revised and therefore were presented to the TUCCS more than once.

87   East Kilbride, Glasgow–Kilmarnock via Barrhead, Glasgow–Edinburgh via Shotts, Kilmacolm, Kyle and Wick/Thurso.

88   http://transformscotland.org.uk/blog/2015/12/08/saving-the-north-berwick-line/ [Last accessed on 15 May 2020.]

Chapter 4

1   Hajducki, A., Jodeluk., M. and Simpson, A., *The St Andrews Railway*, The Oakwood Press, 2008, p. 147.

2   In discussion with the author, 1993.

3   Kennedy, D., *The Birth and Death of a Highland Railway*, John Murray, 1971, p. 158.

4   Hillman and Whalley, *The Social Consequences of Rail Closures*.

5   Ibid., p. 26.

6   Ibid., p. 27.

7   email correspondence with the author, October 2019.

8   'Semi-skilled manual, personal service and unskilled manual', in Hillman and Whalley, *The Social Consequences of Rail Closures*, p. 137.

9   Ibid., p. 60.

10   Ibid., p. 62.

11   Ibid., pp. 66 and 67.

12   Ibid., p. 74.

13   Ibid., pp. 76 and 78.

14   Ibid., p. 87.

15   Ibid., p. 97.

16   Ibid., p. 102.

17   Ibid., p. 106.

18   Ibid., p. 117.

19   Jackson, T., *British Rail: The Nation's Railway*, The History Press, 2014, p. 83.

20   Faulkner and Austin, *Holding the Line*, pp. 42 and 139.

21   Spaven, *The Railway Atlas of Scotland*, p. 197.

22   Gibbons, S., Heblich, S. and Pinchbeck, T., *The Spatial Impacts of a Massive Rail Disinvestment Program: The Beeching Axe*, Centre for Economic Performance, London School of Economics, 2018: http://cep.lse.ac.uk/pubs/download/dp1563.pdf [Last accessed on 15 May 2020.]

23   Modern Records Centre, University of Warwick, ref. MSS.127/NU/MV8/3/24.

24   Additional extracts from the original journal article are contained in chapter 6 of *Waverley Route*.

25   Bradley, *The railways: nation, network and people*, p. 143.

26   Wolmar, *Fire & Steam*, p. 284.

27   Bagwell, *The Railwaymen Volume 2*, p. 156.

Chapter 6

1   A water trough 'is a device to enable a steam railway locomotive to replenish its water supply while in motion. It consists of a long trough filled with water, lying between the rails. When a steam locomotive passes over the trough, a water scoop can be lowered, and the speed of forward motion forces water into

the scoop, up the scoop pipe and into the tanks or locomotive tender.' See: https://en.wikipedia.org/wiki/Track_pan [Last accessed on 8 June 2020.]

2 Young, A., *Railways in Northumberland*, Martin Bairstow, 2003, p. 37.
3 http://disused-stations.org.uk/s/sprouston/index.shtml
4 In discussion with the author in 2020.
5 National Records of Scotland, ref. BR/RSR/4/2307.
6 Modern Records Centre, University of Warwick, ref. MSS.127/NU/MV8/3/64.
7 National Records of Scotland, ref. RCC 9/4.
8 Modern Records Centre, University of Warwick, ref. MSS.127/NU/MV8/3/64.
9 Ibid., ref. MSS.127/NU/MV8/3/376.
10 'BR Scottish Region Sectional Appendix', October 1960 (courtesy of A. Boyd), and Alexander & Nicoll, *The Register of Scottish Signal Boxes*.
11 National Records of Scotland, ref. RCC 4/22.
12 https://www.heraldscotland.com/opinion/14127719.when-the-axe-fell-in-kilmacolm/ [Last accessed on 15 May 2020.]
13 Jones, *Beeching*, p. 89.

Chapter 7

1 Spaven, *The Railway Atlas of Scotland*, pp. 32–33.
2 Marshall, P., *Peebles Railways*, Oakwood Press, 2005, p. 215.
3 BR Scottish Region, 'Working Time Table of Passenger Trains', June to September 1957 and June to September 1961 (courtesy of A. Boyd).
4 Mullay, *Scottish Region*, p. 81.
5 National Records of Scotland, ref. RCC 1/14.
6 Faulkner and Austin, *Holding the Line*, p. 129.
7 Modern Records Centre, University of Warwick, ref. MSS.127/NU/MV8/3/24.
8 Ibid.
9 In discussion with the author in 2019.
10 Modern Records Centre, University of Warwick, ref. MSS.127/NU/MV8/3/24.
11 Ibid.
12 National Records of Scotland, ref. RCC 1/14.
13 The reference to relaying the line strikes a personal chord with me. During family trips on the Peebles line in its last years – usually sitting in the non-smoking section of the DMU, with its driver's eye-view – my father would remark on the conspicuous presence of new concrete sleepers below the rails. It became a family in-joke that if you saw these installed on other rural lines, this was a sure sign that the railway was about to close.
14 In discussion with the author in 2019.

15   As of August 2021, Robert's manuscript had not yet been submitted to a publisher.

16   Marshall, *Peebles Railways*, pp. 217 and 219.

17   Ibid., p. 221.

18   http://disused-stations.org.uk/p/peebles_second/index.shtml

19   Mullay, *Scottish Region*, p. 67.

20   https://en.wikipedia.org/wiki/Level_crossings_in_the_United_Kingdom [Last accessed on 15 May 2020.]

21   Crossing loops/block posts at Leadburn (6 miles, 757 yards), Peebles Engine Shed (9 miles, 418 yards), Peebles Junction (826 yards), Innerleithen (6 miles, 525 yards), and thence an 11 miles, 1,656 yards section to Kilnknowe Junction, as identified from 'BR Scottish Region Sectional Appendix', and Alexander & Nicoll, *The Register of Scottish Signal Boxes*. The loop at Peebles Junction was not a conventional loop for crossing trains on the running lines, but did allow locomotives to run round goods trains in the yard adjacent to the signal box.

22   BR Scottish Region, 'Working Time Table of Passenger Trains', June to September 1961.

23   In discussion with the author in 2020.

24   Ibid.

25   Ibid.

26   Mullay, *Scottish Region*, p. 178.

27   Ibid., p. 50.

28   National Records of Scotland, ref. RCC 2/10.

Chapter 8

1   St John Thomas, *The Country Railway*, p. 61.

2   National Records of Scotland, ref. RCC 1/8.

3   Ibid., ref. SEP 5/28.

4   Byrom, B., *The Railways of Upper Strathearn*, Oakwood, 2004

5   Young, J., *Branch Lines of Strathearn*, Lightmoor Press, 2014, chapter 10

6   http://www.railwaysarchive.co.uk/docsummary.php?docID=13 [Last accessed on 15 May 2020.]

7   *The Scotsman*, 12 February 1966 (author's collection).

8   Modern Records Centre, University of Warwick, ref. MSS.127/NU/MV8/3/299.

9   https://en.wikipedia.org/wiki/British_Rail_Class_121 [Last accessed on 15 May 2020.]

10   Modern Records Centre, University of Warwick, ref. MSS.127/NU/MV8/3/159.

11   Notes of a talk given to the CILT by Stuart Sellar and Neil McDonald of SRPS in Edinburgh on 17 March 2020 (courtesy of J. Yellowlees).

12   National Records of Scotland, ref. BR/RSR/4/2079.

13   Modern Records Centre, University of Warwick, ref. MSS.127/NU/ MV8/3/159.

14   Ibid.

15   National Records of Scotland, ref. RCC 2/11.

16   National Archives, Kew, ref. PREM11/5167 (courtesy of C. Loft).

17   Young, *Branch Lines of Strathearn.*

18   Crossing loops / block posts at Muthill (4 miles, 1,356 yards) and Crieff (3 miles, 1,712 yards), thence 'One Engine in Steam' working to Comrie (5 miles, 1,584 yards), as identified from: 'BR Scottish Region Sectional Appendix', and Alexander & Nicoll, *The Register of Scottish Signal Boxes.*

19   Modern Records Centre, University of Warwick, ref. MSS.127/NU/ MV8/3/159.

20   Byrom, *The Railways of Upper Strathearn*, pp. 139–140.

21   In discussion with the author in 2019.

Chapter 9

1   Thomas and Turnock, *A Regional History of the Railways of Great Britain*, p. 193.

2   In discussion with the author in 2020.

3   The Cruden Bay Hotel was requisitioned by the Ministry of Defence and used throughout the war as a military training centre. By 1945 it required major renovation, never re-opened, and was demolished in the early 1950s. (Courtesy of D. Fasken.]

4   National Records of Scotland, ref. BR/RSR/18/18.

5   Advice from Keith Jones (quoting comment by Doug Flett) via GNSRA chat group.

6   https://www.railcar.co.uk/topic/tail-loads/?page=page-02 [Last accessed on 15 June 2020.]

7   https://railcar.co.uk/type/class-128/ [Last accessed on 15 June 2020.]

8   'BR Scottish Region Sectional Appendix', October 1960.

9   *P&J.*

10   https://www.pressandjournal.co.uk/fp/business/scotland-business/1043455/ peterhead-is-the-undisputed-king-of-uk-fish-landings/ [Last accessed on 15 May 2020.] *P&J*, 1 October 2016.

11   Modern Records Centre, University of Warwick, ref. MSS.127/NU/MV8/ 3/162.

12   Ibid.

13   National Records of Scotland, ref. BR/RSR/4/1357.

14   Ibid.

15   The Manson system was first used in 1889 and in due course was deployed throughout the single-track sections of the GNOSR. See: https://en.wikipedia. org/wiki/Great_North_of_Scotland_Railway [Last accessed on 15 June 2020.]

16 Advice from Keith Fenwick and Keith Jones of the Great North of Scotland Railway Association in 2020 (courtesy of David Fasken).

17 Crossing loops / block posts at Newmachar (5 miles, 404 yards), Udny (2 miles, 1,591 yards), Ellon (4 miles, 1,662 yards), Arnage (3 miles, 1,237 yards *(closed January 1965)*), Auchnagatt (3 miles, 1,345 yards), Maud (4 miles, 237 yards), Strichen (5 miles, 1613 yards), Lonmay (4 miles, 1,735 yards *(closed January 1965)*), Fraserburgh (4 miles, 1738 yards), as identified from 'BR Scottish Region Sectional Appendix', and Alexander & Nicoll, *The Register of Scottish Signal Boxes.*

18 'BR Scottish Region Working Time Table of Freight Trains (Section E)', 9 September 1963 to 14 June 1964 (author's collection).

19 National Records of Scotland, ref. BR/RSR/4/1357.

20 BRB, 'Passenger Services Scotland' timetable, 9 September 1963 to 14 June 1964 (author's collection).

21 In discussion with the author in 2020.

22 National Records of Scotland, ref. BR/RSR/4/1357.

23 Fiennes, *I Tried to Run a Railway,* p. 115.

24 In discussion with the author in 2020. Across Scotland in 1966 (the year after Buchan passenger closure), the availability for service of the 15 surviving original NBL Type 2s (1,000 / 1,100hp Class 21) was 79%, albeit this figure did not take account of 30 locos (presumably the least reliable) 'in store'. The 13 of the original fleet of 58 which had been re-engined since 1963 (and seven more would be completed by 1967) – the Class 29 of 1,350hp, all based in Central Scotland – registered just 65% availability in 1966, the worst of 10 loco classes / sub-classes recorded. This contrast between the two sub-classes adds weight to anecdotal references to the Kittybrewster-based locos being better maintained. By way of further comparison, in 1966 Classes 26/27 recorded 80% availability, while non-inter-city DMUs ranged from 87% to 93%. (BR Scottish Region data quoted in Mullay, *Scottish Region*, p. 183.)

25 In discussion with the author in 2020.

26 'The term "diagram" is used in UK train management to mean "working out what each train [or locomotive] does each day" or a "train duty". The diagram shows where and when each train starts and where and when it finishes each day and what it does in between.' See: http://www.railway-technical. com/operations/working-timetable.html#:~:text=Diagrams,what%20it%20 does%20in%20between. [Last accessed on 15 June 2020.]

27 Sayer, A.P., *The North British Type 2 Bo-Bo Diesel-Electric Classes 21 & 29*, Pen & Sword Transport, 2019, p. 59.

28 Across Scotland in 1966, the 15 remaining non-re-engined NBL Type 2s ranked fifth for reliability across 10 different loco classes / sub-classes. (BR Scottish Region data quoted in Mullay, *Scottish Region*, p. 183.)

29 Modern Records Centre, University of Warwick, ref. MSS.127/NU/MV8/ 3/162.

30 National Records of Scotland, ref. SEP 17/2.

SCOTLAND'S LOST BRANCH LINES

31 Modern Records Centre, University of Warwick, ref. MSS.127/NU/MV8/ 3/162.
32 National Records of Scotland, ref. BR/RSR/4/1356.
33 Modern Records Centre, University of Warwick, ref. MSS.127/NU/MV8/ 3/162.
34 BRB, *The Reshaping of British Railways*, p. 18.
35 National Records of Scotland, ref. RCC 2/11.
36 Ibid., ref. RCC 9/4.
37 *P&J*.
38 In discussion with the author in 2020.
39 *P&J*.
40 Loft, *Last Trains*, p. 192.
41 On the Peterhead branch at the time of passenger closure there were crossing loops / block posts at Longside (7 miles, 735 yards) and Peterhead (5 miles, 1,159 yards), as identified from 'BR Scottish Region Sectional Appendix', and Alexander & Nicoll, *The Register of Scottish Signal Boxes*. On the Fraserburgh line, Arnage and Lonmay signal boxes were closed in January 1965, Newmachar in November 1965, followed by Auchnagatt, Fraserburgh, Strichen and Udny in 1966, Ellon in 1967, and finally Maud in 1969. East of Maud, Longside box was taken out in 1965 and Peterhead in 1966. From 1969 until the 1970 Peterhead freight closure, the Dyce–Maud section was operated under the Telephone & Notice Board arrangement, with train crew communicating with the Dyce box to obtain authority to proceed. North and east of Maud, One Train Working was in force on both 'branches'.
42 Advice from Barbara Buchan, former BR clerk at Fraserburgh, courtesy of John G. Williamson (September 2019).
43 Spaven, *Highland Survivor*, pp. 168, 188 and 189.
44 *BR Main Line Gradient Profiles*, Ian Allan, 2003 impression, Profiles Sc23, Sc24, Sc26 and Sc28.
45 *Britain's Growing Railway*, Railfuture, 2017.
46 Fenwick, K., Flett, D. and Jackson, D., *Railways of Buchan*, Great North of Scotland Railway Association, 2008, p. 62.

Chapter 10

1 https://en.wikipedia.org/wiki/Fife_Coast_Railway [Last accessed on 15 May 2020.]
2 Hajducki, Jodeluk and Simpson, *The St Andrews Railway*, p. 127.
3 Hajducki, A., Jodeluk, M., and Simpson, A., *The Leven & East of Fife Railway*, The Oakwood Press, 2013, p. 173.
4 Ibid., p. 177.
5 Ibid.
6 https://en.wikipedia.org/wiki/Camping_coach [Last accessed on 15 May 2020.]

7   BRB, 'Passenger Services Scotland' timetable, 9 September 1963 to 14 June 1964 (author's collection).

8   'Holiday Haunts by British Railways Scotland 1962' (author's collection).

9   Modern Records Centre, University of Warwick, ref. MSS.127/NU/MV8/3/239.

10 'Holiday Haunts by British Railways Scotland 1962'.

11 In discussion with the author in 2020.

12 Modern Records Centre, University of Warwick, ref. MSS.127/NU/MV8/3/239.

13 National Records of Scotland, ref. BR/RSR/4/2036.

14 Bagwell, *The Railwaymen Volume 2*, p. 153.

15 In discussion with the author in 2020.

16 Bagwell, *The Railwaymen Volume 2*, p. 156.

17 Spaven, *Highland Survivor*, p. 286.

18 The 'past practice' referred to may well have been the type of financial breakdown provided in the case of the 1961 closure proposal for the Peebles line – pre-Beeching and also prior to the implementation of the 1962 Transport Act which would change the terms of reference of the TUCCs. The Peebles example included figures for short-term and long-term cost savings and estimated loss of gross receipts, but no specific data on actual costs or contributory revenue.

19 Modern Records Centre, University of Warwick, ref. MSS.127/NU/MV8/3/239.

20 National Records of Scotland, ref. BR/RSR/4/2226.

21 Ibid., ref. RCC 2/12.

22 Ibid.

23 Ibid.

24 Ibid., p. 181.

25 Ibid.

26 Ibid., p. 182.

27 Hajducki, A., Jodeluk, M. and Simpson, A., *The Anstruther & St Andrews Railway*, The Oakwood Press, 2009, p. 147.

28 Crossing loops / block posts at Largo (2 miles, 1202 yards), Elie (5 miles, 501 yards), St Monance (1 mile, 1,729 yards), Anstruther (2 miles, 874 yards), Crail (4 miles, 1,000 yards), Kingsbarns (2 miles, 1,512 yards) and thence an 8 miles, 1,253 yards section to St Andrews, as identified from: 'BR Scottish Region Sectional Appendix', and Alexander & Nicoll, *The Register of Scottish Signal Boxes*.

29 'BR Scottish Region Sectional Appendix'.

30 Hajducki, Jodeluk and Simpson, *The Anstruther & St Andrews Railway*, p. 185.

31 Hajducki, Jodeluk and Simpson, *The St Andrews Railway*, p.127.

32 National Records of Scotland, ref BR/RSR/18/18.

33 The traditional term, One Engine in Steam, rather than One Train Working, had survived in common railway parlance, despite regular steam operation having long ceased.

34   Modern Records Centre, University of Warwick, ref. MSS.127/NU/MV8/3/542.
35   National Records of Scotland, ref. RCC 4/3.
36   'A diagram is the "job list", listing the trains that you are going to be working with headcodes, what the stops and times are, when breaks are to be taken, who you are relieving (or is relieving you) and any other information relevant to the shift (whether working, assisting or travelling, or taxi to-from the start and finish point.' See: https://www.railforums.co.uk/threads/diagrams.50448/ [Last accessed on 15 May 2020.]
37   National Records of Scotland, ref. BR/RSR/4/1283.
38   Ibid., ref. BR/RSR/4/2290.
39   Ibid., ref. RCC 6/66/1.
40   Ibid., ref. RCC 4/3.
41   Ibid.
42   Hajducki, Jodeluk and Simpson, *The St Andrews Railway*, p. 131.
43   Ibid., pp. 131 and 133.
44   Modern Records Centre, University of Warwick, ref. MSS.127/NU/MV8/3/542.
45   'Since the limitation of mechanical operation restricted the design of track layouts on the one hand, and tended to require more signal boxes, even lightly used ones, on the other hand, there has always been a desire of railway administrations to increase the distance that remote turnouts can be operated. This requires some kind of power operation of points and signals. The principal means of power operation include hydraulic, pneumatic and electric.' See: https://en.wikipedia.org/wiki/Point_machine [Last accessed on 15 May 2020.]
46   In discussion with the author in 2019.
47   Hajducki, Jodeluk and Simpson, *The St Andrews Railway*
48   Spaven, *Waverley Route*, pp. 112–118.
49   Hajducki, Jodeluk and Simpson, *The St Andrews Railway*, p. 148.
50   Modern Records Centre, University of Warwick, ref. MSS.127/NU/MV8/3/551.
51   In discussion with the author in 2020.
52   National Records of Scotland, ref. RCC 4/4.
53   Ibid., ref. BR/RSR/4/1601.
54   Spaven, *Waverley Route*, pp. 68 and 88.
55   Hajducki, Jodeluk and Simpson, *The St Andrews Railway*, p. 188.
56   Hajducki, Jodeluk and Simpson, *The Leven & East of Fife Railway*, p. 188.
57   National Records of Scotland, ref. RCC 4/5.
58   Ibid., ref. BR/RSR/4/1177.
59   Hajducki, Jodeluk and Simpson, *The Leven & East of Fife Railway*, p. 189.
60   In discussion with the author in 2020.

Chapter 11

1   Thomas, J., *The Callander & Oban Railway*, David & Charles, 1966, p. 24.
2   Spaven, *The Railway Atlas of Scotland*, p. 123.
3   Thomas, *The Callander & Oban Railway*, p. 164.
4   National Records of Scotland, ref. SEP 17/2.
5   https://www.gov.uk/government/statistical-data-sets/historical-coal-data-coal-production-availability-and-consumption [Last accessed on 15 May 2020.]
6   Modern Records Centre, University of Warwick, ref. MSS.127/NU/MV8/3/347.
7   Thomas, *The Callander & Oban Railway*, p. 164.
8   BR Heads of Information in NUR archives at Modern Records Centre, University of Warwick, ref. MSS.127/NU/MV8/3/347.
9   National Records of Scotland, ref. BR/RSR/4/2036.
10 Forsythe, R.N., *To Western Scottish Waters*, Tempus, 2000, p. 104.
11 National Records of Scotland, ref. BR/RSR/4/2039.
12 Ibid.
13 National Records of Scotland, ref. RCC 2/12.
14 Ibid., ref. SEP 17/5.
15 Thomas, *The Callander & Oban Railway*, p. 165.
16 Crossing loops / block posts at Doune (3 miles, 1,386 yards), Drumvaich (3 miles, 660 yards), Callander East (3 miles, 1,386 yards) and Callander West (407 yards, with double-track between the two boxes), as identified from: 'BR Scottish Region Sectional Appendix', and Alexander & Nicoll, *The Register of Scottish Signal Boxes*.
17 National Records of Scotland, ref. SEP 17/10.
18 Pottinger was a civil servant imprisoned for corruption in 1974. See: https://en.wikipedia.org/wiki/William_George_Pottinger [Last accessed on 15 May 2020.] He was also distantly related, by marriage, to my father.

Chapter 12

1   Thomas and Turnock, *A Regional History of the Railways of Great Britain, Volume 15 North of Scotland*, p. 180.
2   https://railscot.co.uk/articles/Aberdeen_to_Ballater_by_BMU:_Notes_on_the_Battery_Railcar_Experiment/ [Last accessed on 15 May 2020.]
3   Jones, K.G., 'Thirty Years of Diesels on the Great North', *Great North Review*, No. 96 (Spring 1988), Great North of Scotland Railway Association (courtesy of John G. Williamson).
4   National Records of Scotland, ref. BR/RSR/18/18.
5   https://www.railscot.co.uk/articles/Aberdeen_to_Ballater_by_BMU:_Notes_on_the_Battery_Railcar_Experiment/

6   https://www.railcar.co.uk/type/battery-multiple-unit/operations [Last accessed on 15 May 2020.]
7   In discussion with the author in 2020.
8   *P&J*.
9   *P&J*.
10   Farr, *Stories of Royal Deeside's Railway*, chapter 5 'Anatomy of a Closure'.
11   National Records of Scotland, ref. SEP 17/4.
12   Modern Records Centre, University of Warwick, ref. MSS.127/NU/MV8/3/304.
13   Ibid.
14   Ibid.
15   Ibid.
16   Ibid.
17   Farr, *Stories of Royal Deeside's Railway*, p. 55.
18   In discussion with the author in 2020.
19   Modern Records Centre, University of Warwick, ref. MSS.127/NU/MV8/3/304.
20   Farr, *Stories of Royal Deeside's Railway*, p. 55.
21   Crossing loops / block posts at Culter (6 miles, 1590 yards), Park (3 miles, 537 yards), Banchory (5 miles, 1641 yards), Torphins (7 miles, 313 yards), Lumphanan (2 miles, 1624 yards), Aboyne (5 miles, 947 yards), Dinnet (4 miles, 1031 yards), and Ballater (6 miles, 501 yards), as identified from: 'BR Scottish Region Sectional Appendix', and Alexander & Nicoll, *The Register of Scottish Signal Boxes*.
22   Farr, *Stories of Royal Deeside's Railway*, p. 57.
23   In discussion with the author in 2020.
24   National Records of Scotland, ref. BR/RSR/4/1354.
25   BRB, 'Passenger Services Scotland' timetable, 9 September 1963 to 14 June 1964 (author's collection).
26   National Records of Scotland, ref. BR/RSR/4/1354.
27   https://www.gov.uk/government/statistical-data-sets/all-vehicles-veh01#licensed-vehicles [Last accessed on 15 May 2020.]
28   *P&J*, 24 September 1964.
29   National Records of Scotland, ref. SEP 16/1.
30   Ibid., ref. RCC 2/12.
31   In discussion with the author in 2019.
32   Modern Records Centre, University of Warwick, ref. MSS.127/NU/MV8/3/304.
33   Sayer, *The North British Type 2 Bo-Bo Diesel-Electric Classes 21 & 29*, p. 235.
34   Memorandum of 30 January 1962 from the Office of the Planning Officer to the general manager of BR Scottish Region: 'Introduction of diesel traction: Highland and G.N. of S. areas' (courtesy of Graham Maxtone, Great North of Scotland Railway Association).
35   Sayer, *The North British Type 2 Bo-Bo Diesel-Electric Classes 21 & 29*, p. 235.
36   Ibid.

37 Copy of 'Remembering the Deeside Line', published in the *Great North Review* in 2017, as supplied to the author by Gordon Casely in 2019.

38 In discussion with the author in 2020.

39 Gordon Casely, in discussion with the author in 2020.

40 *P&J*.

41 *P&J*.

42 National Records of Scotland, ref. BR/RSR/4/1256.

43 https://en.wikipedia.org/wiki/Dee_Street_Halt_railway_station [Last accessed on 15 May 2020.]

44 In discussion with the author in 2019.

45 National Records of Scotland, ref. BR/RSR/4/1256.

46 Ibid.

Chapter 13

1 Thomas and Turnock, *A Regional History of the Railways of Great Britain, Volume 15 North of Scotland*, p. 273.

2 Vallance, H.A., *British Branch Lines*, BT Batsford, 1965, p. 193.

3 R.A. (Bobby) Fasken was subsequently the first Secretary of the Highlands & Islands Development Board, where he was a colleague of Frank Spaven, the HIDB's first Planning & Research Officer. Bobby's son, David, and I have been good friends since joining Inverness Royal Academy in 1966, and we have produced two railway books together: *The Insider Rail Guide: Inverness to Kyle of Lochalsh* and *The Insider Rail Guide: Aberdeen to Elgin & Inverness* (both published by Lomond Books).

4 In part, author's private papers; also held at the Highland Archive in Inverness (thought to be in the Frank Spaven collection).

5 Modern Records Centre, University of Warwick, ref. MSS.127/NU/MV8/3/299.

6 National Records of Scotland, ref. BR/RSR/4/2081.

7 https://dictionary.cambridge.org/dictionary/english/nostrum [Last accessed on 15 May 2020.]

8 Welbourn, N., *Lost Lines: Scotland*, Ian Allan Publishing, 1994, p. 72.

9 Crossing loops / block posts at Benderloch (2 miles, 1,228 yards), Appin (10 miles, 836 yards), Kentallen (9 miles, 730 yards) and Ballachulish (4 miles, 1,716 yards), as identified from: 'BR Scottish Region Sectional Appendix'), and Alexander & Nicoll, *The Register of Scottish Signal Boxes*.

10 Kennedy, *The Birth and Death of a Highland Railway*, p. 125.

11 Smith, *The Making of Scotland*, p. 71.

Chapter 14

1 Faulkner and Austin, *Holding the Line*, p. 129.

2 In discussion with the author in 2020.

3   In discussion with the author in 2020.
4   Hillman and Whalley, *The Social Consequences of Rail Closures*, p. 109.
5   In discussion with the author in 2020.
6   Ibid.
7   Spaven, *Waverley Route*, p. 235.
8   Sourced by David Prescott from his copy of the Airdrie–Bathgate Initial Technical Feasibility Report, p. 41.
9   Private research by David Prescott of Allan Rail Ltd. (2017).

Chapter 15

1   *Britain's Growing Railway*, Railfuture, 2017.
2   Spaven, D., *Waverley Route: the battle for the Borders Railway*, Stenlake Publishing, Third Edition, 2017.
3   Informal advice to the author in 2020.
4   https://greens.scot/sites/default/files/Rail%20For%20All.pdf [Last accessed on 23 February 2021.]
5   https://www.nrscotland.gov.uk/statistics-and-data/statistics/statistics-by-theme/population/population-estimates/settlements-and-localities/mid-2016-population-estimates-for-settlements-and-localities-in-scotland [Last accessed on 15 May 2020.
6   BRB, *The Reshaping of British Railways*, p. 4.
7   https://levenmouth.co.uk/ [Last accessed on 15 May 2020.]
8   https://www.eveningexpress.co.uk/fp/news/local/peterhead-and-fraserburgh-most-distant-towns-in-uk-from-rail-network/?sso-c=MC4xNzQ4NDEwMCAxNTE0OTTk0ODYw [Last accessed on 15 May 2020.] *Evening Express*, 7 September 2015.
9   https://www.pressandjournal.co.uk/fp/business/scotland-business/1043455/peterhead-is-the-undisputed-king-of-uk-fish-landings/ [Last accessed on 15 May 2020.] *P&J*, 1 October 2016.
10   The TramTrain concept was pioneered in Germany two decades ago, and a successful British trial has been taking place in the Sheffield / Rotherham area. The core difference is that a TramTrain can negotiate sharper curves and steeper gradients than heavy rail operations, thereby avoiding much of the major engineering which would be needed to get round breaches of old railway alignments by housing, roads, etc. For more information, see: https://www.railway-technology.com/projects/sheffield-rotherham-tram-train-pilot-south-yorkshire/ [Last accessed on 15 May 2020.]
11   For more information on the Ellon rail study, see: https://www.nestrans.org.uk/wp-content/uploads/2017/11/FPASTS-1plus-Ellon-Rail-Study_Final-Report.pdf [Last accessed on 15 May 2020.]
12   For more information on the StARLink campaign, see: http://www.starlink-campaign.org.uk/page1/about.html [Last accessed on 15 May 2020.]
13   Faulkner and Austin, *Holding the Line*, p. 116.

Bibliography

Atlas of Railway Station Closures, Crecy Publishing Ltd., 2018

Bagwell, P.S., *The Railwaymen Volume 2: The Beeching Era and After*, George Allen & Unwin, 1982

British Railways Board, *The Reshaping of British Railways*, HMSO, 1963

Clough, D.N., *Dr Beeching's Remedy*, Ian Allan Publishing, 2013

Farr, A.D., *Stories of Royal Deeside's Railway*, Kestrel Books, 1971

Faulkner, R. and Austin, C., *Holding the Line: How Britain's Railways Were Saved*, Oxford Publishing Co, 2012

Fiennes, G., *I Tried to Run a Railway*, Ian Allan Ltd., 1967

Hajducki, A., Jodeluk, M. and Simpson, A., *The Anstruther & St Andrews Railway*, The Oakwood Press, 2009

Hajducki, A., Jodeluk, M. and Simpson, A., *The Leven & East of Fife Railway*, The Oakwood Press, 2013

Hajducki, A., Jodeluk, M. and Simpson, A., *The St Andrews Railway*, The Oakwood Press, 2008

Hardy, R.H.N., *Beeching: Champion of the Railway?* Ian Allan Ltd., 1989

Hillman, M. and Whalley, A., *The Social Consequences of Rail Closures*, Policy Studies Institute, 1980

Jones, R., *Beeching: the inside track*, Mortons Media Group Ltd., 2012

Kennedy, D., *The Birth and Death of a Highland Railway*, John Murray, 1971

Loft, C., *Last Trains: Dr Beeching and the Death of Rural England*, Biteback Publishing, 2013

Marshall, P., *Peebles Railways*, Oakwood Press, 2005

Mullay, A.J., *Scottish Region: A History 1948–1973*, Tempus, 2007

Railfuture, *Britain's Growing Railway*, 2017

Ransom, P.J.G., *Iron Road*, Birlinn, 2007

Sayer, A.P., *The North British Type 2 Bo-Bo Diesel-Electric Classes 21 & 29*, Pen & Sword Transport, 2019

Simmons, J. and Biddle, G. (eds.), *The Oxford Companion to British Railway History*, Oxford University Press, 2003

Spaven, D., *The Railway Atlas of Scotland*, Birlinn, 2015

Spaven, D., *Highland Survivor: the story of the Far North Line*, Kessock Books, 2016 – awarded '2017 Railway Book of the Year' by the Railway & Canal Historical Society

Spaven, D., *Waverley Route: the battle for the Borders Railway*, Stenlake Publishing, third edition, 2017

St John Thomas, D., *The Country Railway*, Frances Lincoln Limited, new edition, 2011

Thomas, J.A., *A Regional History of the Railways of Great Britain, Volume 6 Scotland: the Lowlands and the Borders*, David & Charles, 1971

Thomas, J.A., *The Callander & Oban Railway*, David St John Thomas, new edition, 1990

Thomas, J.A. and Turnock, D., *A Regional History of the Railways of Great Britain, Volume 15 North of Scotland*, David & Charles, 1989

Welbourn, N., *Lost Lines: Scotland*, Ian Allan Publishing, 1994

Wolmar, C., *Fire & Steam*, Atlantic Books, 2007

Appendix – passenger route closures since the 1923 Grouping

This year-by-year list of withdrawal of regular passenger services over standard-gauge rail routes in Scotland since the 1923 Grouping is based on *The Last Trains Scotland, 1–5*, by W.S. Sellar and J.L. Stevenson (Moorfoot, 1979–83) – courtesy of A.J. Mullay – and has been supplemented by additional intelligence from Andrew Boyd, John Yellowlees and others.

In the case of branch lines, normally only the terminus is shown, while for cross-country routes / main lines the start and end points of service are indicated. LMS routes are shown in standard font, while LNER closures are italicised. Routes which were jointly operated by the LMS and the LNER are shown thus: *[joint]*.

In some cases – e.g., Lanark–Carstairs–Edinburgh in 1966 – only a short track chord (in this case, between Lanark and Carstairs) lost its passenger service. Note that this list may not take into account every instance where a chord has ceased to be used or where a through route serving no intermediate stations has ceased to be used by non-stopping through trains. Withdrawals of local stopping services on surviving cross-country routes / main lines are *not* listed.

Lines subsequently re-opened (partially or wholly) for passenger service are marked with an asterisk. In some cases only a very short section has been re-opened, e.g., from Hamilton to Larkhall (the line originally extending through to Coalburn and Strathaven).

1924   East Kilbride–High Blantyre

1925   *Granton*
      Macmerry

1926 *Charlestown*
Renfrew (Porterfield)

1929 Carmyllie *[joint]*
South Queensferry

1930 Airdrie–Newhouse
Ayr–Turnberry
Bathgate–Blackston
Denny
Dunfermline–Alloa (via Kincardine)
Giffen–Kilbirnie
Bonnybridge
Irvine (Bank St)
Manuel–Coatbridge
Morningside [LMS]
Morningside [LNER]
Ratho–Kirkliston–Dalmeny

1931 Annan (Shawhill)
Bankfoot
Edzell
Fochabers Town
Hopeman
Oldmeldrum

1932 *Boddam*
Gullane
Lauder
Leslie
Uplawmoor–Ardrossan (except boat trains)

1933 *Dolphinton [LNER]*
Fort Augustus
Gifford
Glencorse

1934 *Balloch–Stirling*
      Montrose East

1935 Dalserf–Stonehouse
      Larbert–Bonnybridge Central–Kilsyth *[joint]*

1937 Methven

1939 Balerno–Ravelrig Junction
      Banavie Pier
      Loch Tay
      Strathaven–Darvel
      Uplawmoor–Ardrossan boat trains
      Wanlockhead

1942 *Dalkeith*
      Girvan–Turnberry

1943 Airdrie [LMS]
      Balerno(–Slateford)
      Catrine
      Fort George
      Moniaive

1944 Lybster

1945 Dolphinton [LMS]

1946 Strathpeffer

1947 *North Leith* (from 1952 – during the BR freight-only
      period – known as 'Leith Citadel')

NATIONALISATION

1948 Jedburgh
      St Boswells–Duns

1949 Haddington

1950 Alford
       Auchinleck–Muirkirk
       Bothwell [ex-LMS]
       Holehouse Junction–Rankinston
       Ladybank–Mawcarse
       Peebles (West)
       Portpatrick
       Whithorn

1951 Aberfoyle–Kirkintilloch
       Alyth
       Barnton
       Bothwell [ex-LNER]–Coatbridge Central [ex-LNER]–Blairhill
       Brocketsbrae
       Comrie–Balquhidder
       Duns–Reston
       Fortrose
       Inverbervie
       Kilsyth–Maryhill / Kirkintilloch
       Macduff
       Newburgh–St Fort
       Penicuik
       Perth–Crieff
       Polton
       Selkirk
       Whiteinch (Victoria Park)
       Wilsontown

1952 Brechin–Forfar
       Brechin–Bridge of Dun–Montrose
       Hamilton [ex-LNER]
       Kirriemuir
       Leith Central
       Lockerbie–Dumfries

1954　Alva
　　　Moffat

1955　Arbroath–Guthrie
　　　Blairgowrie
　　　Bothwell [ex-LNER]
　　　Dundee–Newtyle–Alyth Junction / Ardler
　　　Forfar–Broughty Ferry
　　　Ladybank–Perth*
　　　Methil

1956　Airdrie–Bathgate–Newbridge Junction(–Edinburgh)*
　　　Bo'ness
　　　Leuchars–Tayport
　　　Riccarton Junction–Hexham

1959　Clydebank (East)
　　　Dundee (East)
　　　Maryhill–Glasgow (Central Low Level) via Kirklee
　　　Greenock (Princes Pier) – except boat trains

1960　Dornoch
　　　Hyndland (branch terminus replaced by a new station on
　　　　　the 'main line')

1962　Beith
　　　Edinburgh–Peebles–Galashiels
　　　Edinburgh South Suburban Circle
　　　Eyemouth
　　　Leith North
　　　Rosewell (after a short period as a branch following the
　　　　　Peebles closure)
　　　Uplawmoor

1964　Banff
　　　Dalmellington
　　　Darvel

Dumbarton / Dalmuir Riverside /Possil–Glasgow Central Low
  Level– Rutherglen / Coatbridge*
Edinburgh (Princes Street)–Haymarket West Junction (Stirling–
  Edinburgh service diverted to Waverley)
Gleneagles–Crieff–Comrie
(Ardrossan–)Irvine–Crosshouse(–Kilmarnock)
Kinross Junction–Alloa
Kirkintilloch
Langholm
Lossiemouth
Muirkirk
Musselburgh (including the loop line via Piershill and Abbeyhill)
St Boswells–Kelso–Berwick-upon-Tweed

1965 Aberfeldy
      Aviemore–Forres
      Boat of Garten–Craigellachie
      Coalburn & Strathaven*
      Dumfries–Stranraer
      Dunblane–Callander–Crianlarich
      Dundee (West)
      Edinburgh (Princes Street)
      Fraserburgh
      Killin
      Kirkcudbright
      Leven–Crail–St Andrews
      Peterhead
      St Combs

1966 Ballachulish
      Ballater
      Dalry–Elderslie (via Lochwinnoch)
      Glasgow (Buchanan Street)
      Glasgow (St Enoch)
      Greenock Princes Pier boat trains
      Lanark–Carstairs(–Edinburgh)
      Stranraer Town
      Tayport

1967 Renfrew (Wharf)
      (Perth–)Stanley Junction–Forfar–Kinnaber Junction(–Aberdeen)

1968 Ardrossan (Montgomerie Pier)
      Corstorphine
      Elgin–Cairnie Junction (via Buckie)
      Elgin–Keith Junction (via Craigellachie)
      Grangemouth
      Heads of Ayr
      Larbert–Alloa
      Stirling–Alloa*–Dunfermline

1969 (Ayr–)Barassie–Kilmarnock*
      Edinburgh–Galashiels*–Hawick–Carlisle
      Leven
      Newport-on-Tay East
      St Andrews

1970 (Perth–)Bridge of Earn–Kinross–Cowdenbeath

1971 Fairlie Pier

1973 Dalry–Kilmarnock
      (Glasgow Queen Street–)Winchburgh Junction–Dalmeny
        Junction*(–Kirkcaldy)

1979 Bridgeton Central (branch terminus replaced by a new
        station on the 'main line')

1983 (Glasgow Central–)Paisley Canal*–Elderslie Junction–Kilmacolm

1986 Balloch Pier

Index